LUTHERANS IN CRISIS

DAVID A. GUSTAFSON

LUTHERANS IN CRISIS

The Question
of Identity
in the American
Republic

FORTRESS PRESS/MINNEAPOLIS

To my father, DeVore,
who lived his baptism and
was an example to me and many others.

LUTHERANS IN CRISIS
The Question of Identity in the American Republic

Scripture quotations unless otherwise noted are from the New Revised Standard Version Bible, copyright © 1989 by the Division of Christian Education of the National Council of the Churches of Christ in the United States.

Cover design: Pollock Design Team

The persons in the cover photos are, clockwise from upper left, Benjamin Kurtz, Charles Porterfield Krauth, William Julius Mann, and Samuel Simon Schmucker. The text overlay is from the Articles on Faith and Doctrine in the Augsburg Confession (Original: Dresden State Archives).

Library of Congress Cataloging-in-Publication Data

Gustafson, David A., 1942–
    Lutherans in crisis : the question of identity in the American
republic / David A. Gustafson.
        p.   cm.
    Includes bibliographical references and index.
    ISBN 0-8006-2659-1 (alk. paper) :
    1. Lutheran Church—United States—History—19th century.
2. Lutherans—United States—History—19th century.   3. United
States—Church history—19th century.   4. Identification (Religion)—
Case studies.   I. Title

    BX8041.G87   1993
    284.1'73'09034—dc20   92-30397
                                                                      CIP

Manufactured in the U.S.A.   AF 1-2659
97   96   95   94   93   1   2   3   4   5   6   7   8   9   10

Contents

Acknowledgments

Many persons and institutions have made this book possible. My doctoral committee at the Union Institute provided helpful criticisms and suggestions that have made this a better work. To my core faculty member Kevin Sharpe, adjunct faculty members Robert Kolb and James Smylie, and committee members Dominic Fontaine and Edwin Niemi, I express my gratitude.

The library staff at Luther Northwestern Theological Seminary, especially Scott Grorud, facilitated my research by obtaining many books, pamphlets, and other documents. Without their assistance, this book would have taken much longer to complete. I offer them my thanks.

I am grateful to Fortress Press for publishing this work. I am especially thankful to Timothy G. Staveteig, Academic Editor, for his suggestions and encouragement. His eye for details and dedication to excellence have given greater clarity to this book's thesis.

I owe a great debt to my teachers: Pastor Joseph Dahlquist, who faithfully taught me Luther's Catechism; A. R. Pruitt, who shared with a young high school student his love and enthusiasm for history; Arthur Williamson and David Pletcher, who continually encouraged my interest in history at Hamline University; Robert Fischer, who guided my studies in church history at Lutheran School of Theology at Chicago (Maywood) and taught me the value of researching the primary sources; and Paul Sonnack, who was my mentor and friend during my initial graduate studies at Luther Northwestern Theological Seminary.

Words cannot adequately express my thanks to the people whom I serve, the parishioners of Peace Lutheran Church, Poplar, Wisconsin. They have shown constant interest in my pursuits and generously have allowed me freedom in which to work. Every pastor should have the privilege of serving such people.

Finally, I wish to dedicate this book to my partner in marriage, Susan, whose editorial skills, tremendous patience, and unfailing encouragement contributed more to this book than she will ever know. She has been a constant and loving companion through this journey.

Introduction

Americanization and Confessional Identity

Every religious group in the United States, as elsewhere, needs to re-formulate continually just how it should express its distinctive identity and heritage in the face of new questions and alternative answers. This issue was especially important in the middle of the nineteenth century, when more than seven million immigrants arrived in America from various parts of Europe. They brought their languages, cultures, and religious faiths, and sought to maintain these as best they could in their new land.

America, then as now, was dominated by a culturally Protestant majority—a religious establishment and ethos that immediately challenged the cultural and (especially) religious identity of these immigrants. This challenge, termed Americanization, represents the tension between, on the one hand, becoming aligned with this dominant Protestant culture and, on the other hand, seeking to maintain a group's own distinctive substance.

The Lutheran group's struggles over what form its religious identity should take in America presents a clear, even startling, illustration of how Americanization and religious identity stand in tension. The conflict, known as the American Lutheran controversy, refers to more than doctrinal disputes. In addition to grounding their arguments in the Bible, the Nicene and Apostles' Creeds, and the Lutheran Confessions, each side shared a common concern for what would best work in America. For example, should Lutherans conduct revival meetings in addition to or in place of thorough catechetical instruction? On the one side, the American Lutherans advocated that Lutheranism should accommodate itself to the American Protestant establishment. On the other side, confessional Lutherans maintained that Lutheranism should preserve its doctrinal and liturgical distinctiveness as a means of retaining the tradition's Lutheran identity.

Chapter 1 seeks to identify the factors that unified the various strands of American Protestantism. Even though no state church existed in America,

1

nonetheless a consensus was present among the many Protestant groups regarding the value of a civil religion. Mostly a product of the Enlightenment, this religion stressed the importance of good citizenship and a harmonious society. The Protestant majority worked for a broad religious consensus that has a cohesive character, especially when contrasted with Lutheranism. The Protestant majority displayed four broad aspects. First, it was vehemently anti-Roman Catholic. Second, it promoted a strong individualism and emphasized the right to private judgment in matters of biblical interpretation and doctrine. Third, a personal conversion experience—usually accomplished through revivals—was deemed necessary for salvation. Fourth, sacraments were viewed as symbols or testimonies of grace, an understanding much like that of Swiss reformer Ulrich Zwingli, rather than as effective means of grace, an understanding more associated with Martin Luther and John Calvin (even though Calvinism had been a strong religious force in seventeenth-century America). All of these aspects were issues in the American Lutheran controversy.

Chapter 2 explores the concept of Americanization, summarizing several theories that explain how religious groups have experienced and reacted to life in America. Of these theories, Isaac Berkson's community theory seems to best explain the preservation of ethnic identity and adjustment to the American environment. The two main facets of Americanization—adapting to democratic structures and adopting English—were not decisive in the American Lutheran controversy.

Chapter 3 surveys Lutheranism's early years in America, especially 1742–1820. At one limit, Henry Melchior Muhlenberg arrived in America in 1742 and was responsible for bringing stability and organization to Lutheranism. At the other limit, the General Synod was formed in 1820, the first year in which synods joined together to form a unified Lutheran denomination. The intervening years are important because Lutheranism was increasingly moving away from the confessional position (attempting to live out the Lutheran Confessions as founding statements of faith and life) promulgated by Muhlenberg and moving closer to the general civil religion prevalent in America, and especially the views of the American Protestants.

Chapter 4 examines the person and views of Samuel Schmucker, the leader of American Lutherans. Schmucker, through his role as seminary professor in Gettysburg, Pennsylvania, and as the author of many books, was the most influential Lutheran in the United States in the first half of the nineteenth century. What he promoted was a Lutheranism tailored to the American context.

Chapter 5 looks at several other leaders among the American Lutherans: Benjamin Kurtz, Simeon Harkey, and Samuel Sprecher. Although to a lesser extent than Schmucker, these men exercised influence on this movement in the second quarter of the nineteenth century. These three American-born leaders were products of American Lutheranism, so much so that when confronted by aspects of the Lutheran Confessions, for example, they favored their American experience over some of the teachings of those Confessions.

Chapter 6 traces a countermovement, a Lutheran confessional renewal that emerged in Germany around the middle of the nineteenth century. The movement advocated loyalty to the Lutheran Confessions. It was spread to America through immigrants such as Friedrich Conrad Dietrich Wyneken and William Julius Mann and through books.[1] Others, mainly the father-son duo of Charles Philip Krauth and Charles Porterfield Krauth, underwent a change of mind as a result of reading such books and the Lutheran Confessions. Charles Philip Krauth was Schmucker's colleague on the seminary faculty at Gettysburg; his son was a student of Schmucker's.

Chapter 7 documents the events that led up to the *Definite Platform*[2] and the controversy itself. Those who professed confessional loyalty challenged the American Lutherans and advocated that the church in America return to its confessional basis. The *Definite Platform* was the American Lutherans' attempt to make their position the official one of the General Synod and to propose disciplinary actions for any who did not agree. The ensuing controversy was a formal debate over Lutheranism's identity—indeed, its very soul. Only a few small synods adopted the document.

Chapter 8 follows the conflicts that continued after the *Definite Platform* controversy. The American Lutherans tried to maintain their hold on the General Synod, and the confessional party continued to protest the un-Lutheran character of the Synod. In 1864 a new seminary was established in Philadelphia, and in 1867 many pastors and congregations withdrew from the General Synod and formed the General Council.

The Conclusion summarizes Charles Porterfield Krauth's vision for a Lutheran church in America that would be truly Lutheran—that is, confessionally based. This is contrasted with twentieth-century proposals for ecumenical relations and social issues. Once again, the tension between Americanization and religious identity can be observed.

I chose the Lutheran tradition as a subject for five reasons. (1) Most of the Lutheran immigrants arrived after the American Protestant context had

1. For a discussion of the German confessional renewal, see Walter H. Conser, Jr., *Church and Confession: Conservative Theologians in Germany, England, and America, 1815–1866* (Macon, Ga.: Mercer Univ. Press, 1984), 54–96.

2. *Definite Platform: Doctrinal and Disciplinarian, for Evangelical Lutheran District Synods, Constructed in Accordance with the Principles of the General Synod* (Philadelphia: Miller & Burlock, 1855).

been firmly established, so that the contrast between the American Protestant ethos and Lutheranism is apparent. (2) The Lutherans' struggle over the issue of Americanization and religious identity took a public, theological form. (3) Several current issues within segments of this religious tradition can be shown readily to be echoes of this nineteenth-century struggle. (4) A void exists in the current literature regarding this struggle, its context, and its implications. (5) I have a longstanding interest in this segment of American church history. Because this book's burden is to unfold the first three aspects, a few comments may be in order regarding the remaining two.

Surveys of Lutheranism in America have tended to provide only a narration of the events surrounding the American Lutheran controversy without either situating that controversy in its American context or providing a thorough analysis of its implications. Abdel Ross Wentz's book *A Basic History of Lutheranism in America,* for example, devotes portions of three chapters—totaling less than thirty pages—to the controversy, but only three sentences seek to connect it to the issue of Americanization. The magisterial work edited by E. Clifford Nelson, *The Lutherans in North America,* covers the controversy in a portion of one chapter, noting that Lutherans were attracted to revivals, for example, but does not introduce the tension of Americanization until the years 1875–1900, far too late. The only book-length study of this controversy, *The Crisis in American Lutheran Theology,* by Vergilius Ferm, published over sixty years ago, focuses on the controversy surrounding the *Definite Platform,* a document that brought the issues raised by American Lutherans to the fore. Ferm's well-documented study, however, investigates neither the antecedents nor the consequences of this controversy. This book offers a more complete interpretation of the events and issues as a whole.[3]

This book, moreover, is the result of my interest in Samuel Schmucker, leader of the American Lutherans. My Master of Theology thesis dealt with aspects of his theology. This led me to delve into the American Lutheran controversy as the focus for a Ph.D dissertation.[4] Both investigations have led me to a conviction that the tension between context and

3. Abdel Ross Wentz, *A Basic History of Lutheranism in America* (Philadelphia: Fortress Press, 1964), 134; *The Lutherans in North America,* ed. E. Clifford Nelson, rev. ed. (Philadelphia: Fortress Press, 1980); Vergilius Ferm, *Crisis in American Lutheran Theology* (New York: Century Co., 1927).

4. David A. Gustafson, "The Theology of the Church in the Writings of Samuel Simon Schmucker" (Master's thesis, Luther Theological Seminary, St. Paul, Minn., 1973); and "The Americanization of the Lutheran Church: The Mid-Nineteenth Century Controversy between Confessional Lutherans and Proponents of an Americanized Lutheranism" (Ph.D. diss., Union Institute, Cincinnati, Ohio, 1990).

identity is a perennial one among religious groups that seek to maintain their heritage or religious identity.

A word of explanation is in order. The term "American Lutherans" denotes the party that advocated a distinctively American form of Lutheranism, as opposed to those who advocated loyalty to the Lutheran Confessions. "Lutheran church in America" denotes the Lutheran church that exists in America.

1

Religious Identity in Protestant America

*E*very religious group has certain identifying characteristics that define what it means to be a member of that group. These distinguishing marks differentiate one group from another, give significance and meaning to membership in the group, and thereby provide cohesiveness. What adherents believe, say, and do is who they are. Creeds, confessional statements, rituals, and ethnicity, therefore, are defining marks of religious groups.

The early Christian church defined its teachings and confronted heresies by developing credal statements. The creeds affirm the basic truths of the Christian faith. These statements belong to the church universal and have always had a prominent place in the church. The Apostles' Creed is the baptismal creed. The Nicene Creed is the creed recited at the mass. The last of the so-called ecumenical creeds, the Athanasian Creed, has been used at times as a doctrinal test. Creeds have traditionally defined what is Christian and what is not.

Confessional statements, in contrast, differentiate one religious group from another.[1] The Thirty-nine Articles define what it means to be an Episcopalian. Methodism adopted twenty-five of those articles as its doctrinal standard. The Reformed churches have the Second Helvetic Confession. Presbyterians and Congregationalists accepted the Westminster Confession of Faith. In the Lutheran church several documents have been given confessional status, the most important of which is the Augsburg Confession. Occasionally catechisms have served as confessional statements; two examples are the Heidelberg Catechism for the Reformed and Luther's two catechisms for Lutherans. Confessional statements reveal the

1. Texts of the various confessional statements can be found in Philip Schaff, *Creeds of Christendom, with a History and Critical Notes,* 3 vols. (New York: Harper & Brothers, 1877).

nature and character of a religious group and highlight the group's theological focus. Like creeds, confessional statements affirm truths, but they also condemn false teachings—setting limits as to what constitutes the substance of that faith.

Rituals are living expressions of those beliefs and, according to Louis Bouyer, are natural means by which humans discover God and solve the puzzle of their own existence.[2] The mass is a central ritual in Roman Catholicism. The rite of circumcision is a defining feature of Judaism. The silence of a Quaker meeting, even though seemingly without form, is nonetheless a ritual. Variations in ritual may convey certain emphases. Receiving Communion from fellow communicants in the pew conveys a different meaning than does receiving it from a priest or pastor at the altar rail. Believer's baptism conveys a set of beliefs different from those conveyed by infant baptism. Revival meetings communicate a particular view as to how one becomes a Christian. The use of a formal liturgy, such as the mass, demonstrates adherence to the church's tradition; informal worship orders challenge the value of tradition. Rituals communicate certain messages, and those messages are part of the essence of a religious group's identity.

Ethnicity, although not specifically religious, can be an identifying characteristic. For many, ethnic background and religious convictions are intertwined. Wade Clark Roof and William McKinney have demonstrated that certain nationalities tend to belong to certain religious groups.[3] Italians and Irish are most often Roman Catholics. Most Germans are Lutherans. Some groups include their nationality in their name—Greek Orthodox and Dutch Reformed, for example. Being a Jew has both ethnic and religious implications. When ethnic groups came to America, they brought their religious faith with them. It was often difficult to separate their cultural heritage from their religious faith. When immigrants' ethnic identity was threatened or compromised, their religious beliefs were also in danger. Often the language of the homeland was the language of religious ritual. If the language was no longer used in worship, many felt that their faith was in jeopardy.

Religious pluralism is an American phenomenon. European immigrants encountered many and varied religious groups in America instead of a state church to command their loyalty. America offered a variety of choices, and the immigrants were left to decide whether they should retain their

---

2. Louis Bouyer, *Rite and Man: Natural Sacredness and Christian Liturgy* (Notre Dame, Ind.: Univ. of Notre Dame Press, 1963), 3.

3. Wade Clark Roof and William McKinney, *American Mainline Religion: Its Changing Shape and Future* (New Brunswick, N.J.: Rutgers Univ. Press, 1987).

traditional faith, select from among the available options, or abandon religious faith altogether.

The plethora of denominations may have confused the immigrants, but another phenomenon was also present—a Protestantism-in-general that was doctrinally indifferent and presented itself as being thoroughly American. Religious pluralism was offensive to some, and they sought to eliminate it through a broad unity based on agreement on "essentials." Any theological differences between the denominations were minimized in order to achieve the much larger vision of America as a Protestant nation.

Will Herberg has highlighted one aspect of this problem. He maintains that, even though no "common denominator" religion exists in America, there is what he describes as "an organic structure of ideas, values, and beliefs that constitutes a faith common to Americans and genuinely operative in their lives, a faith that markedly influences, and is influenced by, the 'official' religions of American society."[4]

This common religion, however, met with resistance. Herberg describes three types of religious groups that opposed assimilation. The first type consists of churches of immigrant-ethnic background that cherish traditional creeds and confessional statements, including certain Lutheran and Reformed churches and some Roman Catholics. A second type includes religious groups that have an explicit consciousness or theological concern—orthodox, neoorthodox, liberal. A third type are the "religions of the disinherited"—holiness, pentecostal, and millenarian sects (91). Herberg sees this common religion as a challenge and threat to any religious groups that came to America. Encountering this common religion has often meant a loss of religious "substance" because, in America, religion and culture have been so thoroughly fused in the people's experience and tradition (126).

How does a religious group maintain its identity in America? John Murray Cuddihy has written a significant study on this question.[5] Maintaining a distinct identity in America is difficult, he believes, because when immigrants, with their religious traditions, arrive in America, "America teaches them to be discreet. It does so by means of its own unique creation: the denomination, or better, many denominations. This is known as 'pluralism.' America tames religious sects into denominations, bringing them into the respectable middle class. America also tames churches down into denominations" (7). Cuddihy claims that religious pluralism, which in turn

4. Will Herberg, *Protestant-Catholic-Jew: An Essay in American Religious Sociology* (Garden City, N.Y.: Doubleday & Co., 1955), 90.

5. John Murray Cuddihy, *No Offense: Civil Religion and Protestant Taste* (New York: Seabury Press, 1978).

is linked to the denominational structures, is de facto the "established" religion of America.

The result of this "taming" is what Martin Marty has called "a nation of behavers."[6] Religious groups should behave well. They should be tolerant of one another. They should be polite and not pushy. They should stay where they belong, in their own private sphere, and not impose their beliefs on others.

Cuddihy believes that the American denominational system forces religious groups to conform. He states that a denomination is neither a church, which is defined by an adherence to historic creeds and confessions and liturgical continuity, nor is it a sect, which is usually defined by a radical departure from those norms. A denomination is defined by its name rather than by any distinctive theological principle or liturgical forms. It differentiates between religious and secular interests, but it is basically a voluntary association where the individual is bound by personal commitment rather than adherence to any particular set of doctrines. In that connection, Marty notes that denominations are less focused on theology and belief than they are on intention and purpose.[7]

According to Cuddihy, the denomination is the last phase in the evolution of what he calls "a differentiating Protestantism." He equates this development with a form of secularization in which religious differences are minimal and have little or no meaning. The various religious groups seek to fit into the American culture that is generally Protestant in its outlook.

Certain groups do not fit this pattern. Cuddihy comments: "Jews, Catholics and, to some extent, Lutherans find that the cultural situation in America forces on them, *ab extra*, differentiations (like the separation of church and state, of ethnicity and religion, etc.) that they are unprepared for."[8] As far as Cuddihy is concerned, the beginning of the end of any religious group occurs when it allows itself to become another of the many denominations in America. To become a denomination is to lose one's distinctiveness.

The development of denominationalism and the growth of the denominations is the key to identifying what is called American Protestantism. In spite of their diversity, the denominations found that they had more similarities than differences, and what differences they had were regarded as being of little consequence. For all practical purposes, differences played no role in the life of the churches. Many regarded it sufficient to be a Protestant. The dominance of Protestantism confronted every religious

6. Martin E. Marty, *A Nation of Behavers* (Chicago: Univ. of Chicago Press, 1976).
7. Ibid., 5.
8. Cuddihy, *No Offense*, 18.

group that came to America. Every group that cared about its identity and wanted to maintain that identity was forced to struggle with the question of assimilation.

Cuddihy's criticisms and concerns deserve consideration. When confronted by the presence of denominational American Protestantism, a group's religious identity can be lost. Loss of certain identifying traits is inevitable. For instance, after the first generation, a group's native language begins to disappear. Certain ethnic customs may no longer be as important as they once were. The crucial question is, What identifying marks must be maintained?

The theological identity and liturgical substance of any religious group are of primary importance. Roman Catholics can give up Latin in the mass, but the mass itself must be preserved. Lutherans can give up their respective languages but cannot give up their theological concerns—such as justification—without losing the essence of what it means to be a Lutheran. A distinction must be made between essentials and nonessentials, and the essentials must be clearly defined. One thing is certain: when a group's origins are forgotten, its ritual abandoned, and its theological foundations ignored, all that is left is the name.

Protestantism and America

Protestantism has played a significant role in America since the coming of the first settlers from Europe. Jamestown was founded by those who belonged to the Anglican Church, the Established Church of England. The Pilgrims who came over on the *Mayflower* were Separatists who had broken with the Established Church. Massachusetts Bay was settled by Puritans, who were also Separatists. They had left the Old World, which they believed was corrupt and beyond redemption. The aim of what they called their "errand into the wilderness" was to establish a true church and society for the Elect, to build a "city set on a hill." The early settlement of America was seen as a religious pilgrimage.

The theocracy in Massachusetts Bay was an attempt to make this dream a reality. The dream was never realized because many disagreed with the rigid structures and strict rules of that colony. Anne Hutchinson and Roger Williams are two well-known seventeenth-century dissenters. Religious diversity was a feature of American life early on. As time passed, other dissenting groups, including Methodists and Anabaptists, came to America to escape persecution and to practice their faith freely. Their arrival, along with theological disputes among the existing groups, created even more diversity.

In spite of this diversity, the various religious groups shared certain common elements. Foremost was their Protestant heritage. Winthrop Hudson says that the best way to describe the American colonies is that they were "English and Protestant." The vast majority of the colonists were Protestants. For example, in 1775, 98.4 percent of the congregations in the colonies were Protestant.[9]

Unifying forces among the separate groups included religious pamphlets and devotional materials. Other common characteristics were present. According to Jerald Brauer, Protestantism in America can be characterized by a full, free experimentation and an enduring biblicism.[10] American Protestants wanted a fuller manifestation of God's will, and they would experiment with revivals or any other means to achieve that end. They felt free to try anything that might bring them closer to God and to better know God's will. They also made a sustained effort to avoid going beyond the Bible to discover the truth. The slogan "The Bible and only the Bible" reflected a deep-seated American Protestant belief that the Bible was the source of all truth and contained all the answers to the questions of human existence. Brauer maintains that these characteristics distinguish American Protestant groups from their European counterparts and are the keys to understanding Protestantism's role in American history and religious life.

The Protestant population believed America to be the fulfillment of the millennial hope. The millennial vision was of Americans as a chosen people with a mission ultimately to redeem the world. This vision was a predominant, widely advocated concept in American thought. Protestantism, it was believed, was the means by which the millennium would come. Ernest Tuveson argues that the concept of the millennium is a key to understanding the American experience.[11] He describes two views of the millennial mission. On the one hand, some expected that the millennium would be peaceful, working a transformation in minds. They believed that their mission was to expand and perfect society and to eliminate the vestiges of old evils. American energy was to be used benevolently to evangelize the world. On the other hand, others felt that the millennium meant destruction,

9. Winthrop S. Hudson, *American Protestantism* (Chicago: Univ. of Chicago Press, 1961), 4.
10. Jerald C. Brauer, *Protestantism in America* (Philadelphia: Westminster Press, 1953), 7.
11. Ernest Lee Tuveson, *Redeemer Nation: The Idea of America's Millennial Role* (Chicago: Univ. of Chicago Press, 1968), 159. Other important works on this subject are Ernest R. Sandeen, *The Roots of Fundamentalism: British and American Millennarianism, 1800–1930* (Chicago: Univ. of Chicago Press, 1970) and J. F. Maclear, "The Republic and the Millennium" in Elwyn A. Smith, ed., *The Religion of the Republic* (Philadelphia: Fortress Press, 1971).

in which the people would have to participate. The advocates of a destructive and violent millennium questioned whether the chosen nation could avoid such catastrophic occurrences. Tuveson describes the American vision: "What nation is blessed with such experimental knowledge of free institutions, with such facilities and resources of communication, unobstructed by so few obstacles as our own? There is not a nation upon earth which, in fifty years, can by all possible reformation place itself in circumstances so favorable as our own for the free unembarrassed application of physical effort and pecuniary and moral power to evangelize the world."[12]

Sharing this millennial vision, the various Protestant groups worked together to achieve their goal. Protestant denominations maintained their own identities and performed their own special works, but they cooperated in an attempt to achieve a moral society, which they believed to be the common national goal. Lefferts A. Loetscher states that religious liberty opened the way for mutual toleration among the denominations and even occasioned proposals for some loose types of Christian unity during the first half of the nineteenth century.[13]

Support for public schools, Sabbath observance, and temperance are examples of cooperative Protestant efforts. In the words of Robert Handy, "The evangelical vision of Christian civilization was of a free, literate, industrious, honest, law-abiding, religious population."[14] Protestants supported public schools because they believed them to be a means to accomplish the moral and spiritual instruction of children—teaching good citizenship and promoting literacy. Josiah Strong (1847–1918), secretary of the Evangelical Alliance, advocated the use of public schools to salvage children who had not received any direct religious influence at home or through Sunday school. Strong was active toward the end of the nineteenth century, but the views he expressed had been felt by many for a long time.

Noah Webster's dictionary and McGuffey's *Reader* were instruments employed in this effort. The dictionary promoted unity of language while

12. Tuveson, *Redeemer Nation,* 170.

13. Lefferts A. Loetscher, "The Problem of Christian Unity in Early Nineteenth-Century America," *Church History* 32 (March 1963). Loetscher cites three types of unity: (1) federative action by ecclesiastical bodies; (2) organic union—almost always on the basis of minimal tenets of the initiating group; and (3) cooperation by individual Christians in nonecclesiastical organizations.

14. Robert T. Handy, *A Christian America* (New York: Oxford Univ. Press, 1971), 48. For an excellent discussion of the role of the public or common school in this effort, see Robert Michaelsen, "Is the Public School Religious or Secular?" in Smith, *The Religion of the Republic.* Michaelsen points out that in regard to the public schools, to desectarianize was not to dereligionize. He notes that Bible reading and hymn singing were common practices employed in the public schools to help achieve a common morality.

the *Reader* inculcated a common moral background.[15] McGuffey's *Reader*, written by William H. McGuffey (1800–73), was so popular that by the end of the nineteenth century over 120 million copies were in circulation and were helping shape the American mind.[16] Horace Mann (1796–1859), secretary of the Massachusetts Board of Education and known for his views regarding educational reform, was a strong advocate of the public school. He called education the "great equalizer of the conditions of men"[17] and viewed the public school as a means to indoctrinate Americans in the civic religion. Mann had been brought up in strict New England Calvinist orthodoxy, but he rebelled against his religious background and ended up a liberal Unitarian. Mann looked back on his Christian upbringing as a blight on his life, a fact that may explain his strong views in favor of public schools.[18] Parochial schools did exist, but most native-born Americans hoped that these institutions would eventually disappear and that "American" education would overcome both the "immigrant problem" and Roman Catholicism.[19]

Protestants knew they had a great mission to fulfill in America, and they poured their energy and resources into the effort. The great cause was to Americanize the immigrant and every means was used to accomplish that end. America must be Christian and that meant being Protestant. The goal seemed attainable; but then came the great influx of Roman Catholics, immigrants who posed a threat to the Protestant empire.

Characteristics of American Protestantism

Although the various Protestant denominations remained organizationally separate, the differences that once distinguished them had, by and large, disappeared. One could speak of Congregationalists, Presbyterians, and Methodists, but in fact all these shared many characteristics in common. Several characteristics of this generic Protestantism can be identified. The

15. Robert A. Carlson, *The Americanization Syndrome: A Quest for Conformity* (London: Croom Helm, 1987), 32–33. For a work on the impact of McGuffey's *Reader* see John H. Westerhoff, *McGuffey and His Reader: Piety, Morality, and Education in Nineteenth Century America* (Nashville: Abingdon, 1977).

16. Sydney E. Ahlstrom, *A Religious History of the American People* (New Haven: Yale Univ. Press, 1972), 642.

17. Carlson, *Americanization Syndrome*, 42.

18. Ahlstrom, *Religious History*, 412.

19. Many immigrants sent their children to what were called "common schools" but resisted, as much as possible, some of the Americanizing influences. One study on this subject is James S. Hamre, "Norwegian Immigrants Respond to the Common School: A Case Study of American Values and the Lutheran Tradition," *Church History* 50 (Sept. 1981).

following are the most important, all of which were factors in the American Lutheran controversy.

The increase in Roman Catholic immigration threatened the Protestant vision of America and caused much concern among the native-born Protestants. They feared that anti-Protestant, anti-republican, and un-American ideas would infiltrate the nation, bringing barbarism with them. It is difficult to overestimate the anti-Catholic feelings among what was, at that time, still a Protestant majority.[20] What Martin Marty has called the "Righteous Empire"[21] was endangered by the vast numbers of Catholic immigrants reaching America's shores. Rather than attempt to convert the Catholic immigrant, Protestants pushed for immigration laws that would limit the number of Catholics who could come to America.

The number of Roman Catholics who made the trip across the Atlantic rose sharply in the first half of the nineteenth century. From 1800 to 1850, the Roman Catholic population in America swelled from 40,000 to 1,606,000.[22] The First Plenary Council, held in Baltimore in 1829, demonstrated that Roman Catholics were going to be a permanent fixture in America. This meeting of bishops and other religious superiors gave rise to intense anti-Catholic feeling. In 1844 the Methodist bishops stated their conviction that "Romanism is now laboring, not only to recover what it lost of its former supremacy in the Reformation, but also to assert and establish its monstrous pretensions in countries never subject either to its civil or ecclesiastical authority."[23] It was believed that, given a chance, the Roman Catholic Church would wrest control from the Protestant empire, a possibility that should be prevented at all costs.

Many anti-Catholic writings came out of the period from 1830 to 1860. Lyman Beecher, a prominent Congregational minister, preached a series of sermons that resulted in an attack on and subsequent burning of the Ursuline convent in Charlestown, Massachusetts, in 1834. (There is some evidence that he may have been involved in the attack.) In a book published in 1835 entitled *A Plea for the West,* Beecher argued that the Ohio Valley, rapidly filling with immigrants, was a crucial area of competition between Protestant republicanism and Roman Catholic immigrant despotism.[24]

---

20. For a full account of the Protestant reaction see Roy Allen Billington, *The Protestant Crusade 1800–1860: A Study of the Origins of American Nativism* (New York: Rinehart & Co., 1938). For other literature on nativism, see Gerald Grob, ed. *Anti-Catholicism in America 1841–1851: Three Sermons* (New York: Arno Press, 1977); John J. Kane, *Catholic–Protestant Conflicts in America* (Chicago: Regenery, 1955); and Bertrand M. Tipple, *Alien Rome* (Washington, D.C.: Protestant Guards, 1924).
    21. Martin Marty, *Righteous Empire* (New York: Dial Press, 1970).
    22. Ibid., 127–28.
    23. Cited in ibid., 129.
    24. Philip Gleason, "American Identity and Americanization," in Stephen Thernstrom, ed., *Harvard Encyclopedia of American Ethnic Groups* (Cambridge, Mass.: Belknap Press of Harvard Univ. Press, 1980), 35.

Another book published the same year as Beecher's, entitled *A History of the Holy Catholic Inquisition,* used the Inquisition to show American Protestants what Roman Catholicism had done and to warn them to beware lest the same thing happen in America. Published anonymously, it was a compilation from several sources. In an introduction to the work the Rev. Cyrus Mason, pastor of Cedar Street Church in New York, stated: "This is the capital feature of the Romish Church: she is bound in conscience, not only to establish herself, but also, (according to her ability and opportunity,) to drive every other mode of faith from the earth."[25] The introduction accused Roman Catholics of forming military companies and spoke of foreign priests and Jesuits who were infiltrating the country. The Roman church's goal was clear: it was engaged in a plot to take over America.

Occasionally a more moderate voice emerged. Henry Wise, an Episcopal layman, calculated that Roman Catholics were outnumbered twenty-one to one; therefore, there was no reason for concern on the part of Protestants. In 1855 he asked, "Now what has such a *majority* of numbers . . . to fear from such *minorities* of Catholics?"[26] But his arguments proved to be of no avail. The most radical Protestants were convinced that there was a Jesuit behind every bush, seeking to promote Popery; and even many moderates were fearful and watchful of the Roman threat. Roman Catholic immigrants were not as welcome as others because they did not fit into the American (Protestant) scheme and were not believed to share the vision of the Protestant majority.

American Protestantism in the nineteenth century was pervaded by belief in the right of individual or private judgment in matters relating to the Bible and doctrines. Those who advocated this position claimed the Reformation as their source; however, the concept, as it appeared in America, probably stemmed more from the influence of pietism and the Enlightenment. Pietism stressed the individual's religious feelings, while the Enlightenment glorified the individual's exercise of human reason. Thus, evangelicals and deists, though miles apart on many issues, shared the common denominator of emphasizing the rights of the individual and subjective judgment in the determination of truth.

The right of individual or private judgment meant that persons could read and interpret the Bible and decide matters of doctrine for themselves. Church traditions could inform, but they were not determinative. Each individual could judge what was true. This resulted in a broad spectrum

---

25. *A History of the Holy Catholic Inquisition* (Philadelphia: Henry Perkins, 1835), vi–vii.

26. Cited in Marty, *Righteous Empire,* 129.

of beliefs—from Baptists to deists—each claiming legitimacy on the basis of private judgment.

Revivals, or, as they were called, the "New Measures," were an integral part of American Protestantism in the mid-nineteenth century. The phenomenon crossed denominational lines. The emphasis was on a concrete personal conversion experience, and the revival was the means employed to bring about that experience. Revival preaching was highly emotional, aimed at reaching the lost sinner. People were made to feel guilty over their sins, which rendered them lost. Those who were most distressed over their spiritual condition occupied the "anxious bench." The purpose of the revival was to bring people to the point where they would come forward and accept Jesus.

Revivals had been a part of American religious life from the beginning.[27] Their influence extended into political, economic, and sociological realms. Timothy L. Smith has documented revivalism's relationship to social concerns and social reform.[28] In a recent study of revivalism, George M. Thomas argues that revivalism was an expression of a natural order that was centered around the individual and that also acted as a framework for a national morality that would transform American civilization.[29] Converted souls would lead to a renewed America.

Revivals were not without critics. Horace Bushnell (1802–76), a noted Congregational minister, attacked the emotionalism associated with revivals. In his book *Christian Nurture,* Bushnell advocated nurture through education as an alternative to revivals.[30] The most famous assault on revivals came from John Williamson Nevin (1803–86), Philip Schaff's colleague at the German Reformed seminary in Mercersburg, Pennsylvania. In his book *The Anxious Bench,* Nevin claimed that the use of the "anxious bench" produced only temporary emotional feelings instead of lasting regeneration.[31] Revivals had no long-term value. Nevin equated the "anxious bench" with Roman Catholic "quackery" such as pilgrimages. Such practices had nothing to do with repentance and faith. Nevin argued that the teaching ministry, doctrinal preaching, pastoral instruction and visitation—the "system of the catechism"—advanced the kingdom of God better than revivals did.

The view of the sacraments that was prominent in the majority of American Protestant groups was that of the Swiss reformer Ulrich Zwingli

---

27. For a survey of revivals in American religion, see William G. McLoughlin, *Revivals, Awakenings and Reform* (Chicago: Univ. of Chicago Press, 1978).

28. Timothy L. Smith, *Revivals and Social Reform* (Nashville; Abingdon, 1957).

29. George M. Thomas, *Revivalism and Culture Change* (Chicago: University of Chicago Press, 1989).

30. Horace Bushnell, *Christian Nurture* (Hartford, Conn., 1847).

31. John Williamson Nevin, *The Anxious Bench* (Chambersburg, Pa., 1843).

(1484–1531), Luther's opponent at the Marburg Colloquy.[32] Zwingli held that baptism was only symbolic and did not bring about spiritual regeneration. Regarding the Lord's Supper, he believed that the bread and wine were symbols of the body and blood of Christ. Sacraments were frequently referred to as ordinances. Zwingli stressed the commandment and rejected any concept of mystery. He held that ordinances were not unique vehicles of the Spirit's work, and he rejected any authority of the clergy to impart absolution.

Zwingli's views were not accepted by Luther or Calvin, and Lutherans and Reformed in Europe continued to follow the lead of their respective reformers. In America, however, Zwingli's views regarding sacraments gradually came to be adopted. Most of the groups that had been Calvinist became Zwinglian; yet they still thought of themselves as being loyal to Calvin and the Reformed tradition as expressed in the Heidelberg Catechism and the Second Helvetic Confession.

One example of this development is instructive. When Nevin published his book *The Mystical Presence: A Vindication of the Reformed or Calvinistic Doctrine of the Holy Eucharist* in 1846, he argued for a "spiritual real presence" of the body and blood of Christ in the Lord's Supper. In response, Dr. Joseph Berg, pastor of Race Street Church in Philadelphia, accused Nevin of heresy.[33] Eventually, many of the Reformed theologians and the American Lutherans were drawn into this debate. The vast majority of them sided with Berg.

The details of this debate are similar to the details of the debate that later developed between the American Lutherans and their confessional opponents. What is noteworthy is Nevin's observation that American Protestantism had defected from the Reformation position, exemplified by Luther and Calvin, to the views of Zwingli. As a result of that development, Nevin saw no differences between the Reformed and the Baptists.

Lutherans and American Protestantism

Lutheranism in mid-nineteenth-century America was confronted with significant choices. Would Lutheranism continue to speak in its traditional forms and adhere to its confessional understanding, or would it adopt some of the devices of the prevailing Protestantism? This was precisely the issue in the American Lutheran controversy. Members of the newly emerging

32. The Marburg Colloquy, held in 1529, failed to reach an agreement on the real presence of the body and blood of Christ in the Lord's Supper.

33. James H. Nichols, *Romanticism in American Theology: Nevin and Schaff at Mercersburg* (Chicago: Univ. of Chicago Press, 1961), 86.

confessional party, who wanted Lutheranism to witness on its own terms in America, challenged the American Lutherans, who thought that Lutheranism could retain its heritage while speaking and believing like its Protestant neighbors.

The American Lutherans shared the anti-Catholic sentiments that were prominent in American Protestantism, and this bias affected their view of Lutheranism. They felt the Lutheran reformers had not carried the Reformation far enough. The doctrines of baptismal regeneration, priestly absolution, and the real presence of the body and blood of Christ in the Eucharist, along with the liturgical structures, were evidences of "Romish corruptions." The American Lutherans felt that such "errors" needed to be expunged. The confessional party, on the other hand, argued that such teachings showed that Lutheranism did not reject the catholic tradition and that those teachings were essential to Lutheranism's identity.

In rejecting certain teachings in the Augsburg Confession, the American Lutherans argued for individual or private judgment. They argued that there were certain "essential" doctrines that were accepted by all Christians. "Nonessential" doctrines were those over which Christians had disputes. In the matter of nonessential doctrines the individual was free to decide. The American Lutherans regarded doctrines, to use George Lindbeck's categories, as "experimental-expressionist,"[34] meaning that doctrines are derived mainly from individual subjective judgments and experiences.

The confessional party countered by stating that doctrines contained in the Bible and confessed by Christians from the beginning are objective truths to be believed by all. Subjective judgment cannot supersede what the Bible and the tradition (in this case the Augsburg Confession) confess to be true. The statements contained in the Augsburg Confession are objective truths because they are in accord with the Bible and the tradition. During the course of the American Lutheran controversy, the confessional party argued that the entire Augsburg Confession was to be accepted, and that this Confession defined the nature and substance of Lutheranism's identity. The confessional party regarded doctrines, again using Lindbeck's categories, as "dogmatic-propositional"—perspectives unique to the religious community that must be accepted.

The leaders of the American Lutheran party were advocates of revivals. Their arguments for such a practice echoed those of revivalism's American Protestant defenders. This was a heated issue between the American Lutherans and their confessional opponents, whose objections to revivals would mirror those of Nevin. The confessional party advocated catechetical

---

34. George A. Lindbeck, *The Nature of Doctrine: Theology in a Postliberal Age* (Philadelphia: Westminster Press, 1984).

instruction as the means to nurture faith and regarded revivals as un-Lutheran and harmful to people's spiritual welfare. They wanted to maintain Lutheranism's traditional identity as expressed in its confessional statements and liturgical forms rather than resorting to the techniques employed at revivals. These Lutherans felt that Lutheranism could exist in America without succumbing to these devices that were so prevalent in American Protestantism.

Regarding the sacraments, the American Lutherans had abandoned Luther altogether, calling Luther's and the Lutheran Confessions' views of the sacraments "superstition." Baptismal regeneration, absolution, and the real presence of the body and blood of Christ in the Lord's Supper were all rejected. The American Lutherans had accepted the views prevalent in American Protestantism, which advocated a Zwinglian, symbolic view of sacraments, as normative. The sacraments are of the essence of the church. It is no accident, therefore, that much of the debate in the American Lutheran controversy centered around them. The *Definite Platform* was an all-out attack on Lutheran sacramental theology. The sacraments were a dividing line between Lutherans and American Protestants. The *Definite Platform* sought to remove that barrier. The confessional party responded negatively to the *Platform's* proposals because they knew that a significant part of Lutheranism's identity was at stake. If the battle over the sacraments was lost, a key component of Lutheranism's identity would be lost.

Historian Jaroslav Pelikan states that Lutheranism's identity has traditionally been seen in terms of a particular theological stance, as expressed in the Lutheran Confessions, as contained in the *Book of Concord*. He cites Lutheranism's stress on "confessional subscription" and its "scrupulous adherence" to those confessions.[35] What Lutheranism is, then, is defined by what Lutheranism believes and confesses to be true regarding the gospel of Jesus Christ. At stake in the American Lutheran controversy was Lutheran identity, and the debates in that controversy centered around whether Lutheranism should retain its identity on American soil or whether it should become another expression of American Protestantism.

---

35. Jaroslav Pelikan, *Christian Doctrine and Modern Culture (since 1700)*, vol. 5, *The Christian Tradition* (Chicago: Univ. of Chicago Press, 1989), 31, 271.

2

The Process of Americanization

What, precisely, is Americanization? Among the many definitions of the term, two are elemental: instructing immigrants in English, U.S. history, government, and culture; and causing persons to acquire or conform to American characteristics or traits. The first definition refers to instruction or knowledge; the second emphasizes the actual assimilation of outsiders into American life. Just as religious identity is more than knowledge or awareness of a group's beliefs, Americanization means identification with American values. Assimilation, according to historian George Edward Hartman, was believed to be desirable by both the immigrants and longtime residents. It involved not only practical matters such as learning the language, but also capturing new ideals and gaining a fresh outlook on life from an American point of view. If this assimilation was successful, the nation would be unified and the continued existence of the American way of life would be assured.[1]

In the mid-nineteenth century, thousands of people, many of them Lutherans, left their homeland in Europe and came to America. James Hennesy, in his informative work *American Catholics,* states: "American Catholicism has European origins. But it also has a peculiarly American history, continuously in contact with the ideas of democracy, due process of law, representative government, religious pluralism, activism, pragmatism, and all the characteristics of this land, which for so many years knew limitless frontiers, rapidly growing industry, and an aggressive, adventurous population."[2] This statement could also apply to Lutherans. Both Roman Catholics and Lutherans immigrated to America; both brought with

---

1. George Edward Hartman, *The Movement to Americanize the Immigrant* (New York: AMS Press, 1967). This study deals mainly with a later period (post–World War I), but it demonstrates there was a consistency in the goals of the Americanization movement.
2. James Hennesy, *American Catholics: A History of the Roman Catholic Community in the United States* (New York: Oxford Univ. Press, 1981), 4.

them a particular theological and liturgical tradition; both had to deal with the issue of Americanization.

Assimilation, however, has many implications. Once the immigrants arrived in America, how much of their cultural and religious heritage could and should they retain? Could one be an American and not learn the English language? Could a Roman Catholic be a good American and still be obedient to the pope? Could immigrants come to America and still retain customs from the culture of their native land? How many "American traits" was one required to have to be considered American? America has always demanded a certain degree of accommodation from immigrants. The extent of that accommodation is the main issue involved in Americanization.

Theories of Americanization

Several studies have focused on the particularities of the process of Americanization. In 1920 sociologist Isaac Berkson published a major study in which he isolated five theories of Americanization.[3]

Berkson believes America is defined by its commitment to democracy. Democracy, he states, is not to be confused with egalitarianism, or laissez faire, or individualism. Berkson cites John Dewey's statement: "What the modern development has told us of the way of life—our new experiences, knowledges, and ideas unified into a principle—that is democracy" (14). Dewey felt that, through the exercise of democratic ideals, humanity could reach its full potential.

According to Berkson, self-determination is the quintessence of democracy. The ultimate judgment of good and final power over one's own fate rests with the individual. Freedom of options is one definition of democracy, and Berkson uses the word "diversity" to describe this freedom. The individual, however, is not an isolated entity. Interdependence of persons is a necessity; with that interdependence, each person must respect the personalities of others. The final goal of interdependence is the unification of the individual with the world. Berkson says: "Where there is a progressive consideration of uniqueness, a multiplication of diverse possibilities, a growing consciousness of man's interdependence—there does democracy exist" (39). Democracy should not resort to coercion for the sake of order, but Berkson speaks of "social control" in a free state, which is exercised through education, a free press, and free speech (55).

3. Isaac B. Berkson, *Theories of Americanization: A Critical Study* (New York: Teacher's College, Columbia Univ., 1920).

For Berkson, democracy is the measuring-rod for any concept of Americanization. He judges five of the theories he discusses on the basis of that criterion.

The first is simply called the *Americanization* theory, defined as follows:

> The main point is that all newcomers from foreign lands must as quickly as possible divest themselves of their old characteristics, and through intermarriage and complete taking on of the language, customs, hopes, aspirations of the American type, obliterate all ethnic distinctions. They must utterly forget the land of their birth and completely lose from their memory all recollection of its traditions in a single-minded adherence to American life in all its aspects. (55)

Berkson judges this particular scheme as inconsistent with the spirit of democracy. The gift of freedom would be taken away. In addition, the immigrants' past, which is a part of their very being, would have to undergo severe alteration, if not total destruction. Thus Berkson searches for other theories regarding Americanization.

The second theory is called the *Likemindedness* theory. Here the accent is on action in affairs for the common good. Likemindedness is needed to safeguard the existence of the state. Berkson sees problems with this theory because it does not consider the personality of the immigrant and has no concrete concept of what *like* means (65). "Men are thought of as being alike when they look alike, when they dress alike, when they speak the same language, and the external similarities seem to be considered sufficient for bringing about an inner national unity. . . . If all Americans could be made to seem alike, unity would be assured. Similarity will bring about unity somehow, even if in itself it is not unity" (66).

Likemindedness is equated with conformity, which, in terms of society, would lead to standardization.

Berkson is critical of this theory: "The most stupid thing in the 'Americanization' program is the failure to recognize that the morality, folkways, ideas, and aspirations of the immigrant groups could be utilized for the development of true Americans out of immigrants" (68). Instead of attempting to break down the various traits such as language, custom, and spiritual allegiances, it would be far better to allow them to make their contributions to American life. The immigrants must be made to feel American without having to sacrifice the very things that give them their identity. A diversified culture is enriched by the traditions of many people.

A third approach, the *Melting Pot* theory, encourages the severing of past loyalties but welcomes the contributions of the various nationalities. Americanization is not a static set of standards to which everyone must conform but a process that is developing. This theory is less certain that the "typical American" has already evolved. It also does not assume that the acquisition of a new culture is dependent on the destruction of the old.

Pride in one's past contributes to self-respect. The Melting Pot theory is superior to the Likemindedness theory in that it fulfills the democratic ideal, but it is finally inadequate in that, ultimately, each group must give up its identity entirely to become accepted in the life of America. Both the Likemindedness theory and the Melting Pot theory deprive immigrant groups of the right to maintain their heritage.

The fourth theory, which Berkson terms the *Federation of Nationalities* theory, makes the ethnic group a prominent entity that asserts its influence on American life. The Federation of Nationalities theory is based on the assumption that race is ineradicable and the central fact in the person's life. Under this theory, cultures are cooperating but distinct. Selfhood is ancestrally determined. The ethnic background of a person is integrally connected with that person's identity.

Berkson judges this theory to be inadequate because it fails to take into consideration other factors such as environment and the influence of various social institutions. This theory may also lead to a doctrine of ethnic pre-destination. For example, Berkson discusses the stereotype of the so-called Jewish "genius," in which it is assumed that most Jews possess high intelligence as a genetic trait (87). In order for the Federation of Nationalities theory to succeed, there would have to be a complete separation of the nationalities. Clearly this would be impossible in America; ethnic communities, even at this early date, were no longer distinct and isolated.

Berkson favors what he calls the *Community* theory. This approach insists on the value of the ethnic group as a permanent aspect of American life and recognizes the group's aesthetic, cultural, and religious inheritance and national consciousness as the basic factors that contribute to its identity.

The Community theory makes culture the reason for the preservation of the life of the group. It gives the community options in terms of where it should move, how far it should influence its members, how isolated or open it should be. The Community theory makes full provision for the American way of life while allowing the ethnic tradition to contribute its finer points to America. For Berkson, the Community theory maintains a proper balance between preservation of ethnic identity and adjustment to the American scene. To maintain that balance is a challenge to every group of immigrants that makes America its home.

Berkson's study, even though it was done many years ago, is an important look at the various forms Americanization can take. His Community theory is an ideal that he hopes might be achieved in America. Particular cultures and religious groups, he suggests, might live together and yet retain their identity, an identity that would be a contribution to America as a whole. This issue is of particular interest to Berkson because of his concern for the preservation of Jewish religion and culture. That same concern, however, can and should be shared by any group that has a particular identity.

Since Berkson's study, others have raised additional questions regarding the American experience. Some recent studies have asked whether the concept of ethnicity should include racial as well as national differences. Many blacks believe race is a separate issue. They believe that blacks are not imitating various ethnic groups in being accommodated, acculturated, and assimilated into American society.[4] By contrast, they assert that they want to continue to maintain their own autonomy and uniqueness in America.

Another sociologist, Milton M. Gordon, writing fifty years after Berkson, discusses other aspects of Americanization. He contends that three ideologies have competed for attention with regard to assimilation: Anglo-conformity, the melting pot, and cultural pluralism.[5] Anglo-conformity means maintaining English institutions (as modified by the American Revolution), speaking the English language, and following English cultural patterns. Anglo-conformity has been the most prevalent ideology employed to achieve assimilation in America.

The melting pot, in contrast, would bring into existence a new blend, culturally and biologically. The open-door policy of the first three-quarters of the nineteenth century was an expression of faith in the effectiveness of the American melting-pot concept. Gordon cites intermarriage between persons of various ethnic and religious groups as one of the results and a testimony to the effectiveness of the melting pot. These intermarriages took the process of assimilation one more step and were the basis for what was called the "triple-melting-pot thesis"—immigration, acculturation, intermarriage. This was the basic thesis adopted by Will Herberg in his study *Protestant-Catholic-Jew.*

Cultural pluralism, the third concept of assimilation described by Gordon, is defined as a consciousness of the value of the immigrants' culture. This ideology prefers to speak of "integration" of immigrants rather than "assimilation." One becomes a part of the American culture without having to reject one's past. This is most desirable, according to Gordon, and the challenge in America has been and always will be that of reducing ethnic

---

4. For an interesting collection of essays that deal with this issue see Richard J. Meister, ed., *Race and Ethnicity in Modern America* (Lexington, Mass.: D. C. Heath & Co., 1974).

5. Milton M. Gordon, "Assimilation in America: Theory and Reality," in Meister, ed., *Race and Ethnicity*, 85.

discrimination and prejudice, and allowing people to choose how much they stay within or move outside their ethnic boundaries.[6]

Berkson and Gordon suggest the various forms the complex phenomenon of Americanization can take—integration, assimilation, acculturation, and Anglicization, to name only a few. In addition, Americanization may have racial overtones. While Berkson's and Gordon's studies are mainly sociological, with the religious aspect constituting one part of the total picture, religious implications have always been a part of the Americanization issue.

Religious Implications of Americanization

From the beginning, America was an experiment in which people of many races, religions, nationalities, political ideologies, and economic levels came by general invitation from around the world to create a new nation. One of the marks of this experiment was religious freedom. Sidney Mead has stated: "The significance of religious freedom and the relationship between Christianity and American democracy are basic to the interpretation of religious developments in America."[7] Early in the American experiment, tension emerged between freedom and diversity on one hand and conformity on the other.

Those who supported conformity as a method of Americanization denigrated the European state church as well as other European institutions. Sociologically, this conformity stressed the middle class; theologically, it supported a supradenominational Protestantism. This Protestantism was characterized by lay involvement in the governing of the church, and its polity was related to representative government in the civic sphere. Even Methodists and Episcopalians, who had an episcopal form of government, encouraged and allowed for lay representation. Protestantism was also characterized by informality in worship and vehement anti-Catholicism.[8]

The Puritans attempted to establish a rigid system to which everyone would conform, but this effort quickly failed. Scholars disagree as to the reason for this failure. Robert Carlson states that the failure may be evidence that pluralism was a part of American life virtually from the beginning.[9] Frederick Sontag and John Roth, on the other hand, contend that pluralism

---

6. Ibid., 95.

7. Sidney E. Mead, *The Lively Experiment: The Shaping of Christianity in America* (New York: Harper & Row, 1963), xii. See also Sidney E. Mead, *The Nation with the Soul of a Church* (New York: Harper & Row, 1975). This study deals with the tensions between the theology of the republic and that which is professed by the majority of the denominations.

8. Robert A. Carlson, *The Americanization Syndrome: A Quest for Conformity* (London: Croom Helm, 1987), 6.

9. Ibid., 22.

was an evolutionary process that moved purely religious communities toward more secular forms.[10]

The secular model of Americanization is clearly visible in the views of Benjamin Franklin. Franklin advocated that a harmonious society required homogeneity to achieve order and to prosper. With regard to religion, while Franklin believed that others should be allowed to adhere to their individual faith, he preferred a generalized religion that gave the state control and encouraged conformity. In this respect, Franklin was influenced by the Enlightenment, a movement that viewed reason as the main source in determining truth. The Enlightenment challenged traditional doctrines such as the divinity of Christ and the Trinity; it was also a powerful force against the doctrinal particularities of any religious group. Franklin gave monetary contributions to several sectarian groups because he felt that religion—any religion—contributed to order and morality in society. But he cared nothing for particular doctrinal views and deplored doctrinal differences between the various religious groups.

Franklin established charity schools for the German immigrants who were coming into Pennsylvania. The purpose of these schools was to rid the immigrants of their cultural heritage, because Franklin feared the Germans would take over the colony. Christopher Saur, a publisher who was respected in the German community, attacked the motives of such schools. They were terminated in 1763.[11] Another of Franklin's critics was Benjamin Rush, fellow member of the Continental Congress, who chided Franklin ("otherwise an astute statesman and philosopher") for allowing his "Yankee principles" to unite him with the anti-German "wiseacres of the time."[12]

The Revolutionary War, which brought about a new social order, was followed by a major Americanization effort. Franklin's concept of a general religion, which he called "happy mediocrity," became an integral part of American civic religion. Americans sought to develop a secular ideology that could encompass various traits of different Protestant groups. The Americanizers wanted this country to be known as a land of individual freedom based on the Protestant religion, middle-class society, and a republican form of government.[13]

The perceived enemies of this effort were European monarchies, the European social class system, and Roman Catholicism. These institutions, it was believed, had brought Europe to a low and decadent state. In America,

10. Frederick Sontag and John K. Roth, *The American Religious Experience* (New York: Harper & Row, 1972), 14.

11. Carlson, *Americanization Syndrome*, 27.

12. Ibid., 35.

13. Ibid., 29. For an interesting discussion regarding the concept of civic or civil religion in America, see Robert Bellah, *The Broken Covenant* (New York: Seabury Press, 1975).

divided Protestantism was turned toward the interests of the homogeneous state; it was out of this concern and effort that the various interdenominational Protestant organizations arose in the nineteenth century. The stress was on the commonalities rather than the differences between the various religious groups. As an example of the downplaying of religious differences, Robert Carlson cites the relationship between the Lutheran and Reformed churches, where the members' faith and practice had become so similar that they seriously considered merging the two churches.[14]

During the post–Revolutionary War period, Americans took a variety of positions on the question of immigration. Franklin questioned whether the new nation could cope with immigrants of such diverse ethnic and religious backgrounds. John Page, a congressman from Virginia, held an opposite view, advocating that America should be open to the oppressed of all nations. Page told Congress: "It is nothing to us, whether Jews or Roman Catholics settle amongst us; whether subjects of kings or citizens of free states wish to reside in the United States, they will find it in their interests to be good citizens, and neither their religion nor political opinions can inspire us, if we have good laws, well executed."[15] The hope and plan was that these people would become "good Americans." There was no intention on the part of native-born Americans to modify their patterns of life or their Protestant republican ideology. It was the immigrants who were expected to adapt to their new setting.

Lutherans and Americanization

This was the situation Lutheran immigrants encountered when they came to America. Richard Wolf, in his study on the Americanization of Lutherans through 1829, states that the effects of Americanization on Lutherans were evidenced in at least four ways. (1) Cultural diversity broke down theological distinctions. (2) Congregational autonomy led to more democratic procedures that were representative and constitutional in form. (3) Voluntarism (freedom of choice) replaced membership in a state church by virtue of citizenship. (4) A liturgical devaluation resulted in less structure and freer worship forms.[16]

How those Lutheran immigrants would adapt and/or react to that situation formed the basis for the American Lutheran controversy that occurred in the middle of the nineteenth century, a controversy that consumed a portion

14. Carlson, *Americanization Syndrome*, 34.
15. Cited in ibid., 35.
16. Richard C. Wolf, "The Americanization of the German Lutherans, 1683–1829" (Ph.D. dissertation, Yale Univ., 1947).

of the Lutheran church's energies for the better part of forty years. One side advocated that Lutherans must become "American" in order to survive in America, a stance that had profound implications for Lutheran identity. The opposing side rejected the program of the American Lutherans and argued instead that Lutheran confessional identity must be maintained.

When Philip Schaff,[17] an immigrant himself and professor at the German Reformed seminary in Mercersburg, Pennsylvania, returned to Germany in 1854, he gave two lectures in which he described American religious life to an audience that was far removed from America's religious experiences. Schaff was both appreciative and critical. America had no established church, but Schaff claimed that the variety of religious groups that existed in America was not new or unique. He argued that religion in America was "only the rendezvous of all European churches and sects, which existed long before, either as establishments or as dissenting bodies."[18] The difference was that in America the various groups were free, with no hindrance from any secular power; this could be a blessing or a curse. Religious freedom could provide religious groups the opportunity to realize their mission and allow more involvement on the part of the people. Schaff's fear, however, was that in such a situation subjectivity and freedom might turn into isolation, division, and confusion.

Schaff's comments on the Lutherans are worth noting. He divided Lutherans in America into three categories. The New Lutheran party, Schaff said, "is an amalgamation of Lutheranism with American Puritanic and Methodistic elements. It consists chiefly of native Americans of German descent, and hence prides itself on being emphatically the American Lutheran Church."[19] Members of this party recognized only the Augsburg Confession, and then only those doctrines "in a manner substantially correct" in accord with the Bible.[20] This party was to be found in the General Synod. Those whom Schaff called the "Old Lutherans" were recent immigrants, mainly from Saxony, Prussia, and Bavaria. They were loyal to Luther, especially the Luther whom Schaff described as "reactionary, scrupulous, intolerant." They also held to the entire *Book of Concord,* Lutheranism's book of confessions. The Synod of Missouri and the Synod of

17. Philip Schaff (1819–93) emigrated to America in 1843, where he became a professor at the German Reformed seminary in Mercersburg. Schaff, along with John W. Nevin, became a proponent of "Mercersburg Theology." Following his tenure at Mercersburg, Schaff went on to become a professor at Union Seminary in New York City. He was the founder of the American Society of Church History. For a recent biography of Schaff, see George Shriver, *Philip Schaff: Christian Scholar and Ecumenical Prophet* (Macon, Ga.: Mercer Univ. Press, 1987).

18. Philip Schaff, *America: A Sketch of the Political, Social, and Religious Character of the United States of North America* (New York: C. Scribner, 1855), 101.

19. Ibid., 150.

20. For Schaff's description of the situation in the General Synod, see ibid., 152–54.

Buffalo were identified as the "Old Lutheran" bodies. The third group exhibited a "Moderate Lutheran tendency."[21] The Synod of Pennsylvania (Pennsylvania Ministerium) and the United Synod of Ohio were mentioned in this connection.

Schaff noted that changes were taking place. A "higher intellectual life and church activity" was developing among the "Moderates." The study of German theology was growing, many pastors had forsaken their former views, views learned from Samuel Schmucker at the seminary at Gettysburg. Also, Schaff viewed positively the founding of the *Evangelical Review,* a magazine that defended the teachings of the Lutheran Confessions. Because of the renewed emphasis on a distinctly Lutheran theology, controversies had arisen. Even though Schaff regretted the controversies, he felt the results would be for the best because a more self-conscious Lutheranism would arise from them.

The issue of Americanization is obviously complex, and its many-sidedness can be confusing. Americanization involves the assimilation of immigrants into the social structures and culture of a new land. How is the immigrant to deal with this? How much assimilation is necessary for the immigrant to feel at home? To what extent are immigrants required to compromise or lay aside their background, including customs, language, and religious heritage? America challenged immigrants, individually and collectively, with these kinds of questions.

With regard to religious matters, America offered a confusing situation. There was no state church to command people's allegiance and to provide some semblance of order. On one hand, there were the myriad varieties of religious groups, each claiming to possess the truth; on the other hand, a form of civil religion rejected all formal doctrinal claims and attempted to reduce religion to a lowest common denominator.

The concern of this book is a controversy within Lutheranism that had, at its heart, the issue of what it meant to be a Lutheran in America. Other potential studies could deal with related issues. A broader approach might examine the Americanization of Lutheran people as that phenomenon relates to the Americanization of the Lutheran church as a whole.[22] One might also consider the Americanization of the German Reformed church, a group that had similar experiences to the Lutherans. These matters, however, are beyond the range of this volume.

21. Ibid., 151.
22. A recent article calling for more studies of the people's religious beliefs is Jay Dolan, "The Immigrants and Their Gods," *Criterion* 27:1 (Winter 1988). Dolan wonders what differences, if any, there were between people's individual beliefs and the church's doctrinal positions.

John Murray Cuddihy argues that the cultural situation in America forced some religious groups, particularly Jews, Roman Catholics, and Lutherans, to make differentiations.[23] They had to demonstrate their unique qualities to the American culture in which they found themselves. In the American Lutheran conflict, one side would argue, in essence, that Americanization meant selling out, converting from their immigrant, precivil, uncivil religion to the American civil religion, which they *experience* as a religion of civility.[24] The American Lutherans did not advocate a civil religion in Benjamin Franklin's sense of the word, but they did want a Lutheranism that would conform to American Protestantism.

America confronted the historic faiths with denominational pluralism and also with a generic Protestant civil religion. Each religious group had to come to terms with that reality. The choices were to hold fast to one's religious tradition or accommodate to the American religious situation, particularly American Protestantism. Such challenges could result in conflict. For Lutherans in the mid-nineteenth century, the Americanization question took the form of a long and intense theological debate.

23. John Murray Cuddihy, *No Offense: Civil Religions and Protestant Taste* (New York: Seabury Press, 1978), 18.

24. Ibid., 29.

3

Early Lutheranism in America

*F*rom the time they first set foot on American soil, Lutherans had a difficult time maintaining their religious identity. Because of a shortage of pastors, worship services were often infrequent or nonexistent. Children went unbaptized; young people were not instructed in the catechism; people went for long periods of time without hearing a sermon or receiving the Lord's Supper. In these circumstances, many Lutherans lost their faith or joined other religious groups.

Through the efforts of men like Henry Melchior Muhlenberg, churches were eventually established, pastors were provided, and a conscious attempt was made to maintain a distinctive Lutheran identity in the new land. As time passed, however, that identity eroded. The influence of Enlightenment rationalism and the surrounding Protestant groups gradually severed Lutherans from their confessional heritage. By the end of the eighteenth century, the name "Lutheran" was retained, but Lutheran Confessions had no recognized authority and such distinctive Lutheran doctrines as baptismal regeneration, the Office of the Keys, and the real presence of the body and blood of Christ in the Lord's Supper were rejected out of hand. The Lutheran church in America, in its beliefs and practices, had become nothing more than a reflection of the Protestant churches that surrounded it. What was later called American Lutheranism had come into existence.

Lutherans were among the earliest settlers in America.[1] As early as 1624, German and Scandinavian Lutherans sailed to New Netherlands (New York) and located at Fort Nassau. In time, Lutheran numbers increased in that area, but they were not allowed to openly practice their faith. From the outset, Lutherans were treated as outsiders. They had to struggle to

---

1. For a more complete account of the early Lutheran experience in America, see Lars P. Qualben, *The Lutheran Church in Colonial America* (New York: Thomas Nelson & Sons, 1940), and E. Clifford Nelson, ed., *The Lutherans in North America* (Philadelphia: Fortress Press, 1975).

maintain their own religious identity. A strict religious policy in New Netherlands permitted only Reformed services. In 1649, the Lutherans petitioned the Amsterdam Consistory for the right to call a pastor and to publicly exercise their religion. The Consistory failed to act on their request. The request was repeated in 1653, but, under pressure from the Reformed clergy, the petition was rejected outright. The Consistory, however, advised the Lutherans that they could hold services quietly and in private.

Paulus Schrik, a lay leader, began conducting private services in 1655. On February 1, 1656, the New Netherlands Council issued an edict forbidding public or private religious meetings and imposed fines on both the preacher and participants. Lutherans protested, and the directors in Holland who supervised the Dutch settlements in the New World chided Peter Stuyvesant, the governor, and urged him at least to tolerate private services. Stuyvesant ignored the directive, and in 1659 he deported Pastor John Ernst Gutvasser. Another proclamation in 1662 forbade preaching of anything but Reformed doctrine.

When the English took New Amsterdam from the Dutch in 1664 they enacted the so-called Duke's Laws, one provision of which guaranteed freedom of conscience to all professing Christians except Roman Catholics. Lutherans filed a request for a pastor, and on February 19, 1669, Jacob Fabritius arrived in New York City. Fabritius quarreled with civil authorities and scandalized his parishioners by, among many things, excessive "tippling."[2] He was replaced in 1671 by Bernardus Arensius, who served until 1691.

The New York Lutherans then remained without a pastor until 1702, when Justus Falckner was called. On November 24, 1703, three Swedish pastors, acting on the authority of the Archbishop of Upsala, ordained Falckner, the first Lutheran ordination in the New World.

Swedish immigrants came to Delaware in 1638 and founded New Sweden. This settlement was served by Swedish clergy, most notably John Campanius, who was known for his work among the Indians and who translated Luther's Small Catechism into the language of the Delaware Indians. Two churches were consecrated, Holy Trinity (Old Swede's) in Wilmington, Delaware, and Gloria Dei in Philadelphia. The Swedes had to depend on the Church of Sweden for clergy, which proved to be difficult. Eventually, the Swedes established connections with the Anglicans, and, in time, the Lutherans in this region became Anglicans.

German immigrants, particularly from the Palatinate, began arriving in large numbers. Justus Falckner served many German-speaking congregations until his death in 1723, again leaving New York without a pastor.

---

2. Leonard R. Riforgiato, *Missionary of Moderation: Henry Melchior Muhlenberg and the Lutheran Church in English America* (Lewisburg, Pa.: Bucknell Univ. Press, 1980), 45.

His brother, Daniel Falckner, ministered to some of the congregations from 1724 to 1734, but it is unlikely that he was ordained.[3] In 1725 William Christopher Berkenmeyer accepted a call to serve congregations in New Jersey and New York. His pastorate finally gave Lutherans in those colonies some stability.

Most Germans settled in Pennsylvania. The Swedes established several other Lutheran settlements, and sporadic attempts at colonization occurred elsewhere.

In 1681 William Penn received a proprietorship from King Charles II of England. Penn, a Quaker, regarded his colony as a holy experiment of good government and religious freedom. On October 6, 1683, the first wave of German colonists reached Pennsylvania aboard the *Concord*. The number of German immigrants continued to increase, and many congregations were established.

Prior to the arrival of Muhlenberg, John Caspar Stoever, Jr., served many of the congregations that later came to be the United Congregations under Muhlenberg. Stoever arrived in Philadelphia in 1728. As early as 1729 he performed ministerial acts around New Providence, Philadelphia, and New Hanover. Stoever was ordained in 1733 and served as an itinerant pastor, preaching, baptizing, and administering the sacraments. He began to keep church records in the many places he served. He continued itinerant work, never serving a particular parish, until his death in 1779.

John Christian Schultze, the pastor who ordained Stoever, went to Europe to seek funds and to encourage pastors to serve in America. Through Frederick Michael Ziegenhagen, the Court Preacher in London, they were able to make contacts with the University at Halle in Germany. Dr. Gotthilf August Francke of Halle promised to supply congregations with pastors.[4]

Several disputes occurred over the next years, especially involving the handling of the money collected for America and the salary that would be offered to pastors. The United Congregations felt that Francke was too demanding. Finally, when the University of Halle refused to give in, the United Congregations petitioned the Consistory of Hesse-Darmstadt for a pastor.

In August 1742 Valentine Kraft landed in Philadelphia. He claimed he had been sent by the Consistory but had no papers to support that claim. Kraft had been ordained in Germany but later had been dismissed by the

---

3. Ibid., 51.
4. Francke placed several conditions on his support: (1) Ordination would be conferred on pastors prior to departure for America. (2) The United Congregations had to promise obedience and support to the pastors sent to them. (3) A definite salary had to be agreed on beforehand, payable in cash. The United Congregations were obliged to pay travel fare to America and, if the pastor was dissatisfied, return fare to Germany. Ibid., 66.

duchy of Zweibrucken. Once in America, he began to establish himself as head of his own consistory. When Muhlenberg arrived in December 1742, he had to confront Kraft and establish his authority.

The first Lutheran congregations in America had German members and were served by German pastors. Most of the first German immigrants came from southwest Germany, where they had suffered social, political, economic, and religious chaos during the Thirty Years' War (1618–48). But there were other reasons why these people left their homeland. Many of the petty rulers in Germany tried to imitate the splendor of the court of Louis XIV, placing heavy financial burdens on an already impoverished peasantry. High taxes had been levied on the poor by the ruling classes. The nobility used any means to gain land from the lower classes, an injustice that was not redressed in the courts. People who believed they had no future in Germany came to America to start a new life.

The religious situation in Germany was in a state of confusion. The Peace of Augsburg in 1555 provided for toleration between Lutherans and Roman Catholics under the ruling *cuius regium eius religio,* which meant that ruler of the territory determined the religion of the territory. In 1648 the Treaty of Westphalia, which ended the Thirty Years' War, added the Calvinists to the provision for toleration. The problem with this arrangement was that it included no provision to protect those who did not share the ruler's religion. If those who practiced other religions were tolerated, it was only due to the ruler's generosity. If the ruler changed, everything became uncertain. In the Palatinate, for example, no two successive Electors were of the same faith for over one hundred years.[5] This chaotic situation encouraged emigration.

Richard Wolf's dissertation on German Lutherans in America notes that the early German immigrants faced many difficulties. Hundreds died on the way to America. Leaderless, they were left to fend for themselves. Many of the Germans, including children, became indentured servants in order to come to the New World. Many of the children ended up in schools where only English was spoken. It was in the school setting that the younger Germans lost the ability to speak their native language and abandoned other characteristics of German culture (138).

The German immigrants had experienced religious disunity in their homeland, and they found the same situation in America. The early German immigrants' religious life in America was characterized by lack of organization, shortage of pastoral leadership, and lack of financial support.

5. Richard C. Wolf, "The Americanization of the German Lutherans, 1683–1829" (Ph.D. diss., Yale Univ., 1947), 42.

This led to pitiful spiritual conditions. Wolf cites Justus Falckner, the first Lutheran pastor ordained in America, who wrote in 1701:

> The Germans, however, I have spoken of not without cause as merely several Evangelical Lutheran Germans, and not the German Evangelical Lutheran Church: those who are destitute of altar and priest forsooth roam about in this desert . . . a deplorable condition indeed. Moreover there is here a large number of Germans, who, however, have partly crawled in among the different sects who use the English tongue, which is first learned by all who come here. A number are Quakers and Anabaptists; a portion are Freethinkers and associate with no one. They also allow their children to grow up in the same manner. In short there are Germans here, and perhaps the majority, who despise God's Word and all outward good order; who blaspheme the sacraments, and frightfully and publicly give scandal; . . . and herein is the great blame and cause of the lack of establishment of an outward and visible church assembly. (159)

According to Richard Wolf, one of the greatest problems was the shortage of pastors. In New York in 1735 there were only three Lutheran pastors: William Christopher Berkenmeyer, Michael Christian Knoll, and Johann Augustus Wolf. The last of these three worked exclusively in New Jersey. Pennsylvania had only six Lutheran pastors in 1742, the year Muhlenberg arrived, and only one of them was still active (161). As late as 1734 there were only three congregations in that province with an estimated 20,000 Lutheran settlers (168). Preaching stations existed, but they functioned only when a pastor was available. Muhlenberg's description of his own early ministry is typical: "When I first arrived in this land . . . I preached in barns or transparent wooden churches during the cold winters. The poor people assembled from miles round about. They were cold and wet and were poor, their clothes [*sic*]."[6]

Although conditions improved, in many areas German immigrants still had no opportunity to attend services. As late as 1763 Muhlenberg was invited by some English colonists to preach to Germans who were indentured to them. Muhlenberg reflected: "When the service was over . . . Germans gathered around me and wept aloud, partly for joy at having again heard the Word of God and partly for sorrow that they had so little opportunity to hear it."[7]

---

6. Henry Melchior Muhlenberg, *The Journals of Henry Melchior Muhlenberg,* 3 vols. trans. Theodore G. Tappert and John W. Doberstein (Philadelphia: Muhlenberg Press, 1942, 1945, 1958) 1:378.

7. Muhlenberg, *Journals,* 1:661.

These examples illustrate the difficulties early Lutheran immigrants faced in attempting to practice their faith and to retain their identity as Lutherans. Many Lutherans joined other religious groups, especially the Anglicans and Moravians. Others fell away from their faith altogether. Those who remained Lutheran had been separated from their ecclesiastical background and were forced to adjust to America with little support from pastors.

Henry Melchior Muhlenberg

The year 1742 is a milestone in the history of Lutheranism in America, for it was in that year that Henry Melchior Muhlenberg, destined to be called the Patriarch of Lutheranism in America, arrived to serve the United Congregations in the vicinity of Philadelphia.[8]

Muhlenberg was born September 6, 1711, in the city of Einbeck in the duchy of Hanover. Einbeck was known for a medieval shrine that purportedly contained a drop of Christ's blood; the city was also famous for its six hundred breweries.[9] Muhlenberg's father, Nicholas, was a burgher, brewer, cobbler, and a deacon in the Einbeck church. His mother, Anna Maria Kleinschmid, was the daughter of an army officer. There were nine children in the family. Henry's father died in 1723 when the boy was eleven years old.

By 1722 Muhlenberg was receiving tutoring in Greek and Latin. At Easter 1733 he was accepted as a student at the Zellerfelde Latin School. To support himself while a student there, Muhlenberg tutored eighteen young men in catechesis, writing, mathematics, and clavichord.

In 1735 Muhlenberg was granted a scholarship to study at the new royal university at Göttingen. It was there that Muhlenberg was introduced to Halle pietism by some transfer students from Einbeck with whom he struck up a friendship.[10] During this time, Muhlenberg studied theology under Professor Oporin, a moderate pietist. In 1738 Muhlenberg went to Halle and studied under Gotthilf August Francke, son of the famous German

8. An old standard biography on Muhlenberg is William J. Mann, *The Life and Times of Henry Melchior Muhlenberg* (Philadelphia: G. W. Frederick, 1887). Another work, Paul A. Wallace, *The Muhlenbergs of Pennsylvania* (Philadelphia: Univ. of Pennsylvania Press, 1950) devotes only one chapter to Muhlenberg himself and has more material on his children. Riforgiato's *Missionary of Moderation* is an excellent recent biography.

9. Riforgiato, *Missionary*, 17.

10. For background on pietism, see two works by F. Ernest Stoeffler, *The Rise of Evangelical Pietism* (Leiden: E. J. Brill, 1971) and *German Pietism during the Eighteenth Century* (Leiden: E. J. Brill, 1973).

pietist August Hermann Francke. In July 1739 Muhlenberg was sent a call to a church at Grosshennersdorf, and later that year he was ordained.

Muhlenberg has been described as a pietist. Pietism was a movement in the church that stressed a meaningful relationship with God which resulted in an internal feeling of commitment. Pietism exemplified religious idealism, which took the form of a struggle for perfection. This struggle was represented by the "Two Ways," light and darkness. Each person must choose one or the other. Sanctification was shown by good works. Pietism stressed the continual interaction of the Redeemer and the redeemed. In a concept that went counter to Luther's teaching, the experience of justification was changed into one of sanctification. This idea was advocated by another German pietist, Johann Arndt (1555–1621).

Phillip Jacob Spener (1635–1705) originally organized the pietistic movement, stressing preaching and forming conventicles, groups of people who gathered for the purpose of Scripture study and prayer. These activities were intended to promote a greater spiritual consciousness in members of the church. Spener's *Pia Desideria,* published in 1675, is representative of his views.

Although influenced by pietism, Muhlenberg denied that he was a pietist, mainly because he was opposed to pietism's more radical forms, which led some to advocate a concept of "the church within the church" or to separate themselves from the church altogether. Riforgiato, unlike Mann, takes the position that Muhlenberg cannot be classified as a Halle pietist and describes him as a "moderate churchly pietist," one who was concerned for religious experience but who also took seriously Lutheran doctrine and liturgical practices.[11]

Muhlenberg brought order out of the chaos that characterized early Lutheranism in America. He accomplished this through a variety of means: strong use of authority, the ability to compromise, and a certain amount of accommodation to the American setting.

Muhlenberg could be very authoritarian, especially when it came to the integrity of the ministerial office. Immediately after arriving in America, he became engaged in a struggle to gain control over the Hanover and Providence congregations, not yet tainted by the Moravians, and to displace Valentine Kraft, who had taken charge in Philadelphia. Muhlenberg insisted that he was the legally called pastor and refused to accept Kraft's authority. After a heated dispute with Kraft, Muhlenberg gained control within a month. He presented the United Congregations with a document that pledged their subscription on three points: (1) Muhlenberg was the only

11. Riforgiato, *Missionary,* 37.

rightly called pastor in accord with the Unaltered Augsburg Confession. (2) The congregations would obey him and his lawful successors. (3) The congregations would shun anyone whose teachings and ministrations violated the Unaltered Augsburg Confession.[12]

The congregations were not totally positive about making this pledge, but Kraft finally abandoned the struggle. Muhlenberg then confronted the Moravians, a German-speaking pietistic group often in conflict with the Lutherans. In this instance, they had taken a church book and chalice that belonged to the Lutherans. In a related case, Muhlenberg attempted to expose as a liar Count Nicholas Zinzendorf, a Moravian who had come to America from London and who was passing as a Lutheran. Zinzendorf returned to London, but intrusions by Moravians into Lutheran congregations persisted.

Muhlenberg quickly discovered that America was not like Germany, where one could appeal to secular authorities on matters of doctrine. In America, people were free to choose in matters of religion, and most matters were decided by majority rule. Because of congregational strife and because people had to move farther away to escape high rents on land, only about one-half of the parishioners in the United Congregations were still members four years after Muhlenberg's arrival.[13]

It was essential for Muhlenberg to be firm to retain his pastoral authority in the United Congregations. For the most part, however, Muhlenberg was not as heavy-handed as he had been in the Kraft case. He soon realized that an alliance between the church and the government, similar to that in Germany, would never work in America. He opted for more democratic procedures, which meant congregational consent and approval regarding local church concerns, including the selection of a pastor.

Muhlenberg's adoption of democratic methods was one sign of his Americanization. Another was his relationships with other religious groups. To some extent, this can be traced to Muhlenberg's Halle tradition, which showed a broad religious tolerance and paid little attention to denominational labels. Muhlenberg, however, went much further in his relationships with other Christians in America, perhaps because of the cooperation he saw all around him. He would not provide services to another group if a pastor was available, but if one was not present, he would serve as needed. He preached to Swedish Lutherans, Anglicans, and Reformed. He performed pastoral acts for Anglicans, Reformed, Quakers, and even Roman Catholics, as well as for Lutherans.[14]

12. Ibid., 94.
13. Ibid., 96.
14. Wolf, "Americanization," 200.

Muhlenberg allowed clergymen of other denominations to preach in his pulpit. George Whitefield, the English evangelist, did so at least twice. Muhlenberg used a wide variety of worship services. For example, he made use of the *Book of Common Prayer* until Lutheran orders were available. He attended sessions of other groups such as Presbyterians, Anglicans, and Baptists. He was a member of the English Colloquium, an interdenominational exegetical and prayer meeting.[15] These relationships are evidence of Muhlenberg's democratic spirit and show that he was committed to Lutheranism's taking its place alongside the other religious groups present in America.

Muhlenberg brought organization to the Lutheran church in America. He was instrumental in the formation of the Pennsylvania Ministerium in 1748. Very early, the Ministerium exercised authority and ruled against the church council of Lancaster. The Lancaster parish, which had suffered many controversies with the Moravians, advocated that anyone returning to the Lutheran fold should be required to sign what amounted to a loyalty oath. The Ministerium advocated leniency and ordered the Lancaster council to submit, which it promised to do for one year. The Ministerium won this first test of synodical authority.[16]

Muhlenberg's *Journals* are filled with stories about situations in which he was called in to mediate congregational disputes. One of the most interesting stories concerns the Germantown congregation, where in 1753 a dispute arose over whether there should be bells on collection baskets. Those in favor reasoned that the bells would awaken contributors, thus increasing offerings. One church officer, who did not like the bells and thought them sectarian, cut them off the baskets. Many objected that he had no authority to take such an action. The same group that disliked the bells also opposed the Halle pastor, John Frederick Handschuh, who was accused of conducting revivals and preaching excessively emotional sermons. The congregation was split by the dispute. Handschuh was removed from the parish. Eventually, Muhlenberg allowed the opposition group to have the church building, provided they assumed the church debt, gave the Halle pastors who had served there testimonials of good conduct, and permitted an audit of the church books. The opposition group then declared their intention to call a pastor from Brandenburg-Prussia.[17] After meeting with this group, Muhlenberg agreed to release them from their obligations to the Halle pastors.

Disputes did not occupy all of Muhlenberg's time. The constitution of St. Michael's Church in Philadelphia, which was approved in 1762, and

15. Ibid., 213.
16. Riforgiato, *Missionary,* 168.
17. For details of the incident, see ibid., 171–73.

the first constitution of the Pennsylvania Ministerium, ratified in 1781, attest to Muhlenberg's organizational abilities.

It is no exaggeration to say that the Lutheran church in America might not have survived without the labors of Muhlenberg. He saw the need to unite pastors and congregations organizationally so that Lutherans could be ministered to, and he was concerned that Lutheran identity be maintained, both in theology and practice, in America. Muhlenberg envisioned Lutheranism taking its place as a separate church in the new land.

Muhlenberg wanted to establish a seminary in order to provide the church with pastors, but nothing came of this idea because of lack of funds. To meet this need, Muhlenberg began in 1769 to instruct "six seminarists"[18] in preparation for the ministry. This pattern of tutoring was the norm until the seminary in Gettysburg was established in 1826.

It is somewhat difficult to assess Muhlenberg's theology because so much of his time was spent in matters of organization, dealing with congregational disputes and other related problems. William Julius Mann in his work, *The Life and Times of Henry Melchior Muhlenberg,* judged Muhlenberg to be a confessional pietist. Vergilius Ferm, however, contended that Muhlenberg was lax with regard to confessional standards.[19] F. Bente, writing from a conservative, confessional, Missouri Synod vantage point, stated with regard to Muhlenberg and his colleagues: "Their doctrinal position was unmistakably Lutheran, in the sense in which Lutheranism is historically known, and is something individual and distinct, and as such stands in opposition to Romanism on one hand, and to Zwingli, Calvin, and all the other so-called Protestant parties on the other."[20] Even though Bente judged Muhlenberg to be confessional, he felt that Muhlenberg did not see the Confessions as a living power for truth that shaped and directed every aspect of the church's life. He was also critical of Muhlenberg's pietistic emphasis on conversion and his hierarchical approach to the church.[21]

Later interpreters of Muhlenberg have concluded that he was just the person needed for his time, a sound confessional Lutheran, but one who could make the accommodations necessary in this new environment. Richard Wolf comments: "He evidenced an honesty, sincerity and dependability which evoked respect and loyalty of all honest men. He combined within himself the attributes of forthrightness with taste, patience with consistency,

18. Muhlenberg, *Journals,* 2:415.
19. Vergilius Ferm, *Crisis in American Lutheran Theology* (New York: Century Co., 1927), 14.
20. F. Bente, *American Lutheranism,* 2 vols. (St. Louis: Concordia Publishing House, 1919) 1:71.
21. Ibid., 1:73–74.

charity with righteousness, opportunism with integrity and humility with self respect."[22] Proof of Muhlenberg's confessional integrity has been shown in his insistence, when dealing with the United Congregations, that everything be done in accordance with the Unaltered Augsburg Confession. Wolf cites the *Kirchen Agende,* published by the Pennsylvania Ministerium in 1786, one year before Muhlenberg's death, as evidence that Muhlenberg held to an orthodox Lutheran stance on such teachings as baptismal regeneration and the real presence.[23]

Muhlenberg recognized that the church must be Lutheran, but also that it had to be American. The Lutheran church in America could not survive as a mere extension of the church in Europe. He learned English and advocated that English be used as much as possible. Instruction, Muhlenberg said, should "include both German and English, as local conditions make both languages necessary—German for our religion and English for temporal and civic welfare."[24] This statement is interesting as it shows that even Muhlenberg felt that, for Germans, only German was appropriate for worship and religious instruction.

Riforgiato is correct when he states that Muhlenberg was a complex figure, not easily fit into the pietist mold. He points to Muhlenberg's strengths as an organizer, which proved to be his legacy to the Lutheran church in America. Muhlenberg was the person responsible for Lutheranism's planting on American soil. Riforgiato says, "Muhlenberg's Americanization process was a compromise between democracy and authoritarianism, retaining European features without compromising distinctiveness."[25]

Muhlenberg thus maintained a confessional Lutheranism while making the necessary accommodations to the American context. He associated with persons of other religious groups, yet did not compromise his theological integrity as a Lutheran. He maintained a confessional Lutheran stance that established a precedent for Lutheranism in America. He believed that the Lutheran church in America could be both truly American and genuinely confessionally Lutheran. Those who followed Muhlenberg, however, were not always able to walk this narrow path as well as he did.

The Next Generation

The persons and events that followed Muhlenberg did not necessarily follow his vision for Lutheranism in America. Muhlenberg's stance on doctrinal

22. Wolf, "Americanization," 184.
23. Ibid., 430.
24. Muhlenberg, *Journals,* 1:588.
25. Riforgiato, *Missionary,* 96.

matters was strongly and consistently Lutheran. He wanted the Lutheran church in America to hold fast to the pure word of God as it was expressed in the Unaltered Augsburg Confession and the other symbols of the Lutheran church.

Movements, however, in Europe and America, would threaten that vision. Muhlenberg was alarmed at the spread of rationalism among Lutherans in Europe. He reflected, "It now appears that in Europe the Holy Bible . . . is no longer suitable; for it is being twisted, rent asunder, hacked to pieces, and hashed up by half-baked critics."[26] English deism and French rationalism had spread to the shores of America. Many, including people as influential as Thomas Paine, author of *Age of Reason,* and Ethan Allen, Revolutionary War hero, supported these movements.[27]

Even under the pressure of these movements and the stress of the American Revolution, the Lutheran church emerged relatively unscathed. The Lutheran church was gaining strength and stability, but problems did arise. After Muhlenberg's death in 1787, with no one of his stature to assume leadership, independent synodical bodies multiplied. Muhlenberg had envisioned one unified Lutheran church in America, but within a few years several synods were formed: the New York Ministerium in 1786, the North Carolina Synod in 1803, the Ohio Synod in 1818, and the Maryland–West Virginia and Tennessee Synods in 1820. Lutheranism did not have a unified voice. A shortage of pastors continued to be a problem. Several seminaries were established, but they failed. The most significant was Hartwick Seminary in New York.

Another problem was the continued use of the German language. Lutheranism was not reaching non-Germans, and many of the young who had grown up in America began to abandon German in favor of the language of their new land. In 1804 a controversy occurred in Zion Church, a Philadelphia congregation, over the language question. It was suggested that a pastor who could preach in English be called to serve along with the two German pastors. Peter Gabriel Muhlenberg, son of the patriarch, was a key figure in this controversy. He stated that English preaching posed no threat to the doctrinal position of the church. The English-speaking pastor was not called, and some members left Zion Church in 1806 and established St. John's English Lutheran Church.

---

26. Muhlenberg, *Journals,* 1:569.

27. A comprehensive study on this subject is Henry F. May, *The Enlightenment in America* (New York: Oxford Univ. Press, 1976). May treats the Enlightenment as a religion that had adherents from many backgrounds. Another recent study, Edwin S. Gaustad, *Faith of Our Fathers: Religion and the New Nation* (New York: Harper & Row, 1987), discusses the influence of deism on Jefferson, Franklin, and others.

In 1818 members of a German congregation in Philadelphia requested the Ministerium to allow ministers to preach at the parish school in English because younger members of the congregation did not understand German. The Ministerium refused on the grounds that it would be improper to allow visiting preachers to preach in the Philadelphia congregation without the congregation's formal permission; but the Ministerium did recommend that English should be used more frequently, for the benefit of the young.[28] Many opposed the use of English, however, and those congregations where English was used were considered by some to be less Lutheran than those where only German was spoken. In New York progress toward increased use of English came more rapidly than in Pennsylvania. In 1807 the New York Ministerium became the first Lutheran body in America to adopt English as its official language. New York therefore became the primary source of English hymnals, liturgies, and catechisms.

Unionism was one of the important issues that emerged during this period. Muhlenberg maintained cordial relationships with other religious groups, but he was a strong advocate of Lutheran distinctiveness and a respecter of theological differences. Others, however, did not share his views and looked to unionism to strengthen the churches that had been weakened by the American Revolution. In 1781 the Anglicans, who had suffered devastating losses during and after the war, approached the Pennsylvania Ministerium to discuss a union of Lutherans and Anglicans. Nothing came of the discussions, but the two groups continued to have a friendly relationship.

Lutherans had cooperated with the German Reformed Synod in the founding of Franklin College at Lancaster, Pennsylvania, in 1787, but the venture failed for lack of finances, and the college eventually became a local "classical school." In 1817 a union hymnal, *Das Gemeinschaftliches Gesangbuch zum gottesdienstlichen Gebraucht der Lutheranischen und Reformirten Gemeinden in Nord-America,* was published. It had the official approval of the Pennsylvania Ministerium, the New York Ministerium, the Reformed Synod, and the North Carolina Synod. Proposals were made for a joint Lutheran-Reformed seminary, but the project was never realized. At that time there was some commitment to unity, but neither side had the financial means to accomplish projects such as joint colleges and universities that would have made the union a reality.

Although no Lutheran-Reformed union took place, interest in such a venture continued. In the Carolinas, an attempt was made to unite all the German-speaking churches into a body called *Corpus Evangelicum* (evangelical body) or *Unio Ecclesiastica* (unified church). This union was perceived to be possible without either Lutherans or Reformed having to give

28. Wolf, "Americanization," 397–98.

up their confessional positions. Whichever group was in the majority in a particular place would determine which hymnals, catechisms, and so on would be used. The *Corpus* passed out of existence in 1794. Lutherans and the Reformed had the German language in common, but all attempts at union failed because, in the end, Lutherans wanted to maintain their identity.[29]

Many Lutherans remained Lutheran in both doctrine and practice during this period, but there was evidence of laxity and indifference toward doctrine and liturgical practices. One reason for doctrinal disintegration was German rationalism, which came from Halle through the influence of Johann Salomo Semler (1725–91). Semler rejected the pietism of his youth and advocated what he termed *liberalis theologia,* or liberal theology. He called whole parts of Scripture into question and engaged in interesting interpretations of certain biblical texts. For example, Semler interpreted "Christ is a stumbling block to the Jew" to mean that Jesus failed to throw off the yoke of Roman authority.[30] Semler also attacked the church's historical and doctrinal authority and denounced many of its teachings as unfounded and irrational.

Lutherans in America responded to rationalism in several ways. Some were alarmed by it. In 1805 John Christopher Kunze (1744–1807), Muhlenberg's son-in-law and head of the New York Ministerium, wrote to his fellow clergy: "Dreadful as it may seem, it is nevertheless the result of my continuing to read German publications and of my continued German correspondence that I assert, should we send for ten candidates to place them in our vacant congregations, it is highly probable that we would have . . . nine despisers, yea, blasphemers of Christ."[31]

In spite of the fact that rationalism was resisted by many Lutherans, it did have an influence on the Lutheran church. For example, in 1792 the Pennsylvania Ministerium removed all references to the Lutheran Confessions from its constitution. No references to the Confessions can be found in the ordination rites of this period.[32] Rationalism, with its doctrinal indifference, was the prevailing view.

The attitudes of many of the clergy can be seen in *The History, Doctrine and Discipline of the Evangelical Lutheran Church,* by John George Lochman.[33] Lochman was a pastor from Harrisburg, Pennsylvania. In 1818,

29. Ibid., 424.
30. Ibid., 433.
31. Letter to the Ministerium of New York, quoted in Henry Eyster Jacobs, "The Confessional History of the Ministerium of Pennsylvania," *Lutheran Church Review* 17 (April 1898): 365–66.
32. Wolf, "Americanization," 436.
33. John George Lochman, *The History, Doctrine and Discipline of the Lutheran Church* (Harrisburg, Pa.: John Wyeth, 1818).

the year this book was published, he was elected president of the Pennsylvania Ministerium.

In this work, Lochman admitted that he felt comfortable with Calvin's doctrine of the Lord's Supper (60). He credited Arminius with having taught doctrines that "were certainly purely Lutheran" (65). Lochman also rejected any concept of original sin (88), skirted the teaching of baptismal regeneration (102ff.), and viewed the sacraments as necessary only "for those who can have them" (114). Lochman assumed that all distinctions between Lutherans and the Reformed were in the process of disappearing, and he hoped that the spirit of union would continue to spread.

Liturgical practices during this period departed from the classic Lutheran liturgies and moved in the direction of free orders of worship. The Order for Baptism used in the Pennsylvania Ministerium contained neither a renunciation of the devil nor any reference to the Trinity.[34] In the Order for Communion, liberties were taken with the Words of Institution, and the ordination rite contained no reference to the Confessions of the Lutheran church.[35]

Frederick Henry Quitman was a key figure in the erosion of doctrinal consciousness. Quitman came to New York in 1796 and joined the New York Ministerium. He had studied under Semler at Halle and brought his teacher's rationalistic attitudes to America. In 1807 he succeeded John Christopher Kunze as president of the New York Ministerium, a position he held for twenty-one years.

Kunze opposed any and all forms of rationalism, but Quitman's stance was quite the opposite. In 1814 Quitman published his *Evangelical Catechism.*[36] Briefly, this catechism made reason the test of every belief. An example of this can be seen in the following questions and answers from the catechism:

3 Q. Can any rational belief take place without a sure foundation?
  A. No. All unwarranted belief is superstition.
4 Q. Which are the grounds that ought to constitute the basis of rational belief?
  A. Either natural perception and experience; or the authority of competent witnesses; or finally, unquestionable arguments of reason (5ff.).

Quitman said Christ's exhortation, "Be ye perfect, even as your Father in heaven is perfect," is "to exhort us that we should endeavor, as far as

34. Wolf, "Americanization," 441.
35. Ibid., 442.
36. Frederick Quitman, *Evangelical Catechism; or Short Exposition of the Principal Doctrines and Precepts of the Christian Religion, for the Use of the Churches Belonging to the Evangelical Lutheran Synod of New York* (Hudson, N.Y.: Wm. E. Norman, 1814).

it is in our power, to imitate the character of God, or his wisdom, goodness, mercy, justice and truth, and thus continually advance to higher moral perfection" (14).

The emphasis in Quitman's catechism was entirely on reason and morals. Nowhere was it stated that Jesus is divine. He was described as a man with a "divine mission," a moral example to humanity. This was totally consistent with Enlightenment thought. No mention is made of baptismal regeneration. During the Lord's Supper, the Christian was to meditate upon the suffering Savior. Quitman concluded the catechism with a section entitled "Sketch of the History of Religions," which advocated a natural religion.

Whether Quitman acted on his own or on behalf of the New York Ministerium in writing this catechism is unclear. The synod did not meet in 1814. Quitman was on the committee responsible for preparing a catechism and may have assumed approval of his work. In any case, Quitman claimed he had the approval of the Ministerium when his catechism appeared in November 1814.[37]

It is now felt that Quitman was influenced by Semler and by the so-called biblical supranaturalism represented in Germany by Gottlob Christian Storr (1746–1805). Biblical supranaturalism held that both reason and revelation were authoritative for the Christian and that they were in harmony with each other.[38] Quitman believed humans were free agents and claimed the Lutheran church had moved toward an emphasis on free will. Quitman was influential in the New York Ministerium. He advocated, in the name of man's free agency, that any belief was allowable. The authority of the Confessions for the Lutheran church was simply ignored.

Prelude to a Struggle

Of the figures in the American Lutheran controversy, none was more important than Samuel Simon Schmucker (1799–1873). He advocated, more powerfully than anyone else, the position of the American Lutherans. He remains one of the most important figures in the history of the Lutheran church in America.[39]

37. Arthur C. Repp, Sr., *Luther's Catechism Comes to America: Theological Effects on the Issues of the Small Catechism Prepared in and for America Prior to 1850* (Metuchen, N.J.: Scarecrow Press, 1982), 121.

38. Ibid., 124. See also Nelson, ed., *The Lutherans,* 106.

39. An old biography of Schmucker is Peter Anstadt, *Life and Times of the Rev. S. S. Schmucker* (York, Pa.: P. Anstadt & Sons, 1896). This work is important because it cites portions of Schmucker's diary, which is now lost. Two more recent biographies are by Abdel Ross Wentz, *History of the Gettysburg Theological Seminary, 1826–1965,* 2 vols. (Harrisburg, Pa.: Evangelical Press, 1965), and *Pioneer in Christian Unity: Samuel Simon Schmucker* (Philadelphia: Fortress Press, 1966).

Schmucker was the author of more than forty books and pamphlets and was a well-known ecumenical figure. Within the General Synod he was at various times (and sometimes all at once) seminary professor, seminary president, president of the General Synod, and president of the West Pennsylvania Synod. In addition, he was the author of model constitutions for several synods of the General Synod; he prepared catechisms and hymnals for that body; and he helped to found the *Lutheran Observer* and other publications. When the General Synod was in danger of breaking apart because of the withdrawal of the Pennsylvania Ministerium, the largest of the synods, Schmucker's tireless efforts kept it alive. For nearly a quarter of a century he was the undisputed leader of the General Synod of the Lutheran church in the United States. In many respects, one can say that Samuel Schmucker *was* the General Synod.

James L. Haney, Jr., has done a comprehensive job of examining Schmucker's educational background in order to discover who influenced this man and the nature of their influence.[40]

The most important figure in Schmucker's theological development was his father, John George Schmucker (1771–1854), who has been described as "a key figure in Lutheran adoption of methods and goals of evangelical Protestantism."[41] An immigrant to Virginia, John George Schmucker was converted at the age of eighteen and was licensed to preach three years later. During that time, he studied under Justus Helmuth and Jacob Goering. Ordained in 1800, Schmucker became a prominent pastor in Pennsylvania and served for twenty-six years at York.[42]

Helmuth and Goering modified what Muhlenberg had done, altered theological priorities, and attempted to bring Lutherans into closer fellowship with American Protestants. They imparted their views to John George Schmucker, and he, in turn, passed those views on to his son, Samuel Simon.

Justus Heinrich Christian Helmuth (1745–1825) entered the university at Halle at the age of fourteen and eventually earned a degree in theology there. He migrated in 1769 from Germany to Pennsylvania. He began his ministry in Lancaster, Pennsylvania, and was later called as associate pastor to Zion's and St. Michael's in Philadelphia, at that time the largest Lutheran congregation in America. While at Zion's and St. Michael's, Helmuth also

40. James L. Haney, Jr., "The Religious Heritage and Education of Samuel Simon Schmucker: A Study in the Rise of 'American Lutheranism' " (Ph.D. dissertation, Yale Univ., 1968).

41. Nelson, ed., *The Lutherans*, 108.

42. For biographical information see Luke Schmucker, *The Schmucker Family and the Lutheran Church in America* (Luke Schmucker, 1937), 12–20; Wentz, *Pioneer*, 2–3; and Haney, "Religious Heritage," 189–200.

taught Oriental languages at the University of Pennsylvania. In 1784 he was elected a member of the American Philosophical Society. Helmuth was awarded a doctorate of divinity from the university and received the appointment of Professor of Oriental Languages, a position he held until 1791. In 1786 Helmuth became president of the Pennsylvania Ministerium. When John Kunze resigned and Helmuth became senior pastor, he brought in Johann Frederick Schmidt (1769–1812) as his assistant. Helmuth and Schmidt began a theological course for future pastors; John George Schmucker was one of their students.

Helmuth was more tolerant than Muhlenberg. He had been influenced by August Hermann Francke's "right hand," Johann Anastasius Freylinghausen (1670–1739). Freylinghausen's goal was to preach the fundamentals of the Christian faith in clear and simple language. He had an aversion to theological subtleties and confessional polemics.[43]

Helmuth brought the emphasis on the practical to bear on the life of American Lutheranism. Confessional theology was deemphasized to the point that, in 1792, while Helmuth was its president, the Pennsylvania Ministerium dropped all references to the Augsburg Confession from its constitution.[44] Helmuth, however, was not a rationalist. In fact, he was critical of rationalism and joined forces with such well-known American evangelicals as Timothy Dwight (1752–1817), the president of Yale, to combat that movement.[45]

Helmuth was particularly upset with conditions in Philadelphia. As early as 1792, he was shaken by what he perceived to be public blasphemy. Later, he preached a sermon in which he claimed that blasphemy and apostasy had brought divine judgment on the city. The sermon was entitled *A Short Account of the Yellow Fever in Philadelphia for the Reflecting Christian.*[46] In this sermon, Helmuth reflected on what he saw taking place in Philadelphia.

43. Henry Eyster Jacobs noted that Helmuth had close relations with the Moravians, whose aversion to precise theological statements had an influence on him. See Henry Eyster Jacobs, *A History of the Evangelical Lutheran Church in the United States* (New York: Christian Literature Co., 1893), 314.

44. S. E. Ochsenford, *Documentary History of the Evangelical Lutheran Ministerium of Pennsylvania and Adjacent States* (Philadelphia: General Council Publication House, 1912), 250.

45. For a discussion of Dwight's activities against what he called "infidelity," see Stephen E. Berk, *Calvinism versus Democracy: Timothy Dwight and the Origins of Evangelical Orthodoxy* (Hamden, Conn.: Archon Books, 1974), 115–39. Dwight's theology is best described as rational Christianity. He believed that man is a rational being and thus capable of learning the operations of God's natural and moral government. He was also an advocate of prophecy and held to a millennial vision of a worldwide organization of evangelicals who would propagate the gospel and fight infidelity.

46. Johann Heinrich Christian Helmuth, *A Short Account of the Yellow Fever in Philadelphia for the Reflecting Christian,* trans. Charles Erdmann (Philadelphia: Jones, Hoff, & Derrick, 1794).

Philadelphia was the place where a certain class of people had associated themselves for the avowed purpose of blaspheming our blessed Savior. It was gone even so far about two years ago, that a certain preacher had hired a room, wherein he set before his hearers, what he called sermons, or rather poison of seduction, from which many were to imbibe an aversion against the doctrine of Jesus Christ. It was even said, that money had been collected for the purpose of building a proper meeting house, for this new teacher, who denied the God-head of Christ. (19)

Besides the teaching of blasphemy, Helmuth found much wrong in the people's actions, particularly with regard to the Sabbath.

Philadelphia was the place that seemed to strive to exceed all other places in the breaking of the sabbath. It may well be said with propriety, that our sundays and holy days were our most sinful days. Immediately at break of day, the rattling of the carriages began through all the streets. They hurried into the country with their families as early as possible, in order by no means to approach the Deity in public worship, along with other citizens and sincere Christians. . . . A great many who had not the means to ride out into the country on the Lord's day frequented the taverns and beerhouses in the city and vicinity, and there spent their time in the most frivolous discourse, backbiting their neighbors, or even coarsely ridiculing the word of God itself; or they gamed, drank to excess, and frequently quarrelled and fought. (15–16)

For Helmuth, there was no doubt that the epidemic of yellow fever was God's judgment on infidelity and on the impious people of the city. Helmuth stated pointedly: "I am well convinced that the judgment we have lately been afflicted with, was the completion of the threats, which the word of God has denounced against such a city and such a country" (19–20).

Helmuth saw the failure in strict Sabbath observance as a major problem that needed immediate correction. He struck out against theatres, dancing, card-playing, and drinking, all of which he viewed as immoral and as impediments to observing Sunday as a day of prayer and meditation.

Jacob Goering (1774–1807), a pastor in York, Pennsylvania, followed the same basic theological position as Helmuth. He, too, was content to emphasize fundamentals in theology. In answer to the question: "What are the principal and fundamental articles which a minister must teach and the people must believe in order rightly to know and worship God?", Goering recorded in his *Common-place Book:* "The foundation of these articles lies in the doctrines: 1. Of human depravity and its consequent misery. 2. Of

the Redeemer, through whom we are to be delivered from misery.
3. Together with the instruction how to avail ourselves of this Redeemer."[47]

Reformed tendencies in Goering's theology are evident in his explanation of the Lord's Supper:

> We believe that Jesus Christ is really (*wesentlich*) present in the Holy Supper, as God and man; that He is really present, not to the bread and wine, but to the communicants. The bread and wine in the Holy Supper are only consecrated bread and a consecrated cup, with which Jesus Christ stands in no real connection: they are merely bread and wine, and nothing more, and their consecration consists in their dedication to a religious use.[48]

As this statement shows, Goering did not identify the presence of Christ with the bread and wine; his position was far closer to Zwingli than to Luther. Goering wanted fellowship with the Reformed, who shared the German language with Lutherans. Fewer than half of the theologians Goering read were Lutheran, while the others were Church of England, French, Dutch, or German Reformed. He did not read Lutherans of the orthodox tradition.[49] Those theologians who interested Goering advocated church union, the restoration of "primitive Christianity," interpretation of "prophecies" of the Book of Revelation, and harmonization of natural law with biblical revelation. All these interests can be seen in the theology of John George Schmucker.

Under the guidance of Helmuth, John George Schmucker read the pietists Arndt and Spener. Helmuth taught Schmucker about the Bible. Schmucker and all other students tutored by Helmuth were trained to defend Christianity against infidels. They were expected to give evidence of "experimental religion," a conversion experience, usually the result of participating in a revival. This requirement caused the elder Schmucker to have grave doubts concerning the state of his soul. Finally, he experienced manifestations that gave him assurance, and in 1792 he was recommended to the Ministerium for licensure as a "catechist."

John George Schmucker was then assigned to two congregations in York, Pennsylvania, where he was under the supervision of Goering. This internship lasted for a year and a half. During this time he continued to receive instruction in theology and Hebrew. On June 10, 1800, Schmucker was ordained. By this time he was serving a group of churches around

---

47. Charles A. Hay, *Memoirs of Rev. Jacob Goering, Rev. George Lochman, D.D., and Rev. Benjamin Kurtz, D.D., LL.D.* (Philadelphia: Lutheran Publication Society, 1887), 29.
48. Ibid., 38.
49. For a listing and discussion of this subject, see Haney, "Religious Heritage," 176–80.

Hagerstown, Maryland, had married, and had two sons; the second son was Samuel Simon.

In 1817 John George Schmucker was chosen to give the principal address in Philadelphia at the three-hundredth anniversary celebration of the Reformation. Two years later he presented a prospectus for a theological seminary, but the plan was laid aside. Schmucker was a delegate of the Pennsylvania Ministerium at the convention that founded the General Synod in 1820 and by that time was one of the leading churchmen in American Lutheranism.

The elder Schmucker was a supporter of the "New Measures" (revivals) and strongly opposed practices that would be considered amusements. Not long after he came to the parish that Goering had served in York, Schmucker upbraided several members of the congregation for playing cards. He preached against the use of alcohol and advocated "moral reforms."[50] Schmucker's piety, while rooted in German Lutheran pietism, was affected by the practices of various Protestant groups in America.

As early as 1804, Schmucker was designated by the Ministerium as a "teacher for the instruction of young preachers."[51] He was a prolific writer; his most famous work is his two-volume *A Prophetic History of the Christian Religion, or Explanation of the Revelation of St. John,* published from 1817 to 1821.[52] This work was explicitly millennial and concentrated on the historical fulfillment of biblical prophecy. Schmucker believed this proved that the Bible authenticated itself.

John George Schmucker was an advocate of Christian fellowship and believed that doctrinal formulations should not be allowed to get in the way of that goal. Such fellowship was possible on the basis of the "grand truths of Evangelical Christianity." Truth was to be found outside of Lutheranism. Indications that Schmucker identified himself with American evangelical Protestants are present in his millennial views, his practice of revivals, his support for Sunday schools, and his involvement in various missionary and tract societies. Schmucker served as senior vice-president of the American Tract Society and was active in chapters of the Temperance Society and the Bible and Sunday School Society.[53] His theological views and practices would have a vital influence on his son Samuel.

Samuel Schmucker's education began in the family home in Hagerstown, Maryland, where his father served as pastor. When the family moved to

50. Haney, "Religious Heritage," 198.
51. *Documentary History,* 345.
52. John George Schmucker, *A Prophetic History of the Christian Religion, or Explanation of the Revelation of St. John,* 2 vols. (Baltimore: Schaeffer & Maund, 1817–21).
53. Haney, "Religious Heritage," 220.

York, Pennsylvania, where the elder Schmucker was called to serve Christ Church, Samuel enrolled at York County Academy, where he studied from 1811 to 1814. York Academy offered college preparatory work and an education designed to prepare young men for the professions.[54] In 1814 Samuel enrolled at the University of Pennsylvania. The situation there was chaotic because the institution was facing financial and internal problems, but Schmucker was disciplined enough to obtain the best education he could under the circumstances.

During this period, Samuel came into contact with his father's teacher, Justus Helmuth. Although he probably never received any formal instruction from Helmuth, the young Schmucker spent many hours listening to him expound topics such as infidelity (rationalism) and biblical theology. It was Helmuth who saw to it that the young man kept on "the straight and narrow." Years later, Samuel Schmucker was as strict as Helmuth about matters of recreation and entertainment[55] and called Helmuth a "venerable father in Christ."[56]

While at the University of Pennsylvania, Schmucker came under the influence of Frederick Beasley (1777–1845), the provost of the institution. Although an Episcopalian, Beasley was evangelical in his views, especially with regard to the ministry. Beasley reinforced what Schmucker had already been taught by Helmuth and his father. Beasley introduced Schmucker to Scottish Common Sense Philosophy, especially that of Thomas Reid (1710–96).[57] This philosophy was used as an apology against the infidelity that was prevalent at that time. The Scottish philosophers, who attempted to make Christianity credible in the face of Enlightenment criticism, stressed that the validity of an event, a miracle for example, rests on evidence found in human consciousness. If the event was not "real," the observable effects would not have occurred. God would not use events to deceive humanity.

54. Ibid., 225.

55. A revealing portrait of Schmucker was later given by one of Schmucker's first students, who recalled: "He (Schmucker) did not know one card from another. I do not suppose he ever had a dice box in his hand, even for amusement. He knew nothing of chequers or backgammon or chess. He was never in a theatre or circus; never heard an opera. He even doubted the propriety of Christians going to hear a famous violinist in a concert hall, especially if they had appeared on the operatic stage. He never used tobacco in any form. He never drank a drop of strong liquor as a beverage. He never conformed to any modern fashion in dress for fashion's sake, however neat or appropriate it might be." John G. Morris, *Fifty Years in the Lutheran Ministry* (Baltimore: James Young, 1878), 129.

56. S. S. Schmucker, *The American Lutheran Church, Historically, Doctrinally, and Practically Delineated, in Several Occasional Discourses* (Philadelphia: E. W. Miller, 1852), 109.

57. This philosophy was intended to refute the skepticism of David Hume and reflected a conservatism in theology. Recently, however, the Scottish philosophers have been assessed as a "liberal vanguard, even as theological revolutionaries." See Sydney E. Ahlstrom, "The Scottish Philosophy and American Theology," *Church History* 24 (Sept. 1955), 5.

Schmucker later employed these arguments in his own work on psychology and mental philosophy.[58]

Samuel Schmucker left the University of Pennsylvania in 1816 before completing all the requirements in history and advanced composition. Three years later, however, the university awarded him an A.B., *gratiae causa*.[59]

In 1816 Schmucker returned to York and for sixteen months was a tutor at York Academy. During those months, he struggled with a call to the ministry. Schmucker's diary entries reflect his anguish over the fact that he had not had a conversion experience. In one entry, Schmucker wrote: "O Lord God, I am a sinner, and the iniquity of my ways will bring me to eternal ruin, if thy saving hand be not exerted in my favor. Though I am guilty of no crime against the world, or to my knowledge any individual, my heart is yet prone to evil and my ways are far from God."[60]

In 1817 Schmucker journeyed to Louisville, Kentucky, with a friend to see the western mission fields and to visit an old college friend, David Geiger. Sometime during this period some sort of conversion experience must have taken place, although Schmucker never described the event, for when Schmucker returned to York he began to study theology under his father to prepare for entrance into a theological seminary.

Under his father's instruction, Schmucker read some of the Lutheran orthodox divines, particularly Johannes Quenstedt (1617–1688), David Hollazius (1648–1713), and Johann Franz Buddeus (1667–1729). These were the most irenic of the orthodox theologians, but Schmucker thought them too polemical.[61] He turned to later theologians such as Sigmund Jakob Baumgarten (1706–1757), Johann Lorenz von Mosheim (1694–1755),[62] and Franz Vikmar Reinhard (1753–1812). The first two were associated with the Transitional School in Germany, which tried to mediate a course between deism and pietism, while Reinhard was a proponent of Biblical supranaturalism.

The elder Schmucker identified himself with orthodox Christianity in its pietistic expressions. His expression of the "peculiar doctrines of the Christian religion" is revealed in the following statement in his *Prophetic History*, which he was in the process of writing at the time he was tutoring Samuel.

58. S. S. Schmucker, *Psychology, or, Elements of a New System of Mental Philosophy, on the Basis of Consciousness and Common Sense* (New York: Harper & Bros., 1843).
59. Haney, "Religious Heritage," 252.
60. Diary of S. S. Schmucker, Nov. 6, 1816, quoted in Anstadt, *Life and Times*, 33.
61. Haney, "Religious Heritage," 273.
62. Mosheim was very influential in America. Years after his death, there were Mosheim clubs, one of which, under Helmuth's encouragement, met in Philadelphia. See Henry A. Pochman, *German Culture in America* (Madison: Univ. of Wisconsin Press, 1957), 522ff.

These essential points are the doctrine of the Holy Trinity of persons in the undivided Godhead; the incarnation of the Son of God; the expiation of the sin of the world by the Redeemer's sufferings and death; the efficacy of his intercession; the necessary cooperation of the Holy Ghost, in order to become experimentally acquainted with the Spirit and the vital influence of religion, spreading itself over all the power of men's souls, and quickening them into a *divine life;* together with the intimate union, between God and the believer's soul. [63]

Several statements in *A Prophetic History* also reveal that the elder Schmucker had negative feelings toward philosophy and considered it to be a stumbling block in relationship to theology.

The elder Schmucker presented to his son a pietism less conservative than that of Muhlenberg and more in tune with the evangelical theology prevalent in America. The elder Schmucker denied that humanity was totally sinful and allowed for humanity's free agency. He used the term "ordinance" interchangeably with "sacrament." He avoided the subject of baptismal regeneration. In his discussion of the Lord's Supper, he played down any concept of real presence and stressed that the Supper was a remembrance of Christ's death. He was silent regarding the Office of the Keys. Not only were John George Schmucker's views close to those of American evangelical Protestants; his views were also representative of the sacramental theology of many Lutherans in America, including Helmuth and Goering.

The father's anti-Catholic bias was also passed on to the son. *A Prophetic History* reflected the anti-Romanism common in early nineteenth-century Protestant America. Among the American evangelicals with whom the elder Schmucker identified, Roman Catholicism was the enemy, along with rationalist infidelity. Intense anti-Catholicism affected Samuel Schmucker's ideas about the nature of Lutheranism.

The last portion of Samuel Schmucker's education took place at Princeton, where he arrived on August 17, 1818. Schmucker's views had already been shaped by Helmuth and by his father; Princeton would round out his education. [64] He studied under two professors, Archibald Alexander (1772–1851) and Samuel Miller (1769–1850). In Miller and Alexander he witnessed a strong commitment to benevolent societies, missions, and other

63. J. G. Schmucker, *Prophetic History*, 1:129.

64. For a detailed discussion of Schmucker's Princeton experiences, see Haney, "Religious Heritage," 315–467. See also E. Theodore Bachmann, "Samuel Simon Schmucker (1799–1873): Lutheran Educator" in Hugh T. Kerr, ed., *Sons of the Prophets: Leaders in Protestantism from Princeton Seminary* (Princeton, N.J.: Princeton Univ. Press, 1963). Abdel Ross Wentz believes that Schmucker's time at Princeton is the key to understanding his theology. Wentz, *Pioneer*, 26–33.

causes with which he himself later became involved. He was also exposed to the Presbyterian understanding of confessional foundations.

The Scottish Common Sense Philosophy was an important component of Schmucker's studies of theology under Alexander. Schmucker learned that humanity must go behind common sense to discover that its nature has been constituted by God. Humanity has the same sort of evidence for the existence of God that it has for its own will and intelligence. Alexander also influenced Schmucker regarding fundamental and nonfundamental doctrines. Fundamental doctrines are those accepted by all Christians— for example, the Trinity; nonfundamental doctrines are those over which there are differences of opinion—for example, baptismal regeneration. The nonfundamental doctrines should not be allowed to divide Christians. Alexander emphasized that those who believe the fundamental doctrines should be united into one church. This helps explain Schmucker's strong support for ecumenism.

Under the instruction of Samuel Miller, Schmucker learned church history. Like Schmucker's father, Miller believed that the first century was Christianity's golden age. Its worship and discipline were taken over from the Jewish synagogue. The internal life of the church was characterized by piety, harmony, and simplicity. All ordinances, such as the Lord's Supper, were observed with little ceremony. Miller believed that the Presbyterian form of church government was established by the apostles and thus was essential for the well-being of the church.

Miller's comments on Lutherans are similar to those seen later in Schmucker's writings. Miller believed that Lutherans, unlike Luther, were reluctant to make a clean break with medieval Catholicism. He cited as examples continued use of the sign of the cross, private confession, crucifixes and images, the use of wafers, and exorcism. Miller thought that Lutherans in America were more in accord with Luther than Lutherans in Germany. He commented: "In the Lutheran Church in the United States I believe *none* of these *superstitions* are retained, etc. neither exorcism, images, incense, crucifixes. They are all generally *discarded* in our country and even the doctrine of consubstantiation is by no means universally held."[65] Miller said the reason for this was that American Lutheranism was influenced by pietism, which attempted to return to the spirit of Luther. It is probable that Schmucker's later move to revive the Augsburg Confession, the confession most closely identified with Luther himself, as a standard for the General Synod and professors of the seminary at Gettysburg was the result of Miller's influence rather than the influence of his father or Schmucker's father's generation.[66]

65. Cited in Haney, "Religious Heritage," 436.
66. Ibid., 474.

In the spring of 1820, Samuel Schmucker decided to leave Princeton Seminary without having completed the prescribed course of study. One possible reason, mentioned in a letter to his father, is that Schmucker wanted to continue his theological studies in the German language.[67] For whatever reasons, Schmucker's Princeton experience was the end of one phase in his life. That same year, he became involved in the organization of a Lutheran synodical body that would consume his efforts for the rest of his life.

Formation of the General Synod

On October 22, 1820, representatives from the Pennsylvania Ministerium, the Synod of North Carolina, the New York Ministerium, and the Synod of Maryland and Virginia met to draw up a constitution for a General Synod. The synods of Ohio and Tennessee, though invited, were absent.

It was hoped that a confederation of synods could provide organization and resolve disputes. The General Synod was to be advisory in nature. Each member synod controlled its own affairs. The General Synod was to be democratic and American in character.

How Lutheran the General Synod was to be was not clearly defined. "Lutheran" was a part of the name, but there was no defined confessional basis. None of the Lutheran confessional documents was even mentioned. The word "General" meant there was to be no doctrinal standard. Doctrinal flexibility was to be the order of the day.

Not all the synods that gathered in 1820 joined the proposed new body immediately. The New York Ministerium finally joined in 1837. The Synod of Ohio, not present in 1820, decided in 1821 to postpone action for a year. It sent delegates to the 1823 convention but never joined. Then, in 1823, the Pennsylvania Ministerium withdrew from the General Synod.

There were many reasons for the withdrawal. Fears of too much synodical authority were voiced. The language question surfaced, especially the apprehension that English would be imposed on the Germans. The major issue, however, was unionism. Many in the Pennsylvania Ministerium were afraid that a general Lutheran synod would make union with the Reformed impossible. One benefit of the proposed union was preservation of the use of the German language, a concern shared by Lutherans and members of the Reformed churches.

The union desired by some, however, never took place. In 1826 Johann Augustus Probst (1792–1844), a Lutheran pastor from Pennsylvania, published *Die Wiedervereinigung der Lutheraner und Reformirten* (*The Reunion of the Lutherans and the Reformed*), which advocated the abolition

---

67. Cited in Anstadt, *Life and Times*, 61.

of all doctrinal standards and differences that divided the churches. The book praised the Prussian Union and human reason. Probst argued that confessional writings had only historical value and were obsolete. He believed that doctrines such as predestination and the real presence in the sacrament were vestiges of the past and were no longer applicable. The influence of German rationalism was evident throughout this work, which provoked opposition from those in the General Synod who wanted an American *Lutheran* church.

Objections to the General Synod were varied. Some said it was too Lutheran, while others deemed it not Lutheran enough. The Tennessee Synod, for example, objected because the General Synod nowhere mentioned the Confessions and thus was not properly grounded in Lutheran standards. The General Synod constitution did make allowances for a new confession of faith if that was deemed necessary—"perhaps more popular, and suited to the new-fangled opinions of the present age of infidelity."[68] This article of the constitution would later be used to justify the American Lutherans' position.

The departure of the Pennsylvania Ministerium in 1823 almost caused the collapse of the General Synod. At that crucial moment Samuel Schmucker came to its rescue. His *Formula for the Government and Discipline of the Lutheran Church in Maryland and Virginia* became the governing standard for the General Synod. One of Schmucker's concerns was to revive the Augsburg Confession.

Samuel Schmucker, Rev. J. Herbst, and Schmucker's father, John George Schmucker, called a meeting of the Special Pennsylvania Conference, which met at York on October 6–7, 1823. At this meeting the conference asked the Ministerium to reconsider its withdrawal from the General Synod. Consideration of the request was postponed until the next meeting of the Ministerium.

Not to be put off, the proponents of the General Synod left the Pennsylvania Ministerium and formed the Synod of the Evangelical Lutheran Church, West of the Susquehanna, in the State of Pennsylvania on September 5, 1825. This new synod then joined the General Synod.

The General Synod did survive. In 1825 the Synod voted to establish a theological seminary. Provisions were made for a board of directors. Initially this board would be elected by the General Synod but thereafter by the individual synods. The board of directors was empowered to draw up a constitution, and a treasury was established. Samuel Schmucker was elected the seminary's first professor. The constitution of the theological

68. Wolf, "Americanization," 529.

seminary stated the seminary's intentions as follows: "It is designed: 2. To provide our churches with pastors who sincerely believe, and cordially approve of the doctrines of the Holy Scriptures, as they are fundamentally taught in the Augsburg Confession."[69] The wording here is significant because Schmucker and the American Lutherans later claimed that this formula, with its stress on fundamental doctrines, proved that the constitution of the seminary had not been violated.

Henry Eyster Jacobs, early twentieth-century Lutheran historian, gave this evaluation of the General Synod:

> The General Synod must be regarded as a very important forward movement, and its influence as beneficial. . . . The General Synod was a protest against the Socinianizing tendency in New York and the schemes of a union with the Reformed in Pennsylvania and with the Episcopalians in North Carolina. It stood for the independent existence of the Lutheran Church in America, and the clear and unequivocal confession of a positive faith.[70]

The General Synod was an extension of Muhlenberg's vision. It was democratic and thus American in its organization. The Augsburg Confession was "brought out of the dust," which gave the synod a confessional undergirding, but it was still intended to be an American Lutheran church.

During this period of roughly eighty years, many changes took place in Lutheranism in America. The 1742 arrival of Muhlenberg signaled the beginnings of an organized church on American soil. Muhlenberg gave a genuinely Lutheran witness. He made certain accommodations to the American situation, but this complex figure maintained confessional fidelity with regard to such doctrines as baptismal regeneration and the real presence of Christ in the Lord's Supper.

A noticeable decline in Lutheran identity occurred in the next generation. The Confessions were not even mentioned in synodical documents and ordination rites. The church was concerned with rationalism, imported from Germany and France. Lutherans joined forces with American evangelicals to combat rationalism.[71] As a result, Protestant agreement was emphasized and doctrinal differences were deemed unimportant. Many Lutherans in America had ceased to believe in such "nonessentials" as certain teachings regarding the sacraments.

69. Cited in ibid., 548
70. Jacobs, *History,* 361–62.
71. American evangelicalism in that period has been described as "an amalgam of denatured Calvinism, revivalism, and liturgical Zwinglianism." Nelson, ed. *The Lutherans,* 206.

George Lochman, Justus Helmuth, Jacob Goering, and John George Schmucker were among those who disregarded doctrinal differences between Lutherans and American evangelical Protestants. They denied certain distinctive Lutheran teachings. They became involved in revivals and were active in many of the newly formed Protestant societies. These four men were all advocates of a Protestant union and were vehemently anti-Catholic. They wanted Lutheranism to take its place with the other Protestant groups. The final goal was a nation for Protestants, ruled by Protestants. The Americanization process had become a reality; Lutheran identity had undergone a change.

Samuel Simon Schmucker was the central figure in the American Lutheran controversy; the General Synod was the battleground. Schmucker's emphasis on the difference between "fundamental" and "nonfundamental" doctrines, his anti-Catholicism, and his Zwinglian sacramental theology were characteristic of many Lutherans in America and were similar to the beliefs of the evangelical Protestants. With Schmucker's vision for American Lutheranism and for a united Protestantism in America, the basics of what would come to be called American Lutheranism were in place.

Benjamin Kurtz

Charles Porterfield Krauth

William Julius Mann

Samuel Simon Schmucker

4

Samuel Schmucker: Leading Voice for American Lutheranism

*I*n the early 1800s Lutherans were not only becoming accustomed to living in America; they were also taking on some of the characteristics of their evangelical Protestant neighbors. The seeds of what came to be known as American Lutheranism were being sown. To understand American Lutheranism it is necessary to examine the early writings of Samuel Simon Schmucker, its most important figure and leader.[1]

Schmucker came to the rescue of the newly formed General Synod when it was struggling for survival. He emerged as the leader of that ecclesiastical body. As professor at the seminary at Gettysburg, he influenced hundreds of students who went on to serve parishes in the General Synod.

Early in his tenure as professor, Schmucker began publishing works to benefit his students and fill the void in English theological texts. In 1826 Schmucker translated a recently published German work, Gottlob Christian Storr's *Lehrbuch der christlichen Dogmatic* (*Handbook of Christian Dogmatics*), which represented the biblical supranaturalism of the Old Tübingen school.[2] Carl Flatt, a colleague of Storr's, supplied additional notes and articles. This is an interesting work because it advocates some of the teachings that Schmucker later put forward as marks of American Lutheranism.

Storr and Flatt, like Schmucker, used the term "ordinance" in place of "sacrament." The closest this volume comes to speaking of baptismal re-

---

1. Selections from the *Collected Papers of Samuel Simon Schmucker,* located in the Library Archives at the Lutheran Theological Seminary in Gettysburg, Pennsylvania, will not be included in this study. The author examined the inventory of this collection and discovered nothing that was not already expressed in Schmucker's published writings.

2. Samuel S. Schmucker, *An Elementary Course of Biblical Theology Translated from the Work of Professors Storr and Flatt,* 2 vols. (Andover: Flagg & Gould, 1826). For a discussion of biblical supranaturalism, see chap. 2, note 50.

generation is as follows: "Little children are indeed unable to worship God. But they are capable of receiving the grace of God, which is secured to them by baptism" (2:302–3). In the discussion of the Lord's Supper, the doctrine of the real presence is nowhere denied or affirmed (2:317–28).

Schmucker added an appendix on the Eucharist in which he stated that the Lutheran view is the most consistent with the Scriptures. He defined presence as "the power to exert an influence at a particular place" (2:333). He went on to say that a person can exert influence in a particular place without being locally present in that place. Christ may be symbolically present in the Eucharist without being locally present. Schmucker believed he was refuting the Reformed objections against the Lutheran position (2:332–33), but it is not at all clear that his position was distinctly Lutheran.

An Elementary Course of Biblical Theology proved to be too difficult for many of Schmucker's students to understand because their educational backgrounds were inadequate; so he wrote a textbook of his own, *Elements of Popular Theology,* which first appeared in 1834.[3] This work was the first dogmatics text written for Lutherans in America. It went through several editions and exercised great influence on the pastors trained at the seminary where Schmucker taught.

Elements of Popular Theology summarizes Schmucker's theological views in a systematic fashion, views that he would hold his entire life. The work is patterned after the twenty-one articles of the Augsburg Confession that the General Synod had adopted, omitting the condemnatory clauses and the entire catalog of Abuses Corrected. Schmucker explained that ministers were not required to agree with everything in the twenty-one articles, only the fundamental doctrines. He did not say, however, what the fundamental doctrines were.[4]

Much of the book defines the doctrine of God. For example, an entire chapter was devoted to the basis for rational belief in the Trinity. In discussing the meaning of revelation, one comment of Schmucker's is particularly revealing:

> In short, if God sees fit to grant to mankind any additional information beyond what the heavens and the earth and the structure of the human soul afford, the most suitable method of this accomplishment so far as we can see, would be this: To communicate those truths which will of course be reasonable in themselves, to one or more suitable individuals; appoint them to teach these doctrines; attest the unity of their mission by satisfactory

---

3. Samuel S. Schmucker, *Elements of Popular Theology, with Special Reference to the Doctrines of the Reformation* (Andover: Gould & Newman, 1834).

4. Samuel S. Schmucker, *Elements of Popular Theology* (Philadelphia: S. S. Miles, 1845), 50. All references to *Elements of Popular Theology* will be from this edition.

evidence, and provide for accurate transmission of these truths and evidences to all future generations for whom they were intended. (22)

Schmucker's emphasis on the reasonableness of truth was prominent in his discussion of various doctrines and was a criterion for what constituted a fundamental doctrine. Schmucker repeated that conviction later in the work: "a divine revelation cannot contain anything which is contrary to the plain indisputable dictates of reason" (73).

Schmucker was opposed to any form of a doctrine of election. He stated adamantly: "Calvinism is again reviving in the church, both in Europe and America; but the doctrine of Melanchthon, or what is essentially the same, the doctrine of the Arminians, on this point, is predominant; and the theory of absolute predestination is generally regarded, by the laity at least, with horror" (109). Schmucker's equating Melanchthon's teaching with that of the Arminians, who believed that man possessed free will in all things, is evidence that he was speaking from his American context, not from the language and doctrine of the Augsburg Confession, of which Melanchthon was the author. Melanchthon's statements in the Augsburg Confession are not Arminian. Schmucker also cited, with obvious approval, a statement about free will written by a Dr. Mayer, a former professor from the German Reformed seminary in Mercersburg, Pennsylvania.[5]

This dogmatics text has no chapters regarding Christology or justification. A brief explanation affirms Christ's divinity and his return to render judgment. Justification is explained in just three pages (169–71). In contrast, six pages are devoted to angels, and fifteen pages to the "Decrees and Providence of God." Fully nineteen pages deal with different aspects of civil government, including "The Principles of the American Revolution" and slavery. The millennium receives sixteen pages of explanation. The inclusion of these topics would seem to indicate the influence of American Protestant theological and social issues.

Justification is described as the imputation of Christ's righteousness to the sinner. Schmucker concluded his brief treatment of the subject by stating that justification takes place "when the sinner first attains a living faith in the Redeemer" (171). As to when that happens, Schmucker was not specific.

Schmucker treated the sacraments in a symbolic way. Baptism was the symbol of natural depravity, and the Lord's Supper was symbolic of Christ's death. Although he used the term "means of grace," he was inclined to

---

5. A reference to Lewis Mayer, whom Sydney Ahlstrom described as "a self-educated, somewhat rationalistically inclined pastor." Sydney E. Ahlstrom, *Religious History of the American People* (New Haven: Yale Univ. Press, 1972), 616.

view the sacraments as "symbols of grace" because they represented rather than actually imparted God's grace.

Schmucker defended the baptism of infants because it is "a duty obligatory upon all, who have the opportunity to receive it; and upon them alone" (240). Also, Schmucker interpreted Christ's command "to all nations" to mean infants. Schmucker believed that the apostles themselves had introduced infant baptism and cited historical data to support his argument: Justin Martyr, Ireneus, Origen, Augustine, and even Pelagius (260–62). Schmucker believed that baptism was symbolic only, figuratively representing the process of spiritual purification.

Schmucker looked to the later Melanchthon and not to Luther for support of his theology of the Lord's Supper. He pointed out that Melanchthon rejected the substantial presence of the body and blood of Christ and instead affirmed what Schmucker described as the "virtual" or "influential" presence (300–301). Schmucker claimed that Lutheranism left each individual free on this matter. He explained that most Americans held the Melanchthonian or Calvinistic view of Christ's presence in the Supper.

With regard to absolution, Schmucker said that the Reformers denied that the ordained priest had the authority to forgive sins. He pointed out that private confession had been eliminated, and the closest practice to it was the custom of the person coming to speak with the pastor before communing. Schmucker treated absolution as the restoration of church privileges rather than the act of the pastor forgiving the penitent in the stead of Christ (310).

Schmucker presented a liberal picture of Lutheranism in his *Popular Theology:* "It embraces all those principles and precepts of permanent obligation, which are contained in the New Testament, and such other regulations as are dictated by reason but adapted to the genius of our free republican institutions, and calculated most successfully to advance the cause of Christ" (217).

This first American Lutheran dogmatics gave few indications of being specifically Lutheran. Reason was regarded as a higher norm for belief than the Augsburg Confession. Specifically Lutheran teachings were denied. Schmucker believed that only an open and free Lutheranism could be successful in America. This would become the conviction of the American Lutheran party.

Schmucker's Anti-Catholicism

Samuel Schmucker was vehemently anti-Catholic, an attitude learned from his father as well as his other teachers. Schmucker's anti-Catholic views played an important role in his attitude toward the Lutheran Confessions and Lutheran identity. Most American Protestants were anti-Catholic and were fearful of a Catholic takeover of America. One historian has commented: "By the middle of the 1840's the American churches were able to present a virtually united front against Catholicism. Swept away by the pleas of organized nativists, they had accepted the challenge to make America the scene of a new Reformation in which Popery would be driven from the land and the work of Luther and Calvin brought to a successful end."[6]

American Protestants organized voluntary societies designed to combat the Roman challenge. The American Tract Society, founded in 1826, was particularly aggressive. Schmucker was a member of this society and served as a vice-president for eight years.[7] He joined Lyman Beecher and a number of other noted Protestant leaders in a scheme to evangelize all Italy and convert the country to Protestantism, which would bring down the Vatican.[8]

Schmucker's nativist and anti-Roman feelings were expressed in three works. The first was *Discourse in Commemoration of the Glorious Reformation of the Sixteenth Century,* presented before the Evangelical Lutheran Synod of West Pennsylvania in 1837.[9] This work was widely received and went through four editions in two years.

Schmucker began by stating that, in his opinion, American citizens were unaware of power of the papacy. He intended to show that the papacy was a corruption of apostolic Christianity, and he hoped that, after hearing the evidence, Catholics would unite with Protestants in denouncing the papacy as a threat to human liberty.

Schmucker believed the Reformation freed people from bondage and was the work of God. Prior to the Reformation the pope had used his claim of the power to forgive sins to enslave half the civilized world. As the result of the Reformation the papacy had lost its power, and it trembled at the voice of earthly monarchs. Because of the Reformation, the papacy would never again rise to power.

The two hundred years prior to the Reformation was a time of preparation for this glorious event. The first objections to the papacy arose at universities such as those in Paris and Prague. A partial reformation had begun in

---

6. Roy Allen Billington, *The Protestant Crusade, 1800–1860: A Study of the Origins of American Nativism* (New York: Rinehart & Co., 1938), 181.

7. Abdel Ross Wentz, *Pioneer in Christian Unity: Samuel Simon Schmucker* (Philadelphia: Fortress Press, 1966), 262.

8. John R. Bodo, *The Protestant Clergy and Public Issues, 1812–1848* (Princeton: Princeton Univ. Press, 1954), 82, note 69.

9. Samuel S. Schmucker, *Discourse in Commemoration of the Glorious Reformation of the Sixteenth Century* (New York: Gould & Newman, 1838).

Bohemia. The Inquisition in Spain was an example of papal despotism. Schmucker described the popes of the period before and during Luther's life as a "disgrace to humanity" (14–15). Councils such as Pisa (1409) had decreed a reformation in the church, but such efforts were often defeated by the intrigues of the popes. Revival of knowledge and culture was an important factor in the movement toward the Reformation. Many enlightened minds satirized the ignorance of the priests and the superstition that abounded in the church. Although Schmucker recognized that the process which brought Luther to the point of reformation was gradual, he staunchly maintained that it was God-guided (21).

Schmucker thought certain features of the Reformation were particularly commendable. One was free access to the Word (25). Christ told those who would follow him that the truth could be found in the Scriptures. In contrast to this, Rome had for centuries elevated tradition and the decrees of councils until they were on the same level as the Scriptures. Schmucker maintained that this was the practice of the Roman church until it became official teaching at the Council of Trent (28). Prior to the Reformation the common people had almost no access to the Bible and little opportunity to study it. Schmucker believed that the Bible and the Reformation went hand in hand. He was willing to grant that Roman Catholics now had the Bible available to them, but only in a corrupted version. Also, the Roman Catholic version added several books (the Apocrypha) "which do not belong to the Word of God at all" (30). Schmucker noted that the Roman church opposed Bible societies, but in Protestantism the word of God was welcomed. The Reformation, in fact, returned the Scriptures to the laity. Schmucker stated:

> Forget not that the Reformation conferred on you this delightful privilege. Does this word enable you daily to hold communion with the men of God who wrote as the Holy Ghost inspired? Do you peruse the predictions of the ancient prophets, or read the very letters which the apostles wrote to the first churches, thus enjoying the privileges of the primitive Christians? Do you find the precious Bible evinced a book divine by its elevating, transforming, beautifying influence on your soul? Then forget not, that for all these high and holy privileges, your gratitude is due to the glorious Reformation by which God delivered your fathers from Papal darkness and superstition. (33–34)

For Schmucker, the primary feature of the Reformation was the restoration of the Bible to its place of chief importance in the life of the church.

The second important feature of the Reformation was that it delivered the church from doctrinal and practical corruptions. Instead of worshiping God through the mediation of saints, angels, or the Virgin Mary, Protestantism restored the privilege of worshiping God alone. Schmucker explained that many of the saints were historically doubtful and others had led illicit lives; "What worshipper of the true God can reflect without horror on the idea of paying religious veneration to such monsters of iniquity!" (37) The Reformation restored the church to the "primitive, simple ordinances of the Gospel" instead of corrupted sacraments (39).

In an interesting comment, coming from one who was a professed Lutheran, Schmucker claimed that the Reformation restored the concept that the Eucharist is an ordinance to "commemorate the dying love of the Savior, and to serve as a pledge of his spiritual presence and blessing on all worthy participants" (41) He also stated that the Reformation did away with the sacramental structure of the church and denied the remission of sins through priests and papal indulgences. Schmucker asserted that the papacy was guilty of promoting sin because the more sins committed, the greater profit for the Roman church. The requirement of celibacy caused even greater corruption in priests, monks, and nuns. Schmucker painted a picture of innocent women being sexually abused by priests and monks after they had been lured into the convents under the guise of living a secluded religious life (45–47). He admitted that the Reformation had led to reforms in the Roman church, and cited the deportment of priests in America as an example. In Catholic countries in Europe, however, few changes had occurred.

A third feature of the Reformation was that it promoted freedom of conscience and freedom from religious persecution. Schmucker charged that the Roman church had forced people to surrender all reason in order that they might believe only what the church taught. The Roman church had specifically disobeyed Christ's command to search the Scriptures. Its people were also forbidden to read other theological works. Schmucker claimed that the Roman church considered it a profound duty to compel all others to accept its faith and would stop at nothing—inquisition, torture, even death—to force people to come under its rule (76). In contrast to this, he maintained that the Reformation accepted conscience rather than the church's dictates as authoritative. Civil authorities and ecclesiastical authorities were to remain in separate realms, which meant that civil authorities were to have no jurisdiction in the church. Schmucker drew from this the conclusion that heresy is an intellectual matter and ought not be dealt with by the civil authorities or by the sword. He claimed that Protestants persecute only when something goes against their principles; Catholics persecute when something goes against their creed (95).

The final feature of the Reformation was the fact that it freed the civil authorities from papal tyranny. The Protestant churches, said Schmucker, are governed by "the fixed principles of reason and scripture" (96). In contrast to this, the Roman church demands unconditional obedience and discourages individuals from making their own judgments. Protestants are thus much more free in the area of civil rights than are their Roman counterparts. Schmucker cited several reasons for this: (1) The pope claimed jurisdiction over all civil government. (2) He attempted to overthrow rulers who did not swear allegiance to him. (3) Priests served the pope rather than the civil authorities, and priests and nuns were protected in many places from prosecution by the civil magistrates (101–26).

Schmucker concluded his discourse by stating that it was the Reformation that opened the eyes of Europe to the subtle papal treachery. Unlike Romanism, Protestantism always vowed loyalty to the government and has not infringed upon the rights and liberties of men. He called on America to watch Rome closely. Schmucker described the Jesuits as a "standing army of foreign allegiance in our midst" (131). All politicians, statesmen, and Christians of every denomination were urged to unite so that the Word of God might be "gotten out," that people might search the Scriptures and think for themselves.[10]

The Glorious Reformation is more an anti-Catholic polemic than a general discourse on the Reformation. One historian has said that it was "entirely anti-Roman."[11] It presented many nativist attitudes, particularly the opinion that the Roman church was authoritarian and would stop at nothing to gain control over Protestant America. Schmucker believed that the Reformation freed people from Roman tyranny and restored apostolic principles. In these attitudes he reflected what the great majority of American Protestants thought about religious events of the sixteenth century.

A second work that reflects Schmucker's anti-Catholicism is a discourse delivered at the English Lutheran Church in Gettysburg on February 2, 1845, *The Papal Hierarchy, Viewed in Light of Prophecy and History.*[12] The text on which this discourse was based was Daniel 7:23-26:

> Thus he said: "As for the fourth beast, there shall be a fourth kingdom on earth, which shall be different from all the kingdoms, and it shall devour

10. Roman Catholics did not sit idle in the face of the Protestant polemics. During the early and mid-1830s, Roman Catholics answered Protestant anti-Catholic claims in several spirited exchanges. The most famous of these was a series of debates between John Hughes, who later became Archbishop of New York, and John Breckenridge, a Presbyterian pastor in Philadelphia. See Billington, *Protestant Crusade,* 62–66.

11. Billington, *Protestant Crusade,* 181.

12. Samuel S. Schmucker, *The Papal Hierarchy, Viewed in Light of Prophecy and History* (Gettysburg, Pa.: H. C. Neinstedt, 1845).

the whole earth, and trample it down, and break it to pieces. As for the ten horns, out of this kingdom ten kings shall arise, and another shall rise after them; he shall be different from the former ones, and shall put down these kings. He shall speak words against the Most High, and shall wear out the saints of the Most High, and shall think to change the time and the law; and they shall be given into his hand for a time, two times, and half a time. But the court shall sit in judgment, and his dominion shall be taken away, to be consumed and destroyed to the end."

Schmucker stated that the four beasts represent empires. The first empire is Babylon. The three kings or empires after it are the Medes, the Greeks (Alexander), and Rome. The ten horns referred to could only represent Rome because after the death of Theodosius, the empire was divided into ten kingdoms. The prophecy, Schmucker claimed, indicates that the Son of Man would come during the reign of the fourth beast or kingdom. Christ came during the period of the Roman Empire. The little horn (Dan. 7:8, 20) was to come out of the Roman Empire and after 536 A.D., the date of the foundation of the tenth kingdom. Since the "Mohammedan Kingdom" did not come out of Rome, Schmucker said that he was forced to come to the conclusion that the little horn must be the "Romish papacy" (12).

Schmucker cited five traits or marks as proof that his interpretation was correct. In the first place, the papacy acquired control over much of the territory. Daniel 7:8, 20 was used to support this view. The triple crown that the pope wears symbolizes the three kingdoms he has subdued (Dan. 7:8). A second trait of the little horn is that in it "were eyes like the eyes of a man" (13). Schmucker maintained that this indicates that the papacy possesses worldly vision and insight; it knows what everyone is doing. In this context, the Jesuits were the pope's main agency of espionage. The third trait of the little horn is that it has a mouth capable of speaking prophecy and uttering great things—"he will make pompous, sacrilegious and arrogant assumptions of dignity and power" (15).

Schmucker concluded that this must represent the papacy. He asked,

Where in the history of the civilized world, can we find a king or an emperor, who makes pretensions at all comparable to those of this pretended successor of the meek and lowly Jesus? What can be more disgusting to a person imbued with the humble spirit of Christianity, than the pompous and even blasphemous titles and forms of address, claimed by these arrogant pontiffs, and cheerfully given by their submissive, servile and abject subjects. (15–16)

The pope is not content to be ruler of the church; he must be ruler over the earth as well, and so he exercises authority over kings and princes. The incident of Henry IV standing in the snow for three days at Canossa is proof of that.

The fourth mark of the little horn is that "he shall seek to change times and laws." The pope claims to be the head of the church when Christ is its head. Schmucker listed many ways in which the church changed both God's laws and church customs: papal infallibility, image worship, celibacy of priests, auricular confession, Purgatory, the Word of God being kept from the people, transubstantiation, and the denial of the cup to the laity (19–20).

The final mark is that the little horn will make war against the saints of the Most High. Schmucker maintained that the "Romish hierarchy" had persecuted the saints of God. The example he used was the "infernal inquisition," which he claimed was made a permanent part of the church by the Fourth Lateran Council in 1215. Those who opposed the Roman church were put to death—1,500,000 Jews in Spain, 3,000,000 Moors, the St. Bartholomew's Day massacre of French Protestants, and over a million Albigenses and Waldenses (23–25).

Schmucker analyzed the biblical prophecies and explained how they related to the Roman church of that day. No Roman Catholic, however, should take this unflattering analysis as a personal affront, Schmucker claimed. He was only doing his duty as God had called him to do it. He explained that he was concerned over the increasing number of the "worshippers of this papal beast" in the United States, an obvious reference to the increased immigration of people from predominantly Roman Catholic countries. Schmucker was particularly suspicious of the Jesuits. If Americans were not on their guard the papacy would take over.

Finally, the prophecy could reveal the nature of measures called for by the great emergency that Schmucker saw. He did not advise personal animosity toward the papists but instead toward their errors. Pastors should preach the gospel more powerfully than ever. In addition, books and pamphlets should be distributed to Catholics so that they could see their errors. Schmucker closed this discourse with the assurance that enlightened Catholics would be led to the truth by such means.

This pamphlet reflected the anti-popery common among the nativists of that time. Schmucker's use of prophecy also reflects the influence of his father. The Bible, especially the prophetic books, could be used to prove that the papacy was the anti-Christ and that the Roman church stood against everything Jesus and the apostles intended. This discourse was popular enough to be reprinted the same year it appeared; it was also translated into German.[13]

The last of Schmucker's three anti-Roman works was a fifty-eight-page pamphlet, *Elemental Contrast Between the Religion of Forms and of the Spirit*.[14] This was an expansion of another discourse given before the Synod of West Pennsylvania. In addition to presenting Schmucker's anti-Roman bias, it gives a clear picture of his vision for Protestantism.

Schmucker began by contending that there are two forms of religion, ecclesiastical organization, and action that are at odds with each other. They could be seen as forms versus spirit, works versus grace, authority versus liberty—or, more directly, the Romish and Protestant systems (4). As in his two previous anti-Catholic works, Schmucker accused the Roman church of not regarding the Bible as the only sufficient rule for faith and practice. In addition to the Bible, the Roman church had added the Apocrypha and the authority of the church fathers. Rome regarded the church as infallible, outside of which there is no salvation; the ministry was believed to be a divinely appointed priesthood; the sacraments were efficacious in themselves; justification was by works; and conversion and regeneration were never addressed to the people (6–9). This formal system, Schmucker claimed, demanded absolute obedience and deprived the laity of their right to search the Scriptures. The Reformers, Schmucker contended, rejected this whole system (9).

Schmucker attacked not only the Roman church; he included the Puseyites, members of a party within the Anglican (Episcopal) church, whom he regarded as being nothing more than Romish people who had not left the Protestant ranks.[15] Schmucker also criticized the "church development" concept,[16] which he contended gave the church the opportunity to justify all her errors.

13. Wentz, *Pioneer*, 261.

14. Samuel S. Schmucker, *Elemental Contrast Between the Religion of Forms and of the Spirit, As Examined in Popery on one Hand, and Genuine Protestantism on the Other* (Gettysburg, Pa.: H. C. Neinstedt, 1852).

15. The term "Puseyite" refers to one of the leaders of the Oxford Movement, Edward Pusey (1800–82). The Oxford Movement advocated catholic reforms within the Church of England and also had an impact in America. Works on the Oxford Movement are numerous. The best source is Owen Chadwick, *The Victorian Church: Part I, 1829–1859* (London: A & C Black, 1966). For an example of American anti-Puseyism, see a book written by an Episcopalian: Ira Warren, *The Causes and the Cure of Puseyism: Or, the Elementary Principles of Roman Error Detected in the Liturgy, Offices, Homilies, and Usages of the Episcopal Churches of England and America; With a Proposed Remedy* (Boston: Crocker & Brewster, 1847).

16. Probably a reference to the work of John Henry Newman (1801–90) whose book *Essay on the Development of Doctrine* (London, 1845) advocated that all doctrines existed from the beginning but, because of heresies and other circumstances, doctrines had to be

Unlike the Roman church, Protestantism regarded the Scriptures as the sole norm for the faith and life of the church; and this, said Schmucker, was the "grand characteristic feature of Protestantism" (14). The church consists of individual believers who hear the Savior's word and use his ordinances faithfully. In Schmucker's eyes the difference between the two systems was clear. In the Romish system the sinner gains access to Christ through the church; in Protestantism the sinner gains access to the church through Christ. In the Roman church, the person is received unconverted; in Protestantism, the person is not received until his mind has been enlightened. Protestants view the ministry as an office to which people are appointed to preach the word and dispense the sacraments. The Holy Spirit works through these means to save sinners. By contrast, the Roman church interposes the priest between Christ and the believer. Forgiveness is not received directly from God but through the forgiving power of the priest (16–17).

The Protestant system makes the sacraments exhibitions of divine truth while in the Roman church they are indispensable channels of divine grace. This, argued Schmucker, results in a dependence on ritual (17). Finally, regarding justification, the Protestant system makes pardon a forensic and instantaneous act of God where the believing sinner is released from all penalties. This, said Schmucker, is the "touchstone of Protestantism" (17–18). The members of the Roman church who need pastoral care are enslaved to the priests who hold them in captivity, whereas in Protestantism the minister constantly points the people to Christ in order that regeneration and conversion might be accomplished.

Romanism is not the Christianity of the Bible; Protestantism is. In opposition to both Rome and the Puseyites, Protestantism regards the Bible as sufficient and infallible for faith and practice, and as the principal means of grace. Schmucker was willing to grant that both Rome and the Puseyites believed this, but their traditions contradicted that truth. He accused them both of denying the Scriptures to their people and of looking to the church fathers in addition to the Scriptures. Schmucker claimed that the fathers contradicted themselves, and much of the information known about them was apocryphal. Councils have not always been correct either. Schmucker pointed out, for example, that the Council of Nicea almost embraced Arianism (23).

---

commented upon, explained, interpreted, and applied. For Newman, a "new revelation" was impossible because the "idea" was present from the beginning. For a discussion of this topic, see Nicholas Lash, *Newman on Development: The Search for an Explanation in History* (Shepherdstown, W.V.: Patmos Press, 1975). Newman was a leader in the early days of the Oxford Movement but became Roman Catholic in 1845.

Schmucker offered four proofs for his contention that Protestantism is the Christianity of the Bible. First, since the Bible was written in human language, it must be interpreted like other works. Rome interpreted the Scriptures incorrectly and thus it had become corrupt. Schmucker cited the commission of Christ as proof that the Word of God is the chief means of grace. He felt that preaching was more important than baptizing; but baptism was an important ordinance because it showed the depravity of humanity and the necessity of purifying influences of the Holy Spirit (27–28).

A second proof that Protestantism, and not Rome, is the Christianity of the Bible is seen in Protestantism's views of the church. Schmucker contended that the church is not an organic whole; the plan of the apostles was to found several independent congregations. No trace of synods or councils can be found until the second century. Schmucker distinguished between the visible and invisible church, a distinction he said was a cardinal principle of Protestantism (33). The fact that Christ condemned the Pharisees and Paul spoke of "circumcision of the heart" was evidence enough that there were those in the visible church who did not belong to the invisible church.

Schmucker's third argument was that Rome's idea of infallibility has no foundation in the Scriptures. Rome had most often invested infallibility in the hierarchy, but there had been many disputes over the location of infallibility, and that proved to Schmucker that Rome's claims were wrong. He asked, "How can a body that is made up of fallible parts be itself infallible?" (36). Christ never pronounced the church infallible, so such could not be the case.

The final argument was that Rome's legislative power to establish doctrines and creeds proves her unscriptural character. Schmucker used the Immaculate Conception of the Virgin Mary as an example of unscriptural dogma (38). Acts such as this showed that the original "inspired ideal" of the church had been lost.[17] Schmucker lamented that, the longer Christianity was in existence, the longer the list of required beliefs grew.

Schmucker attacked both Romanism and Puseyism with regard to their views on the ministry. He rejected their concept of apostolic succession, which regarded that succession as a channel of ministerial authority and blessing. He cited a list of abuses committed by those who had sat in Peter's chair and argued that their actions were not consistent with the teachings of the Bible. There were no such offices as popes and bishops in the first centuries, so apostolic succession cannot be true. Schmucker was particularly critical of the practice of private confession, which he

17. Schmucker, *Elemental Contrast,* 39. This "inspired ideal," according to the footnotes, was belief in the statement "Jesus is the Christ, the Son of God."

said had no biblical foundations. Priestly absolution he regarded as a "Scriptural abomination" (45). Schmucker believed that a minister could declare pardon, but the minister could not apply it unconditionally in the form of absolution. As far as Schmucker was concerned, an absolution would do no more good than a declaration of pardon, because only a converted person could be pardoned.

Schmucker's attack extended to the Roman and Puseyite view of the sacraments. He referred to disagreements over the number of sacraments and their influence. He pointed out that, in the Scriptures, previous moral qualification is required—faith is demanded. The sacraments cannot work independently (51). Those whose baptism was described in the Scriptures believed before baptism took place. With regard to the Lord's Supper, Paul enjoined examination on the part of the recipient. Schmucker said that the Romans and Puseyites were wrong in speaking of the sacraments as effecting a change. He asked how a physical act on the body could purify the mind (51). Proper views and feelings are necessary, whereas Rome and the Puseyites rely on forms. Mere external rites can be performed by the impenitent and unbelieving, Schmucker said, but they are to no avail because there is no moral preparation and conversion (52).

Schmucker's final assault was on the Roman doctrine of justification. Rome and the Puseyites believe in works-righteousness, he argued, as evidenced by the numbers of prayers, Ave Marias, attendance at mass, and other works designed to gain God's favor. This emphasis on works, said Schmucker, "generates spiritual pride and fosters ignorance of the plan of salvation through Christ" (54). It also serves to treat all in the church as good Christians and thus blur the distinction between the visible and invisible church. In contrast to this are the five features of apostolic Christian evangelization: the apostles preached the Word; they gave to awakened souls specific instruction as to what they should do; they introduced awakened sinners to the invisible church by the ordinance of baptism; the apostles continued to watch over and edify the new converts; and having received children by baptism, they labored faithfully to train them in the faith (55–56).

Schmucker closed by telling his audience that they should faithfully guard and adhere to the primitive, apostolic, inspired model of Christianity, and that the religion of forms should be resisted and preached against as being "ruinous to the soul" (58). The doctrine of individual responsibility is important and should be kept. The church should guard against ministers who exalt their office by ceremonies, forms, and robes. Finally, Protestants should ignore their minor differences and unite against the common foe.

The three previous works leave no doubt about Schmucker's feelings toward Roman Catholicism. Like most American Protestants of his day, he viewed the Roman church with disdain and believed that institution was a threat to what he perceived to be a Protestant America.

The theology Schmucker propounded in these works is perfectly consistent with that found in his previously published articles. This theology was evangelical American Protestantism more than Lutheranism, especially in its stress on the need for conversion, its distinction between the visible and invisible church, and its sacramental theology.[18]

One new issue was Schmucker's desire for a pan-Protestant union in America that would exemplify the unity Christ desired for his church and that would also serve to stand against the Roman threat. Schmucker was serious about such a union, which he proposed in an 1838 work.

Schmucker's Fraternal Appeal

Although he was a Lutheran, Samuel Schmucker's associations were by no means limited to other Lutherans. Throughout his career he was a staunch advocate of and worker for a union that would encompass all Protestant denominations. His early education at Princeton had put him in contact with men such as Robert Baird (1798–1863) and Charles Hodge (1797–1878), who were destined to become leaders in other denominations.[19] These relationships probably stirred Schmucker's interest in ecumenical affairs.

Schmucker was active in what Charles I. Foster has called the Evangelical United Front.[20] This was not one unified organization but a group of voluntary societies that involved most Protestant denominations. Denominational differences were overlooked in order that Bible distribution, printing of tracts, promotion of Sunday schools, temperance, and other causes might be advanced. Four societies received Schmucker's special attention: the American Bible Society (organized in 1816), the American Education Society (1813), the American Sunday School Union (1824), and

18. In the Augsburg Confession, Article VII, the church is specifically defined as a visible and audible community of believers where the Word is preached in its purity and the sacraments are rightly administered. Article VIII allows that there are hypocrites in the church, but no distinction is made between a visible and invisible church.

19. Robert Baird, a Presbyterian, was Schmucker's roommate during his second year at Princeton. Baird would later occupy positions of leadership in Christian social reforms such as temperance and antislavery. He was also involved in the American Sunday School Union. Charles Hodge, also a Presbyterian, later became a professor at Princeton Seminary. Staunchly conservative, he reacted against the sectarian spirit of the times. Other contacts made by Schmucker were William B. Sprague, a Congregationalist, and two future Episcopalian bishops, John Johns and Charles P. McIlvane. See Wentz, *Pioneer,* 30.

20. For a history of this effort, see Charles I. Foster, *An Errand of Mercy: the Evangelical United Front 1790–1837* (Chapel Hill: Univ. of North Carolina Press, 1960).

the American Tract Society (1826). Schmucker contributed his time and talents to all of these, for he saw them not only as tools for Christian evangelism but also as agents for the reform of society.

Closely related to Schmucker's interest in the various evangelical societies was his concern for missions. Schmucker, Abdel Ross Wentz argued, was one of those most instrumental in transforming the concept of missions from a private, individual matter to an area of activity for the entire church.[21] Paul Kuenning's recent study, *The Rise and Fall of Lutheran Pietism*, discusses the involvement of pietists in the various social causes of that day, especially abolition of slavery.[22] Although European Lutheran pietists who influenced Schmucker had sensed long ago the responsibility of the church in the area of missions, that concept was never fully realized because of the church-state relationship that prevailed in Germany. The situation in America, however, was entirely different; there was no state church, support of churches was voluntary, and clergy and laity were recognized as equal. The General Synod sponsored missionaries who went to all parts of the world.[23] Schmucker focused on America as the leading nation in the establishment of a worldwide communion of saints. He felt this was Christ's intention for his church on earth. Protestantism must unite under one banner to create this communion of saints. Various denominations carried out their individual work in missions, but many efforts were interdenominational. Missions and ecumenical cooperation were linked.

Unlike many who were concerned for unity but did little to promote it, Schmucker drew up and submitted plans to the various Protestant denominations. The *Fraternal Appeal* was his formal proposal for that union.[24]

Before he presented his plan for the unity of the Protestant churches, Schmucker enumerated a series of reasons why this unity should take place. He began by arguing that there is nothing in Scripture about sectarian parties in the church of Christ. The person who reads the sacred record, Schmucker said,

> . . . finds nothing there of Lutherans, of Presbyterians, of Methodists, of Episcopalians, of Baptists. But he sees that when the formulation of such

21. Wentz, *Pioneer*, 265.

22. Paul P. Kuenning, *The Rise and Fall of Lutheran Pietism: The Rejection of an Activist Heritage* (Macon, Ga.: Mercer Univ. Press, 1988).

23. Wentz, *Pioneer*, 267.

24. Samuel S. Schmucker, *Fraternal Appeal to the American Churches with a Plan for Catholic Union on Apostolic Principles* (New York: Gould & Newman, 1838). Quotes from this work are from the second edition, published in New York by Taylor & Dodd in 1839. *Fraternal Appeal* was the first work of its kind and "provided the arguments for the 20th-century ecumenical movement. He did work that did not need to be done again." Ruth Rouse and Stephen Charles Neill, eds., *A History of the Ecumenical Movement, 1517–1948* (Philadelphia: Westminster Press, 1967), 245.

parties was attempted at Corinth, Paul deemed it necessary to write them a long letter and besought by the name of the Lord Jesus Christ to have no divisions among them. The Christian is therefore constrained to mourn over the desolations of Zion and to meet the solemn inquiry: cannot a balm be found for the ulcerous divisions which deface the body of Christ? (10)

Schmucker fully admitted that these denominations or divisions in Protestantism had diversities of opinion on some nonessential points, and so all of them must be partially in error. This, however, did not mean that the body of Christ should be torn into various segments; rather, the segments (denominations) should be united in "that bond of fraternal love" (12).

Schmucker discussed the fact that Saint Paul forbade the separation of Christians into various sects, and recommended that the people of the many denominations in the United States follow Paul's admonition. When a Christian was expelled from one group or denomination he could easily join another, Schmucker said, because their beliefs were similar. He concluded that there were no fundamental differences, only insignificant ones.

Schmucker asked how the divisions between denominations could be pleasing in the eyes of God. He then addressed an appeal toward the unity of the churches:

> It would seem then to be irresistibly evident that the unity of the church ought to be sacredly preserved by all who love the Lord Jesus; and without stopping at this stage in our investigation to ascertain all the precise features of this unity, which will hereafter appear, it is evident that the union inculcated by the apostle is such as is inconsistent with the divisions which he reprobates, and such divisions substantially are those of the present day, which are all based on some difference of doctrine, forms of government, or mode of worship among acknowledged Christians. (19)

Christians are to follow the example of the apostles. Schmucker recognized that there were differences among the first Christians, but none of those differences was cause for division in the church. For example, he regarded the dispute about circumcision between the Jewish and Gentile converts in the early church as being far more important than anything that separated the various Protestant denominations in the nineteenth century (20). In the days of the apostles there were many churches. Each had been influenced by an individual apostle, yet all were Christian. "In short, Christians in those days were called Christians and nothing but Christians, and one Christian Church was distinguished from another only by the name of the place in which it was located" (23).

Rather than perpetuating the existing denominational divisions, Schmucker stated, the emphasis should rest on the unity of the body of Christ. He did not call for organizational unity, which would not be practical or necessary, but there could be a unity in the sense previously described. Sectarian divisions served only to "destroy that community of interest and sympathy of feeling which the Savior and his apostles so urgently inculcated" (24). The existence of many denominations resulted in nothing but bitterness and rivalry. Consequently, Schmucker asked, "If one denomination suffers, fails of success or meets with disgrace in some unworthy members, do not the surrounding denominations rather at least tacitly and cheerfully acquiesce if not rejoice, hoping that thus more room will be made and facility offered for their own enlargement?" (25).

Denominational divisions also impeded the impartial study of the Scriptures by pastors and laity. Doctrines can be divided into those that are undisputed and held by all in common, and those that are disputed. It is the disputed doctrines that distinguish denominations from each other. Each denomination tried to defend its own opinions and refused to open itself to other views. This resulted in denominational pride and roadblocks to the study of the Bible. It also led to controversies that agitated the church and left Christ in the background.

Schmucker believed Protestantism was originally a unified protest against Rome. The split that followed the Reformation had brought nothing but strife and enmity to the church.

Having given evidence of the need for unity, Schmucker offered his plan for achieving it. Any plan for Christian union, he argued, must be based on apostolic principles and must be in accord with the New Testament. A union of Christians must also leave the individual rights of Christians untouched. With these principles in mind, Schmucker submitted four attributes of Christian union.

1. It must require of no one the renunciation of any doctrine or opinion believed by him to be scriptural or true.
2. It must concede to each denomination or branch of the church of Christ the right to retain its own organization, or to alter or amend it at option, leaving everything relative to government, discipline, and worship to be managed by each denomination according to its own view for the time being.
3. It must dissuade no one from discussing fundamentals and nonfundamentals in the spirit of Christian love, and amicably showing why one believes some nonfundamental opinions held by any of others are incorrect.
4. The plan must be applicable to orthodox denominations,[25] to all that are regarded as portions of Christ's visible church on earth. (88–89)

25. A possible clue to what Schmucker meant by "orthodox" can be found in the *Fraternal*

Schmucker stated that each denomination in the union should keep its own system of doctrines and organization. Others (he does not specify who) had advocated that, if a union were to take place, all denominations involved should abandon their own system and unite under one rule. Schmucker said it was too late for such a union. Also, the weaknesses of the denominations would be revealed as each had to give up its own cardinal principles. Moreover, a new hierarchy would result. The breaking up of the denominations would not lead to unity; rather, to suddenly unsettle established habits of the community would lead to confusion and unrest (93).

Schmucker advocated that no member of this union, whether clergy or lay, should be disciplined for holding a doctrine of another denomination, unless that member is guilty of bad conduct or follows the rules of discipline or worship of that other denomination. Rather than chastise a person who has fallen into evil ways, the church should try to help restore the person fully to the faith.

The church could still be a unified body despite differences in points of doctrine. The laity are able to live harmoniously among themselves in their secular lives, although they might differ somewhat in religious doctrine; Schmucker argued that ministers and churches should be able to do the same. As long as there were fundamental agreements in doctrine, unity was possible. If people are truly brothers and sisters, they should not condemn one another, even if they disagree about some doctrines.

Schmucker believed that churches belonging to this union should adopt a creed that would include only the doctrines mutually held by all. The first part of this creed would be the Apostles' Creed. The second part, called the "United Protestant Confession," consisted of sections from the creeds of Protestant churches.[26] These included the Thirty-nine Articles of Religion from the Episcopal church, the Methodist Discipline, the Westminster Confession of the Presbyterian church, and the Lutheran church's Augsburg Confession. If a section that contained a disagreeable article was chosen from a particular creed, the disagreeable words of that article would be expunged.

The purpose of this creed was twofold. First, it would keep heretics out of the church of God (109). A creed provides a principle by which individuals can be judged to be of the faith or not. If one did not adhere to

---

Appeal, 99. An "orthodox" denomination is that which accepts Christ as Lord and the divine inspiration of the Scriptures. This excluded the Roman Catholic church because, in Schmucker's eyes, it did not have access to the Word of God.

26. The text of the "United Protestant Confession" consisted of twelve articles as follows: the Scriptures, God and the Trinity, the Son of God and the Atonement, Human Depravity, Justification, the Church, the Sacraments of Baptism and the Lord's Supper, Purgatory, Liberty of Conscience, Civil Government, the Communion of Saints, and the Future Judgment and Retribution. Schmucker, *Fraternal Appeal,* 129–35.

this creed, that person would be excluded from the church. This creed, however, did not include beliefs that were exclusive to any one of the denominations; only matters concerning the fundamental faith were important. Other articles were seen as too trivial to deserve disciplinary actions (110).

The second purpose of the creed was to maintain the great and acknowledged truths of Christianity (110). Prominence should be given only to undisputed doctrines; being undisputed, they are "certainly true" (111). Protestants acknowledge that persons will be saved even if they deny the disputed doctrines. Consequently, only the undisputed doctrines are important. These undisputed doctrines, said Schmucker, "are the principal means which effect the good accomplished by all the different sects, the principal means of conversion, sanctification, and salvation" (113).

This creed would not only serve the various denominations in the United States; it would also serve as a bond for true Christians throughout the world. This creed, Schmucker pointed out, was much more than the apostles ever required; yet all Christians could believe in it.

Sacramental, ecclesiastical, and ministerial communions were to be free in the prescribed union of churches. Each group would keep its own practices in its worship life. However, members of one church in the union would be allowed to enter another church in order to worship. Clergy would also be allowed to interchange pulpits occasionally, and all members of the clergy would be considered equal. In order to express unity, Schmucker suggested that all denominations participate in an annual joint communion.

All denominations in this union would act in accord as far as possible in all matters of concern for Christianity. It would be the duty of all denominations in Christ's church to exercise influence on the secular society in order to promote love on earth. All groups within these denominations would adopt the catholic principle of action and cooperate in social endeavors.

The Bible should be the major textbook for all denominations. This did not mean that other works were not allowed. Other texts were needed to provide instruction of the people, yet the Bible was to be the most important book. The more the Bible was used, the more ministers would concentrate on the Word of God instead of engaging in sectarianism. Missionaries belonging to the Protestant union were to profess only the Bible and the Apostolic Protestant Confession of the union. Schmucker contended it would be better for the heathen to have a Bible-centered religion and never hear the names of Calvin and Luther.

Schmucker argued against having one representative body. None existed at the time of the apostles, and the proposed union had no need of any. A national organization would only increase in power, which would eventually take away the freedom of the individual conscience.

In 1839 Schmucker sent out petitions asking for the opinions of various denominations regarding his proposed union. The reaction was quite wide informal acceptance and the formation of the interdenominational American Society for Christian Union, which distributed copies of the *Fraternal Appeal*. Some of the best-known church leaders in the United States signed the petitions. In its convention at Chambersburg, Pennsylvania, June 1, 1839, the General Synod adopted resolutions recommending the plan to the various synods.[27] Yet the plan was never adopted. Wentz stated that the major reason was that too many divisions had arisen within, not just between, the various Protestant bodies—for example, the split that resulted in Old School and New School Presbyterians and the North-South cleavages among the Baptists and Methodists. In addition, the rift that would erupt into the American Lutheran controversy was beginning to appear by the late 1830s.[28]

The *Fraternal Appeal* is an important document for two reasons. It demonstrates Schmucker's serious commitment to church unity, but his hope for unity was limited. The Roman Catholic church was excluded, and Schmucker made it abundantly clear that the Protestant union was designed to stand against Rome, to prevent Rome's expansion in the United States and in the rest of the world.

The *Fraternal Appeal* is also important because it shows how Schmucker's distinction between fundamental and nonfundamental doctrines could be put into practice. The emphasis was on a unified American Protestantism that would result in America being a Protestant nation. If only the various denominations would cooperate with each other, that goal could be attained. Seen in this light, the *Fraternal Appeal* is an example of Schmucker's attempt to adapt to the American (Protestant) religious climate.

Schmucker's dream never became a reality. In time his own church began to take its confessional stance very seriously. Then Schmucker's distinction between fundamental and nonfundamental doctrines was no longer considered applicable; in fact, it was regarded as lax, even heretical.

Although the *Fraternal Appeal* had implications for the world, it was primarily an American plan, a pan-Protestant union to ensure that America would continue to be a Protestant nation and thus fulfill its destiny. Schmucker is to be commended for his ecumenical concerns, but his lowest-common-denominator approach could not accomplish his vision. He failed

27. *Proceedings of the Tenth Convention of the General Synod of the Evangelical Lutheran Church, in the United States, Convened at Chambersburg, Pa., June, 1839,* 19.
28. See Wentz, *Pioneer,* 281–82.

to see that theological differences are to be taken seriously and that confessional statements are more than reflections of a past, Old World view. As the Lutheran church in America as well as the Reformed and Episcopal churches underwent a renewal of confessional consciousness,[29] his vision fell by the wayside.

The American Lutheran Church

Thus far, the views of Samuel Schmucker have been seen in their broader context. His textbook *Elements of Popular Theology,* written early in his career, contained the theological positions he held his whole life, but at that time they did not carry the label of American Lutheranism. The *Fraternal Appeal* also demonstrated certain of Schmucker's lifelong attitudes toward doctrines, but this work gave little insight into his understanding of Lutheranism.

His specific thoughts about the Lutheran church became evident in a series of articles that date from the early 1840s to the early 1850s. By that time many in the General Synod were showing a greater appreciation for the Lutheran Confessions and were advocating that they be taken more seriously in the life of the Lutheran church in America. This situation forced Schmucker to go on the offensive, defining and arguing for an American Lutheranism and opposing the stricter views of the confessional proponents.

The aforementioned articles were published in 1851 as *The American Lutheran Church.*[30] Two of Schmucker's friends, J. B. Butler and David Harbaugh, students at Wittenberg College in Springfield, Ohio, were the compilers. The volume contained three discourses, "Retrospect of Lutheranism in the United States" (1841), "Portraiture of Lutheranism" (1840), and "The Patriarchs of American Lutheranism" (1845). In addition, it contained a reprint of an article in Charles Philip Krauth's *Evangelical Review* of July 1851, "The Nature of Christ's Presence in the Eucharist." Another reprint was from the April 1851 number of the *Evangelical Review,* "The Vocation of the American Lutheran Church." Finally, a previously unpublished article by Schmucker, "The Doctrinal Basis and Ecclesiastical Position of the American Lutheran Church," was included.

---

29. For a discussion of this renewed confessional consciousness, see Walter H. Conser, Jr., *Church and Confession: Conservative Theologians in Germany, England, and America, 1815–1866* (Macon, Ga.: Mercer Univ. Press, 1984).

30. Samuel S. Schmucker, *The American Lutheran Church, Historically, Doctrinally, and Practically Delineated, in Several Occasional Discourses* (Springfield, Ohio: D. Harbaugh, 1851). Quotes from this work are from the fifth edition, published in Philadelphia by E. W. Miller in 1852.

"Retrospect of Lutheranism in the United States," originally a sermon Schmucker preached at the opening of the General Synod meeting at Baltimore in 1841, was an indirect appeal for a distinctive American Lutheranism. Schmucker pointed to the "practical piety" of Muhlenberg and his successors.

Most of the sermon recounts the history of Lutheranism in America— the early congregations, pastors, and important events. Schmucker emphasized the hardships that had been endured and the labors of so many that had brought about the growth and progress of Lutheranism in America. He lauded the present work of the General Synod, especially its government, the books containing "pious and evangelical hymns" it had published, and the maintenance of parity of laity and ministers.

Schmucker called attention to the Franckean pietistic tradition of Muhlenberg and the other early Lutheran pastors who had come from Germany. He took great pains to demonstrate Muhlenberg's concern for the conversion and care of souls. He emphasized throughout the sermon that the General Synod could only prosper by remembering and being faithful to its past.

"Portraiture of Lutheranism," stated pointedly that Lutheranism in America had made improvements over the Lutheranism of the past. This discourse was originally given on the occasion of the dedication of the First English Lutheran Church at Pittsburgh, Pennsylvania, in 1840. Schmucker began by speaking of Reformation in Germany, but he said little about Luther other than that he had challenged a corrupt Roman church. Far more attention was given to pietists such as Spener, Francke, and Arndt who wrote, lived pious lives, and performed acts of love.

To Schmucker, the Reformation was not a finished event; it was ongoing, and there was always room for improvement. He then enumerated seven improvements that he regarded as important. The first was that the church fathers were now rejected and ignored. He found the Reformers in error because they looked to and quoted the fathers. "The writings of the fathers instead of being good authority for Scripture doctrine, are a perfect labyrinth of theological errors, from which it is impossible to escape with safety, and in which we look in vain for that unanimous consent which Rome has so loudly boasted" (60).

The second improvement that Schmucker saw concerned the doctrine of the real presence. Schmucker claimed that in the Lutheran church of his day positions on this subject differed; "all are permitted to enjoy their own opinions in peace" (63). He pointed out "cheerfully" that other Protestant churches had rejected the Reformers' teachings on the real presence with less controversy than the Lutheran church had. Schmucker stated that, in his opinion, the bread and the wine are "merely symbolic representations of the savior's absent body" (63).

A third improvement Schmucker listed was the abolition of private confession and absolution as a means of preparation for reception of the Lord's Supper. He felt that a formal declaration of forgiveness, conditionally made, was sufficient to "intelligent minds."

The fourth improvement was the rejection of what Schmucker called "the Papal doctrine of baptism." For Schmucker this meant especially the rite of exorcism. He maintained that, while Luther and the Reformers rejected exorcism, they still upheld the idea of natural depravity.

A fifth improvement Schmucker recognized in the Lutheran church was a "systematic adjustment" of its doctrines. Schmucker used Luther's doctrine of free will as an example. He thought that Luther had originally gone too far on that subject, advocating an Augustinian view of predestination. Schmucker claimed that Luther, under the influence of Melanchthon, later adopted a more moderate view that allowed for some free will; doctrines continued to be adjusted when necessary.

As a sixth improvement, Schmucker cited a better and more rigid system of church government, which was accomplished by meetings designed to provide practical preaching and convert sinners. This is an obvious reference to revivals. In an interesting statement, Schmucker commented that the setting in America lends itself to achieving such ends.

The final improvement was that ministers were not expected to be bound to any "human creed." The Bible and the "substantial correctness" of the Augsburg Confession were all that were required (68). Assent to the "fundamental doctrines" of the Augsburg Confession was required, but Schmucker did not enumerate what those "fundamental doctrines" were.

"Portraiture of Lutheranism" is important because it spells out clearly what the American Lutherans believed, especially that the Reformation was not finished and that improvements had been made.[31] Another point worth noting is that Schmucker believed this was the way Lutheranism had developed on American soil, and he was obviously pleased with the results. When Schmucker gave this discourse in 1840 most of his audience was probably in agreement with him. By the time it appeared in *The American Lutheran Church* a little over ten years later, the response was not nearly so affirmative.

Schmucker's third discourse, "The Patriarchs of American Lutheranism," reveals his attitude about the early Lutheran leaders in America. In this discourse, delivered before the Historical Society of the Lutheran

---

31. Vergilius Ferm stated that *Portraiture* was the first time the name American Lutheranism was used, to distinguish its character from confessional Lutheranism, which was becoming more prominent. Vergilius Ferm, *The Crisis in American Lutheran Theology* (New York: Century Co., 1927), 131.

Church in the United States during the session of the General Synod at Philadelphia, May 17, 1845, Schmucker attempted to show that American Lutheranism was a logical development for the American situation and that the patriarchs were in essential agreement with it.

Schmucker contended that the American church, which included all denominations, was in a transition state. All immigrant churches except the papal church had thrown off their allegiances to foreign powers and had adopted self-government. This movement was also a time of development: "The state of the church in any particular age, is so ordinarily in some degree the result of gradual development under the various influences in which she is placed, and in which the gospel is called to act on the minds of her members" (92). Schmucker felt this was particularly true in America. He heartily approved of the pietistic influence in Lutheranism in America, the separation of church and state, and the religious situation in general, especially cooperation between various denominations.

Schmucker claimed that Muhlenberg and his contemporaries were the legitimate ancestors of American Lutheranism and were "ardent friends of spiritual religion and of scriptural religious revival" (93). Schmucker credited their pietistic background for their spirituality. In America, this led to adjustments, mainly seen in worship customs. Holy days were reduced to Christmas, Good Friday, Easter, Ascension, and Whitsunday (103). The long form of the liturgy was used only on special occasions. Schmucker cited Muhlenberg as the chief source of these changes. The major adjustment was the holding of prayer meetings, and for Schmucker that was proof that the Lutheran fathers in America were amenable to revivals (106).

Schmucker believed that Lutheranism in America was consistent with the ideas of the Reformers (pietists such as Spener, Francke, and Arndt) and Muhlenberg and his colleagues. He was concerned over the "ultra Lutherans" who would "roll back the wheels of time about three hundred years" (92). He wanted Lutheranism to be "the friend of spiritual religion and religious revival" and earnestly desired that Lutherans would cooperate with other Protestants "in advancing the mediatorial reign of our blessed Master, and preparing the way for the second glorious coming of the Lord" (119).

Little needs to be said about "The Nature of Christ's Presence in the Eucharist," because it repeats the same arguments Schmucker had used before. One fact is evident: for Schmucker, reason and common sense played an important role in the task of biblical interpretation. For example, he admitted that the "Romish doctrine" regarding the Words of Institution is the only literal one, but it contradicts the senses and is, therefore, unacceptable (125). This doctrine also contradicts human experience, which says that a substance cannot be in more than one place at a time (128–29). Schmucker's position is as follows: "The expressions from which some would deduce another design, 'are not the bread and wine *the communion* of the body and blood of Christ,' have been explained above, we think, satisfactorily. They teach that the bread and wine bring us into solemn, spiritual, mental communion, or recollection of, the reflection on the Savior's body and blood, broken and shed for us on the cross" (148–49). It is clear that, for Schmucker, the bread and wine are only symbols of the Lord's absent body and blood. In taking that position, Schmucker admitted being partial to Zwingli (154).

A lengthy discourse, "The Doctrinal Basis and Ecclesiastical Position of the American Lutheran Church," spelled out Schmucker's positions and constituted a confessional history of Lutheranism from 1740 to 1850. Schmucker contended that the Lutheran church in America dropped the binding nature of all the Confessions and only demanded faith in the Word of God. Individuals were free to believe or reject certain teachings as a matter of conscience—"In matters not prescribed by the Word of God, I am bound by no other obligations than those which I personally assumed" (159–60).

The General Synod accepted the Augsburg Confession as its basis, but each individual was free to reject any parts of it. Schmucker stressed that the church is people rather than things. Thus, the people and not confessions decide what takes place in the church. Creeds are only binding on those who wrote them and no one else. The church could decide to accept certain doctrinal standards, however. In the case of the General Synod, Schmucker stated: "We, therefore, after much and prayerful study of this subject, in light of scripture and history, approve the use of the so-called Apostles' Creed, the Nicene Creed, and the fundamentals of the Augsburg Confession, as an expression of the prominent truths we believe the Bible to teach, and as tests of administration and discipline in the church" (169).

Schmucker claimed that Muhlenberg did not believe that all parts of the Confessions required belief and that the fathers of American Lutheranism relaxed the standards with regard to the symbols. He also argued that many pastors and lay people did not believe certain portions of the Augsburg Confession; therefore it would be folly to bind people to all the articles. Schmucker believed that Scripture and reason teach that God acts with each individual as a moral agent; thus, "each individual member of the church is bound to search the Scriptures and to believe and act for himself" (191).

Confessions should not impede relationships with other Protestants. Here Schmucker employed some of the same arguments he used in the *Fraternal*

Appeal. He saw the mission of the Lutheran church in America as follows: "On this broad basis of Protestantism the American Lutheran churches are still standing; charitable and liberal in matter of minor importance, they are willing to aid in leveling down the partition walls, which are now separating Protestant from Protestant" (204).

Schmucker was aware of objections to the General Synod's position. He defended the Synod as being Lutheran, in spite of the fact it did not accept every article of the Augsburg Confession. The General Synod was Lutheran because it had not denied the Bible or the doctrine of justification. The Confessions were "useful exhibitions" but not binding on one's conscience. As for the rejection of baptismal regeneration and the real presence, Schmucker claimed that such a rejection removed "remnants of Romanism" from the Augsburg Confession.

For Schmucker, freedom in America included freedom with regard to religious matters. By taking the position that the Bible and individual consciences determined truth, American Lutherans were throwing off the bonds of the Old World where Lutherans were enslaved. In America, they could use the Scriptures in freedom (244–46).

The last discourse, "The Vocation of the American Lutheran Church," reveals Schmucker's vision for American Lutheranism. The chief vocation of the Lutheran church was to develop an *American* character. Schmucker rejected a close connection between the state and the church, as had developed in Germany. American Lutheranism's main task was to throw off all authority and get back to the Scriptures. This did not exclude eliminating or altering the Lutheran Confessions.

Schmucker noted all manner of errors in Lutheranism's history. He deplored the number of confessions that had become authoritative for the Lutheran church. He claimed that Luther's rejection of Zwingli was a mistake. With the adoption of the Formula of Concord (1577), the Lutheran church forsook theological liberty. Schmucker regarded the Formula as "a document of suppression" (264). Schmucker pointed to the fact that the General Synod had adopted the Apostles' and Nicene Creeds and the Augsburg Confession, but parts of the Augsburg Confession can be rejected. On the whole, Schmucker regarded confessions with suspicion. The American Lutheran church should continue to rely on the Bible, which can be interpreted by the individual using reason and the dictates of conscience.

A prolific writer, Schmucker more than anyone else gave shape to the concerns and views of the American Lutheran movement. Certain themes appear in virtually all his writings. He was vehemently anti-Roman. He saw in the Augsburg Confession and other confessional documents remnants of Catholicism that had to be purged. On this point he differed markedly from his confessional opponents. His understanding of Lutheranism came not from Luther or the Confessions of the Lutheran church, but instead from the pietistic movements in Germany; that understanding, in turn, was influenced by the American religious environment and his contacts with American evangelical Protestants.

For the source of the church's beliefs, Schmucker appealed to the Augsburg Confession, but with limits. The real authority lay in the Bible, interpreted through the eyes of reason and individual conscience. He stressed the need for conversion, a change of heart that was reflected in a person's moral conduct. That change was to be accomplished through prayer meetings, otherwise known as revivals. Many rejected doctrines such as baptismal regeneration, absolution, and the real presence. Here Schmucker appealed to human reason and to the individual right to decide one's own beliefs. Creeds and confessions were vestiges of the past, products of the Old World. In America, religious liberty prevailed. The individual interpreting the Bible was capable of deciding what were the truths of Christianity.

The influence of Schmucker and his views can be measured by the fact that his *Popular Theology,* which was not particularly Lutheran in its emphasis and content, was read by seminarians at Gettysburg for at least thirty years. They, in turn, passed on what they had been taught to the laity in the General Synod. The theology they communicated was consistent with what was known as American Lutheranism.

The American experience convinced Schmucker that Lutheranism needed to adapt to the American religious situation, which meant that it must relate to the various evangelical Protestant denominations and must accept what was perceived to be a Protestant doctrinal consensus. Every one of the discourses that appear in *The American Lutheran Church* states that conviction forthrightly. The agenda of American Lutheranism was to bring Lutheranism into the American Protestant fold.

Samuel Schmucker was not the only advocate of that position. Other well-known, influential persons promoted the American Lutheran cause. Their writings merit examination.

5

More Voices for American Lutheranism

*A*lthough Samuel Schmucker was the most prominent of the American Lutherans, many others advocated American Lutheranism. Literally hundreds of pastors who had been trained by him at Gettysburg shared his vision of a Lutheran church that was truly American in character. The vast majority of these pastors never achieved any measurable prominence and spent their years serving parishes within the General Synod.

Other American Lutheran partisans, however, were prominent figures. Although their literary output was nowhere near that of Schmucker, they were staunch defenders of the cause of American Lutheranism.

Benjamin Kurtz

Next to Samuel Schmucker, the most important person in the American Lutheran party was the fiery, tempestuous Benjamin Kurtz (1795–1865). Kurtz, a colleague of Schmucker's, and editor of the *Lutheran Observer,* was an adamant defender of American Lutheranism.

Kurtz was the grandson of the Rev. John Kurtz, who came to America in 1745 as an associate of Henry Melchior Muhlenberg and was the first pastor ordained at the meeting that formed the Pennsylvania Ministerium in 1748.

By age fifteen, Benjamin Kurtz was an assistant at the Harrisburg Academy, where he gave private instructions in Latin and Greek. He was licensed in 1815 and later became pastor of the English Lutheran Church in Baltimore, where he was very influential. Kurtz was a zealous advocate of catechetical instruction, and on one occasion is said to have confirmed one hundred and fifteen members.[1]

1. Charles A. Hay, *Memoirs of Rev. Jacob Goering, Rev. George Lochman, D.D., and Rev. Benjamin Kurtz, D.D. L.L.D.* (Philadelphia: Lutheran Publication Society, 1887), 110–11.

Kurtz was a firm believer in revival meetings and conducted them in his parish. He especially directed his revivals at the young. In spite of much opposition, he also introduced more frequent preaching in English, temperance reform, prayer meetings, and a Sunday school.

In 1825 Kurtz was selected to go to Germany to solicit funds for the newly proposed seminary. His travels were difficult, but he made numerous contacts during his two years in Europe (most of the time spent in England and Germany). He returned with nearly ten thousand dollars for the new seminary plus six thousand volumes for its library.

Following his return from Europe, Kurtz became pastor at Hagerstown, Maryland, where he remained until he was called to serve at Chambersburg, Pennsylvania, in 1831. In 1833 he resigned this call because of ill health. That same year Kurtz became editor of the *Lutheran Observer,* a position he would hold for twenty-five years. In 1834 Kurtz was called to a professorship at the seminary in Gettysburg and subsequently to a chair at Pennsylvania College, both of which he declined. In addition to his work on the *Observer,* Kurtz was twice elected president of the General Synod.

When Kurtz took over the *Observer,* it was a floundering publication. He immediately changed the newspaper into a folio that was published weekly. During his tenure as editor, the subscription list rose from about seven hundred to almost eight thousand.[2] As editor Kurtz defended the cause of American Lutheranism, and through this made both friends and enemies. John G. Morris, another General Synod pastor and an acquaintance of Kurtz's, claimed that Kurtz, through his tabloid, had more influence in the General Synod than anyone else.[3]

Kurtz's combative personality was displayed not only in the pages of the *Observer* but also in other areas. John G. Morris stated: "He was a hard man to preach to, and seldom listened to any man's sermons with any degree of patience."[4] Kurtz was remembered as an "able disputant" but not easily open to others' views. Another of Morris's observations is worth noting: Kurtz did not frequently attend services in Lutheran churches because the preaching did not suit his taste. He was not easily satisfied.[5]

The subject of revivals was frequently treated in the *Observer.* Samuel Schmucker, it has been noted, also favored revival meetings, but they were accorded less prominence in his writings than in Kurtz's. Revivals had been a part of Lutheran life in America for some time. They were a means

2. Hay, *Memoirs,* 154.
3. John G. Morris, *Fifty Years in the Lutheran Ministry* (Baltimore: James Young, 1878), 136.
4. Ibid., 137.
5. Ibid.

to achieve conversions, a concern for both Lutheran pietists and American evangelicals. The interest in revivals is an example of how some Lutherans had accommodated to the American religious scene.[6]

Kurtz's agenda regarding revivals appeared in the first issue of the *Observer* after he became editor (May 1, 1833). He stated that it was his intention to be a "decided, independent, and fearless" advocate of what were called the "New Measures." From that point on, issue after issue contained articles defending the practice of revivals in the Lutheran church. Kurtz stressed that it was important to hold protracted meetings and that the sermons preached at such meetings should be enthusiastic and full of conviction in order to win immediate conversions. The lost sinner must know there was a need to be saved and a way by which that could happen (Aug. 3, 1837). Preaching should be practical so that the gospel would be driven into the hearts of its hearers in a "simple, direct, and pointed manner, with the view of promoting immediate conviction and conversion" (March 25, 1834).

When the confessional Lutherans began to attack the proponents of revival meetings as un-Lutheran and even heretical, Kurtz and the other American Lutherans defended themselves. They referred to the *"collegia pietatis"* in Germany as forerunners of the meetings in America (*Lutheran Observer,* Nov. 24, 1843). They also claimed that revivals were not anti-scriptural, and thus it was not wrong for Lutherans to apply such a means to save sinners. In the Jan. 26, 1844, issue of the *Observer,* Kurtz stated: "The question of doctrine has been fully met, and revival men are found to hold the doctrines of the Bible, while their enemies are found to belong to one of three classes, viz.: First, to those who believe in faith without works; or second, to those who believe in works without faith; or third, to those who are infidels." As far as Kurtz was concerned, no true Christian would oppose revivals.

By the 1840s revivals were becoming less common, and many former advocates no longer supported them.[7] Noting this trend, Kurtz lamented in the *Observer:* "The time was when [revivals] held a most prominent place in the affections of the good; when their very name was cherished with a sacredness which was well suited to their sacred character; when they were deemed essential to the growth and prosperity of the church,

6. For an account of Lutherans and revivals in America, see David H. Bauslin, "The Genesis of the 'New Measure' Movement in the Lutheran Church in This Country," *Lutheran Quarterly* 40 (July 1910), 360–91 and Frank H. Seilhammer, "The New Measure Movement Among Lutherans," *Lutheran Quarterly* 12 (May 1960), 121–43.

7. Seilhammer, "The New Measure Movement," locates the first Lutheran revivals in 1804 and sees them on the decline after 1842 until the beginning of the Civil War, when they passed out of prominence.

and especially to the salvation of the world. But alas! a change has taken place" (Jan. 19, 1849). Kurtz was convinced that revivals were good for sinners and therefore good for the church.[8] He never ceased defending the practice, even when he encountered great opposition. As late as 1863, in a sermon preached at Newville, Pennsylvania, entitled "Experimental (not ritual) Religion, the One Thing Needful," Kurtz attacked uniformity in mode of worship and liturgical services in general. What was needed, he said, was "experimental religion" because it would increase membership and give power to families and congregations.

With regard to other doctrinal views, Kurtz maintained that the Bible is the only infallible standard of faith and practice. An editorial, "Creeds and Confessions," in an 1840 issue of the *Observer* expressed his position well:

> These documents or standards, as they are usually termed, have been a prolific source of strife and persecution in the Christian church, and are likely so to be, as long as they remain in force in all their accustomed *minutiae* of subordinate and detailed doctrine. In great and fundamental principles, the intelligent and pious may indeed be expected to coincide, but in the numerous small and unimportant points which enter more or less into the creeds of different individuals, it is impossible for all to think alike; nor is it important that they should. (Aug. 21, 1840)

Kurtz's position was that everything beyond fundamental principles should be reserved to individual judgment.

For Kurtz, the Symbolical Books were only exhibitions by the Reformers of the truth of God's Word "as they understood it." He claimed that when he was ordained in 1815 he was never asked any questions about the Lutheran Confessions, nor did he make any promises in regard to them, not even the Augsburg Confession. If these requirements had been in effect, Kurtz stated frankly, he never would have become a minister.

Kurtz considered doctrines such as baptismal regeneration and the bodily presence of Christ in the Lord's Supper as "unscriptural and dangerous." He regarded baptism not as initiatory but as a ratifying sacrament, "the Sign and Seal of the Covenant of Grace."[9] Children are entitled to membership in the church, not on account of their baptism but by their inclusion

8. In 1843 Kurtz prepared a statement on the "New Measures" for the Synod of East Pennsylvania. As a result, the Synod approved protracted meetings and various means by which a pastor could judge the spiritual state of his people. Revivals, including the "anxious seat," were approved but avoidable noise and confusion, such as more than one person praying at a time, were discouraged. It was also stated that the pastor should conduct the activities at such a meeting.

9. Hay, *Memoirs*, 180.

in the covenant of grace. Adults become members of the church by their conversion. Kurtz also regarded the Lord's Supper as "the Sign and Seal of the Covenant of Salvation by faith in Christ." Christ is present in some way but not corporally.

Kurtz was strongly in favor of a union of the Lutheran and Reformed churches. He was intensely anti-Roman, and anything relating to Roman Catholicism (ritual, chanting, even the wearing of a gown in the pulpit) was to be avoided.

Kurtz and his journal also played a part in the controversy over the *Definite Platform* (see chap. 7). During that controversy, he vigorously defended the entire American Lutheran vision for the General Synod.

Kurtz is remembered for other works, including the two-volume *Theological Sketch-Book* of sermon outlines on various subjects.[10] Which of these sermons are specifically Kurtz's is unknown, but they are in agreement with his theology. A portion of a sermon subtitled "Invitation to Come to Christ," based on Revelation 22:17, contains a strong tone of exhortation that would be applicable to revivals.[11] The sermons are arranged in topical order, beginning with The Holy Spirit and proceeding with God, Christ, Man, the Way of Salvation, the Means of Grace, Exhortations, The Work of Grace, Christian Graces, Christian Duties, Warnings, The Consequences of Sin, and The Blessedness of Religion. Conversion is distinguished from regeneration. No connection is made between regeneration and baptism. With regard to the Lord's Supper, the real presence is denied.

Kurtz's most famous work is a book intended for the laity, *Why Are You a Lutheran?*[12] which went through several editions. This book is revealing of Kurtz's theology. Early in this work, Kurtz denied that Lutherans believe and teach doctrines such as the real presence and absolution by a pastor, citing Johann Lorenz von Mosheim, an eighteenth-century Lutheran divine, and Samuel Schmucker in his footnotes. He also argued against the notion that Lutherans were closer to Rome than to other Protestants.

Kurtz cited nine "prominent doctrines" as characteristics of Lutheranism. (1) doctrine of the Trinity; (2) universal depravity of mankind; (3) deity of Jesus Christ; (4) atonement of Christ; (5) deity of the Holy

---

10. *Theological Sketch-Book, or Skeletons of Sermons Carefully Arranged in Systematic Order So as to Constitute a Complete Body of Divinity; Partly Original but Chiefly Selected from Simeon's Horae Homileticae and Skeletons; Sketches of Sermons; Pulpit Assistant; Benson's Plans; Preacher Pulpit, and other approved publications,* 2 vols. (Baltimore: Publication Rooms, 1844). No author's name is listed in these volumes. Hay, *Memoirs,* 211, credits them to Kurtz. These volumes are very scarce. The author is indebted to Scott Grorud of the library staff at Luther Northwestern Seminary, who procured copies from the Harvard College library.

11. *Theological Sketch-Book* 2:37–41.

12. Benjamin Kurtz, *Why Are You a Lutheran?* (Baltimore: T. Newton Kurtz, 1843). All quotes from this work are from the thirteenth edition, published in 1869.

Spirit; (6) justification by faith; (7) good works; (8) ministerial office and means of grace; (9) future judgment and retribution. Kurtz stated that these are "the doctrines of the Reformation" that all the Reformers confessed. With regard to church government, Kurtz wanted no part of bishops or any other form of hierarchical rule. He spoke with pride about a congregational system of governing, parity of ministers, and the fact that the synod had only an advisory role. The purpose of the General Synod was to promote harmony, administer educational institutions, prepare hymnbooks, and sponsor missionaries. He stated: "This system, while it guarantees to ministers equality of rank and privilege and protects them in all their just claims, abundantly secures to congregations and individual members every exercise of power and immenity [*sic*] to which they are entitled" (41).

Kurtz reacted against all ceremonial in liturgy and maintained that as little form as possible should be used. This attitude, he felt, coincided with the early church, especially as portrayed in the New Testament. He made it clear that ministers were free to dispense with all but the simplest forms.

Although Kurtz believed that Protestants were in basic doctrinal agreement, he recognized that there were some differences between denominations. Lutherans and Calvinists disagreed about predestination, for example; Lutherans and Baptists had opposing views on baptism but Kurtz defended the practice of infant baptism against the Baptists, citing New Testament references to baptism of households. Kurtz also pointed out that the baptism of the Philippian jailer and his family occurred in prison and thus could not have been baptism by immersion (84). Lutherans differ from Methodists regarding the possibility of perfection. Kurtz cited Jonathan Edwards, who warned against false delusions regarding pardon and the inward presence of the Spirit. Kurtz contended that the Spirit always acts on people from the outside. In opposition to the Episcopalians, Kurtz argued against a threefold office of ministry and apostolic succession. "They (Lutherans) regard the apostles as extraordinary officers of temporary standing, and at their decease the ministry of such officers was superseded. Hence, after the death of the twelfth, the church had no more apostles in the technical sense of the word. There was no 'official' succession; when the original apostles died, the office ceased" (97). Kurtz argued that in the New Testament bishop and presbyter were one person and that the church should follow this precedent to avoid a ministerial hierarchy. All evidence from the fathers in favor of a hierarchy is excluded "because our religion is a religion of the Bible" (106).

A large section of the book is devoted to conferences or experience meetings. Kurtz commended Spener's accomplishments in Frankfort and

Francke's work at Halle as examples to Lutheranism in America. In America protracted meetings were appropriate. "They are in accordance with the constitution of the human mind, and founded on the soundest principles of mental philosophy" (160). In a protracted meeting, awareness and conversions can be accomplished in a matter of days, while the same task would take months if it were done only on Sundays.

Kurtz highly approved of confirmation, which he saw as an opportunity for conversion and for young people to affirm the promises others had made for them when they were baptized. In the case of adults, confirmation allowed those who were anxious concerning their spiritual condition to become Christians. Kurtz's arguments for confirmation are interesting, considering that the rite had no biblical foundation. It did not matter that Rome practiced it and that it was not appointed by Christ or the apostles. Kurtz accepted confirmation because it accomplished conversion and served as a sign of spiritual awakening. Confirmation also provided the transition from childhood to adulthood.

Kurtz concluded the book with a discussion of the Eucharist, emphasizing the "remembrance" aspect of this sacrament and to whom it should be offered. Kurtz said that only a few—"a precious few, and they mostly from Europe"—believe in a "peculiar" mode of the divine presence in the Eucharist. Concerning Lutherans in America: "The generally received opinion is, that the bread and wine remain unchanged in the Lord's Supper; that they are merely symbolic representations of the Savior's body" (223). Kurtz recognized what Article XI of the Augsburg Confession said, but he was of the opinion that the author of that document meant a spiritual presence. He also defended the right of American Lutherans to tone down the language of the Augsburg Confession in their own way.

The fact that *Why Are You a Lutheran?* continued to be published in new editions after Kurtz's death is evidence of his widespread influence. Kurtz could be an abrasive person, but the force of his arguments spoke to many. He was a force to be reckoned with.

Simeon W. Harkey

Simeon Harkey (1811–89) was an advocate of American Lutheranism, active in the General Synod's affairs during the middle of the nineteenth century; yet he has not received much attention.

Harkey began his studies at Gettysburg Seminary in 1832 and was graduated from that institution in 1834. He was thus a member of one of the first graduating classes and had studied under Samuel Schmucker. Following his graduation, Harkey filled the pulpit at St. Matthew's in

Philadelphia. The previous pastor, Charles Philip Krauth, had become president of the newly chartered Pennsylvania College.

Harkey was licensed by the Maryland Synod in 1834 and called to Williamsport in that state. Later he went to Frederick, Maryland, and served there for fourteen years. During that time he was elected president of the Maryland Synod. In 1850 Harkey was called to a professorship at Illinois State University. He taught at that institution from 1852 to 1867. He also served two terms as president of the university, 1856–58 and 1860–65. Following his teaching tenure, Harkey served parishes in St. Louis, Missouri, and in Washington and Knoxville, both in Illinois.[13] He was also the editor of a magazine, the *Olive Branch.*

Harkey was noted for favoring revivals. In 1843 he proposed to the Maryland Synod that it publish a monthly periodical to be called the *Revivalist,* which would "be devoted to the history and defense of genuine revivals of religion, revival intelligence, the best measures and means of promoting and managing revivals, and in general, to the furtherance of practical godliness among all classes of men."[14]

Harkey was one of the authors of the "Abstract of Doctrines and Practice of the Evangelical Lutheran Synod of Maryland." In 1843 a resolution was put forth that the Maryland Synod should go on record as favoring the "new measures." After much discussion, the resolution was dropped. In 1844 the convention passed a resolution that a committee of three be appointed "to prepare a summary of the doctrines and usages of the church, within the limits of this Synod, and report at our next meeting."[15] Two of the committee members were Benjamin Kurtz and Harkey.

When the report was submitted in 1845, the positions taken were decisively those of the American Lutherans. The topics covered were regeneration, sacraments, and the Symbolical Books. In every case, the report reflected the positions taken by Samuel Schmucker, positions that were well known throughout the church. The Maryland Synod Abstract was never adopted because many of the clergymen in Maryland had moved toward a more conservative confessional stance. This document is important, however, because it was a preview of what was to come. In fact, many regard it as the forerunner of the *Definite Platform,* which appeared ten years later.[16]

13. The source for most of this material is J. G. Jennson, *American Lutheran Biographies; or Historical Notices of over Three Hundred and Fifty Leading Men of the American Lutheran Church from Its Establishment to the Year 1890* (Milwaukee, 1890), 286–87.

14. *Proceedings of the Twenty-fifth Annual Session of the Evangelical Lutheran Synod of Maryland. Held at Westminster, Carroll County, Md., October, 1843,* 14–15.

15. *Proceedings of the Evangelical Lutheran Synod of Maryland, Held at Middletown, October, 1844,* 11.

16. Adolph Spaeth, *Charles Porterfield Krauth,* 2 vols. (New York: Christian Literature Co., 1898), 1:114. Vergilius Ferm, *The Crisis in American Lutheran Theology* (New York: Century Co., 1927), 165, agrees with this assessment.

Harkey was the author of several articles and two books. In his work on justification, published long after the controversy over the *Definite Platform,* Harkey explains his belief that a decision is involved in the matter of justification: "The pardon becomes ours by faith, by accepting it as offered, and when we accept it."[17] Harkey took the position that people are rational and responsible agents. Humans cannot take the initiative but they do have the freedom to respond to what God offers.

The work that is most revealing of Harkey's theology is *The Church's Best State or Constant Revivals of Religion,* published in 1843.[18] In the preface, Harkey cited the opinion of Princeton professor Archibald Alexander that constant revivals were more in the church's interests than "temporary excitements." He decried the numbers of people who were ignorant of "experimental religion" and stated that the church must carry out its mission to serve such lost souls. "If therefore, the church as the instrument in the hands of God, does not labor for and effect the generation and sanctification of souls, what good does she accomplish for the spiritual instruments of men? None at all. She might as well have no existence" (9).

Harkey contrasted the spirit of revival to ceremonies and "frigid orthodoxy." Ceremonies, he declared, cannot change the heart of sinful people so that they will love God, have true religion, and be saved. Only a spirit of repentance and conversion, which comes about as a result of revivals, can bring people to God. The new creation that is necessary is not natural but spiritual. Harkey continued: "To go still farther: a man may be convinced and not converted; he may be alarmed and not have the fear of God in his heart; he may receive the word with joy and be a stranger to the comforts of the Holy Ghost" (27).

Citing Schmucker's *Popular Theology,*[19] Harkey said that regeneration consists of call, illumination, conviction, penitence, faith; he added that sanctification is subsequent to regeneration (29–30). Baptism is nowhere mentioned in this process. Faith is described as "that voluntary act of the illuminated and evangelically penitent sinner, by which he confides in the mercy of God through Christ for salvation, on the terms offered in the gospel" (33). Sanctification is viewed as "a progressive conformity to the divine law and an inercoming [*sic*] ability to fulfill its requisitions wrought in the faithful believer by the Spirit of God, through the means of grace" (34).

17. Simeon W. Harkey, *Justification by Faith as Held and Taught by Lutherans* (Philadelphia: Lutheran Board of Publication, 1875), 24.

18. Simeon W. Harkey, *The Church's Best State or Constant Revivals of Religion* (Baltimore: Publication Rooms, 1843).

19. Pp. 166–67.

Revivals are the work of God, Harkey said, and thousands of genuine conversions had occurred during their course. If a conversion later proved to be spurious, it was because the persons involved were deceived or acted as hypocrites. Not everything that passes for a revival is genuine. Harkey cited the Campbellites and Shakers as examples of false revivals. Revivals should promote not "animal excitements," Harkey said, but "intelligent excitement," which occurs when people contemplate their sin and the awful judgment that awaits the unrepentant sinner. Tears of agony are signs of such excitement.

Harkey cited many biblical examples of excitement—for instance, Elijah and John the Baptist. Paul's entire ministry was described as "an uninterrupted scene of excitement and religious revivals" (57). Harkey was willing to admit that "animal excitements" were a part of a genuine revival— "unless men were angels!" The real marks of false revivals were disorder and confusion, according to Harkey. Such events produced no good fruits. God is not the author of confusion. Noise, confusion, and disorder are unscriptural, unnecessary, and do great injury to the work of the Holy Spirit and to the subjects involved.

A true revival involves many factors. The first is that professing Christians are quickened and revived—"a great searching of heart." Results are seen at the communion table and prayer meetings. Second, hypocrites and formalists are brought to a "saving acquaintance with the Lord." Finally, sinners are awakened and converted. Harkey asserted that "revivals are the best state and most glorious state of the church this side of heaven itself" (79).

Genuine revivals are not confined to certain intervals or short periods of time. Harkey explained: "Whenever an evangelical sermon is preached, a prayer meeting held, and the ordinances of God's house administered faithfully and sincerely, are we not to expect God's blessing, and as the immediate result, the building up of believers, and the conversion of sinners?" (95).

Harkey was aware of the controversy concerning "Old" versus "New Measures," but he claimed to favor neither. Any measures that resulted in the regeneration of souls, with God's approval, were good enough. He encouraged protracted meetings as long as they were orderly and suited the needs of the situation. He saw an important connection between revivals and catechetical instruction but even more so between revivals and the Sunday school.

Prayer meetings were integral to the existence of revivals in that revivals arose out of prayer. Prayer meetings were the very atmosphere of revivals, and as long as there was constant prayer there would be no backsliding.

Harkey suggested that there ought to be at least three prayer meetings a week in every congregation—one male, one female, and one general meeting (132). Harkey noted that, among Lutherans, protracted meetings were held in connection with Communion seasons (usually twice a year, but three or four times a year in some congregations) and prior to confirmation. Such meetings provided opportunities for young people to be converted.

There was, however, one basic prohibition: revivals should not be designed to produce excitement and emotional outbursts. If a meeting got out of control it should be stopped. Meetings should be characterized by silence and order. Harkey's advice was that the awakened should be invited up in front of the whole congregation after the sermon. He did not approve of them kneeling at the "mourner's bench"; he deemed this a disgusting display.

Harkey concluded *The Church's Best State* with an appendix on justification. He took a Lutheran viewpoint until he got to the question: "How are we justified?" In his answer he stressed human feelings and actions— "we must feel our need for Christ" (193). Among the "means of grace" Harkey included prayer meetings, catechetical classes, and Scripture reading along with the preaching of the Word and the Lord's Supper. "These are called 'means of grace,' because it is by them that God communicates his grace to the souls of his children, and instructs, enlightens, confirms, and leads them" (211).

The last chapter, "How Churches Can Help Ministers," was taken from Charles G. Finney's *Lectures on Revivals*.[20] Earlier in the work Harkey showed the influence of Finney in advocating that converted people should be brought into the church's fellowship as quickly as possible. In this final chapter, members are implored to support their minister through decent pay, prayer, and work in the life of the local church.

Harkey's views were unmistakably in accord with those of Schmucker and Kurtz. His work on revivals is the best statement of what the American Lutherans believed regarding that subject. However, Harkey was to have little impact when the *Definite Platform* controversy came in the 1850s. He supported the document and its proposals, but his professorship in Illinois put him far from the center of the action.

Samuel Sprecher

The final advocate of American Lutheranism considered here is Samuel Sprecher (1810–1906). Sprecher attended both the college and seminary

---

20. Charles G. Finney (1792–1875) was the best known revivalist of that period. He devised the techniques to get the best results in a revival, and his methods have been used ever since.

at Gettysburg, where he studied under Samuel Schmucker, who made a lasting impression on him. More than sixty years after meeting Schmucker, Sprecher said: "He was one of the best and most earnest men I ever knew. I never knew any man, who was so constantly absorbed by his work, or one who seemed so perfectly to understand what he was called to do, and who so constantly had it in view, and so perseveringly labored to accomplish it."[21] Sprecher married one of Schmucker's sisters.

Although he admired Schmucker, the most influential person in Sprecher's young life was Benjamin Kurtz. When Kurtz was installed as superintendent and professor at the Missionary Institute at Selin's Grove, Pennsylvania, it was Sprecher who gave the main address. Reflecting on Kurtz's preaching, Sprecher said:

> From his lips dropped the first sermon to which I was a conscious listener.
> It was on the text: "I know you, that you have not the love of God in you;"
> and though I was but a child, it made an impression on my mind of a special
> work of grace in the soul, which has never left it. Indeed, I owe it to a
> charge produced by his instrumentality in the religious character of my native
> place, that I stand . . . this day as an evangelical Christian.[22]

Sprecher expressed admiration for the "moral heroism" of Kurtz when his innovations were opposed.[23] Sprecher stated that he had experienced conversion at one of Kurtz's revivals. Even though Kurtz was accused of having become a Methodist, Sprecher judged that such revivals had contributed to the extension of the church and made the congregations "soundly evangelical."

After Sprecher completed his seminary training at Gettysburg in 1836, he served parishes in Martinsburg, West Virginia, and in Harrisburg and Chambersburg, Pennsylvania. He is most noted, however, for his position as professor at Wittenberg College and Theological Seminary in Springfield, Ohio (1849–84). This school had been founded by those who wanted

21. Peter Anstadt, *Life and Times of the Rev. S. S. Schmucker* (York, Pa.: P. Anstadt & Sons, 1896), vi.

22. Samuel Sprecher, "Address and Charge Delivered at the Installation of Rev. Dr. Kurtz as Superintendent and Professor of Missionary Institute, in Selin's Grove, Pa," in *Addresses, Inaugurals and Charges, Delivered in Selin's Grove, Snyder Co., Pa., September 1st, and November 24th, 1858, in Connection with Laying the Cornerstone, and the Installation of the Evangelical Lutheran Missionary Institute, Together with an Appeal in Behalf of that Institution* (Baltimore: T. Newton Kurtz, 1858), 25–26.

23. Sprecher listed those innovations as preaching in English, holding prayer meetings, founding Sunday schools, conducting revival meetings, and being active in the temperance movement.

to practice a more "American" form of Lutheranism, which meant preaching in English, using the "New Measures," and having a more liberal attitude toward the Lutheran Confessions. The so-called English Synod had broken from the Joint Synod of Ohio in 1840 and stopped its support of the Joint Synod's seminary in Columbus.

The school began in Wooster, Ohio, in 1842 but was permanently established at Springfield in 1845. In 1843 Ezra Keller, a friend of Sprecher's, was called to be professor of theology. Before he died of typhoid fever in 1848, Keller asked the board of directors to call Sprecher to succeed him.[24] Under Keller, Wittenberg was known as the "Revival College," and Sprecher was called to continue that emphasis.

Sprecher believed that in the General Synod there should be "unity in fundamentals" but "diversity in non-essentials." He regarded the Augsburg Confession as the standard for Lutherans, but claimed that one need not follow all its distinct "doctrinal peculiarities." He was concerned with the increased influence of those who held a much more conservative view regarding the Lutheran Confessions.

It was Sprecher who convinced Samuel Schmucker, his brother-in-law, that the American Lutherans needed a standard that would more clearly define their position. He recognized that tensions were increasing between the confessional party and the American Lutherans. Choices had to be made. In 1853 Sprecher said: "I do not see how we can do otherwise than adopt the Symbols of the Church, or form a new symbol which shall embrace all that is fundamental to Christianity in them, rejecting what is unscriptural, and supplying what is defective."[25]

In June 1855, some of the proponents of American Lutheranism met informally while the General Synod was in session at Dayton, Ohio. Again, Sprecher argued for a statement that would provide theological guidance. He pointed to the situation in Ohio, where American Lutherans had withdrawn from the conservative Joint Synod of Ohio to form English synods, as evidence of the need for such a statement. It was agreed that Schmucker should draw up a statement for the smaller synods in Indiana, Ohio, and Illinois. After Schmucker wrote the statement, he sent it to Sprecher for review. In September 1855, the *Definite Platform* was distributed to the clergy of the General Synod. Sprecher was not the author of this work but a prime mover in its inception.

The interrelationships among the chief advocates of American Lutheranism contributed to their common perception of Lutheranism. Samuel

24. Ray Franklin Kibler III, "Samuel Sprecher: An American Lutheran Theologian," (Master's thesis, Luther Northwestern Theological Seminary, 1982).

25. Spaeth, *Charles Porterfield Krauth,* 1:347. Spaeth does not cite his source for this quote.

Schmucker was the key in that he was a close friend of Benjamin Kurtz and the theological mentor of both Simeon Harkey and Samuel Sprecher.

Out of their common perceptions emerged a unified "American" prescription for Lutheranism. The American Lutherans felt that if Lutheranism was going to be a vital force in America it must make certain accommodations to the American scene. Each of the men advocated revivals as a means of bringing about spiritual conversion and increasing church membership. Each also had a strong aversion to forms and ritual in worship, which were seen as "Popish."

The most important similarity was their beliefs regarding the sacraments. Although the American Lutherans defended the practice of infant baptism, they rejected any concept of baptismal regeneration. No spiritual transformation occurred in baptism; that was accomplished through the individual's conversion experience. The American Lutherans rejected absolution as a means of forgiveness, saying that forgiveness can only come from God. A general declaration of grace was the most they would allow. Finally, they rejected the doctrine of the real presence of the body and blood of Christ in the Lord's Supper, claiming that such a belief was absurd and against all reason.

The American Lutheran leaders were vehemently anti-Roman, and they sought to rid Lutheranism of its "Romish vestiges." They regarded the Reformation as unfinished; America offered the opportunity to accomplish its completion. Such a completion would put Lutheranism in agreement with other evangelical Protestant churches in America. The American Lutherans saw that certain Lutheran "peculiarities" conflicted with "fundamental" doctrines that united all Protestants. Since such "peculiarities" were "nonfundamental," they could be left to the individual to accept or reject or they could be disregarded altogether.

What was called American Lutheranism had been developing within the Lutheran church in America since the latter part of the eighteenth century. It had been expressed in sermons, discourses, and articles. Through the influence of Samuel Schmucker, it had been taught to hundreds of pastors at the Seminary in Gettysburg; the pastors, in turn, disseminated its views into the churches of the General Synod. The American Lutherans offered a series of proposals that they claimed would make Lutheranism thoroughly American. That vision ultimately became the object of the greatest controversy ever experienced by Lutheranism in America.

6

The Renewal of
Confessional Lutheranism

*T*hrough the first four decades of the nineteenth century, the American Lutherans were the dominant force in the General Synod,[1] but times were changing. Lutherans were again beginning to find their identity on the basis of the Lutheran Confessions. The change in that direction was gradual. By the 1850s, when the controversy over the *Definite Platform* occurred, Lutheranism in America had taken on a greater confessional consciousness and was beginning to evidence a stronger Lutheran identity.

The Changing Situation in Germany

In the eighteenth century, Lutheranism in Germany was under the domination of rationalism, which emphasized the subjective, idealistic, naturalistic, and rationalistic aspects of religion. This influence has been previously noted in reference to the changes that took place at the University at Halle, and its effects in America were exemplified by Quitman's *Evangelical Catechism* (see chap. 3).

The first signs of reestablishment of Lutheran identity came in a sermon preached on Reformation Day 1800 by Franz V. Reinhard (1753–1812), a professor of theology and ethics at the University of Wittenberg. The English text of this sermon can be found in a collection edited by Carl S. Meyer.[2] Reinhard observed that the Lutheran church was moving further and further away from the "real teaching of Luther"; if Luther returned

---

1. Wentz maintains that the advocates of American Lutheranism were a minority within the General Synod. See Abdel Ross Wentz, *A Basic History of Lutheranism in America* (Philadelphia: Fortress Press, 1964), 131. This estimate is questionable when one considers the overriding influence of Samuel Schmucker, the fact that the American Lutherans dominated the General Synod's leadership, and their control of the publications such as the *Lutheran Observer*.

2. Carl S. Meyer, ed. *Moving Frontiers: Readings in the History of the Lutheran Church— Missouri Synod* (St. Louis: Concordia Publishing House, 1964).

from the grave, Reinhard alleged, he would not recognize the church's teachers of that day as members of the church he had founded (62–63). Even the doctrine of justification had become a stranger in the church that bore Luther's name.

> Now, my brethren, that may sound rather strange to you, for we hear less and less of *this* doctrine, especially in the church which supposedly has come into existence through it. If we may believe a large group of her most famous members, it is a very dangerous *error* to want to be right with God and eternally blessed without merit and merely by grace; on the contrary, one must help oneself and become worthy of salvation through one's virtue (62).

Reinhard noted that most Lutherans in his day considered the doctrine of the free grace of God to be "doubtful and unprovable" and thought that Luther himself would reject it for "the privilege of living in our enlightened age."

Reinhard's message was clear: This doctrine cannot be forgotten. Reason cannot deny that all people are sinners and "are without the glory which they should have before God." Reinhard called on his hearers to reject the rationalism that had taken over the church and return to the message of the gospel as Luther and those who followed him had proclaimed it.

The second indication of a Lutheran confessional revival came in the person of Claus Harms (1778–1855), who attacked the plan for a Prussian Union Church. Because of the influence of rationalism, all distinctions between Lutheran and Reformed had disappeared. Some felt it would therefore be possible to construct a union of the German Protestant churches, with a doctrinal base so minimal that it could be accepted by Protestants of all views.

As early as 1798, King Friedrich Wilhelm III of Prussia attempted to bring about such a union. Finally, in 1817, the year of the three-hundredth anniversary of the Reformation, a union Communion service was held in the palace at Potsdam. In a decree issued September 27, 1817, the king stated that a union of the Lutherans and Reformed would be a "God-pleasing work." He added: "But no matter how strongly I desire the Reformed and Lutheran churches in my territories to share my well-grounded conviction, I respect their rights and freedom and have no intention of forcing anything upon them by my decree and decision."[3]

Harms's reaction was sharp and came in the form of his *Ninety-five Theses*, published in 1817.[4] These *Theses* represent the end of a long

---

3. Cited in Meyer, *Moving Frontiers,* 59.
4. Meyer, *Moving Frontiers,* 66–69 lists many of the Theses. The English translation of the complete text of the *Ninety-five Theses* is found in H. E. Jacobs and John A. W. Haas, eds., *The Lutheran Cyclopedia* (New York: Charles Scribner's Sons, 1899), 512–14. The following quotes from the Theses are from *Moving Frontiers.*

spiritual road for Harms. He had been educated under the influence of rationalism but broke with it. A friend loaned him a book of Schleiermacher's, which Harms spent the better part of a day and a night reading and rereading. Finally, he walked through a section of the city of Kiel— the path of the "still ones," those who disagreed with rationalism and adhered to the biblical faith. During that walk, Harms stated, "all at once I recognized that all Rationalism, and all Aestheticism and all self-knowledge and all self-doing are meaningless in the work of salvation. The realization that our salvation must have another source struck me like a bolt of lightning" (65). When Schleiermacher's sermons appeared in print, Harms reflected, "Oh, how [eagerly] I reached for them! And, oh, how mistaken I was! He who had conceived me had no bread for me" (65–66).

The *Ninety-five Theses* were directed against the errors and confusion of the church of that day. Harms stated he was willing to explain them or defend them, and he requested all genuine Lutherans who agreed with him to give him support. Harms lamented that "Lutheranism is reformed into paganism, and Christianity is reformed out of this world" (66). With regard to the proposed union, Harms wrote, "To say that time has removed the wall of separation between Lutherans and Reformed is not to speak correctly. The question is: Who have fallen away from the faith of their church, the Lutherans or the Reformed? Or both?" (68) Harms affirmed, "If the body and blood of Christ were present in the bread and wine at the Marburg Colloquy in 1529, this is still true in 1817" (68).

Harms believed this union could only happen in a church that had fallen into theological and doctrinal ruin. When the Scriptures and the church's confessional statements are disregarded, truth no longer matters. When reason is allowed to reign, humanity becomes its own God or God is humanity's own invention. The *Ninety-five Theses* were a powerful call for reform and renewal within the Lutheran church. As for the plan of union, Harms stated: "They want to make the Lutheran Church rich by an act of union (Copulation) as if she were a poor hired girl. Just don't consummate the act over Luther's bones! That would bring them back to life and then—woe to you!" (68).

King Friedrich Wilhelm III did not give up his plans for a Lutheran-Reformed union. On April 4, 1830, the tricentennial observance of the Augsburg Confession, he issued an edict stating that the power of the state would be used to enforce a union Agenda (liturgy) and to introduce the Reformed practice of the breaking of bread in the communion. Differences in the names of evangelical congregations were to be abandoned. What happened in Prussia spread to all Germany: a systematic attempt to unite Lutherans and Reformed was under way.

The union met with opposition. Many confessional Lutherans refused to enter into it. Johann Gottfried Scheibel (1783–1843), a pastor in Breslau in Silesia was suspended as a result of his opposition to the union. Many pastors were imprisoned for refusing to conduct services according to the union Agenda. Laity who refused to cooperate with the union had their homes confiscated and sold by the government. When Lutherans in Breslau petitioned for a separate Lutheran church, they were denied. With conditions like these, and no hope in sight, many Germans who opposed the union came to America.[5]

In 1840, however, the government began to reverse these pro-unionist policies. When Friedrich Wilhelm IV came to the throne in Prussia, one of his first actions was to revoke the suspensions of pastors who had refused to comply with the Union Church. The General Concession of 1845 allowed Lutherans to organize free churches without loss of privileges. Organizations had to be approved by the state, but Lutherans did not have to contribute to the state church.

In 1843 Heinrich Schmid's *The Doctrinal Theology of the Evangelical Lutheran Church* was published in Germany.[6] A compilation of theological statements drawn from the writings of Lutheran theologians of the sixteenth and seventeenth centuries, this book had a great effect on the Lutheran church in America. Although it was not translated into English until 1875, the German volume was read by many pastors in America.

The Henkel Family

Confessional Lutheranism was present in America in the early decades of the nineteenth century. Perhaps the best example of its presence is seen in the work of, not one person, but an entire family, the Henkels. The central figure in this remarkable family was Paul Henkel (1754–1825). His great-grandfather had emigrated from Germany before Muhlenberg and organized Lutheran congregations in Pennsylvania.

Paul Henkel traveled in Virginia, Ohio, North Carolina, Kentucky, and Tennessee preaching and administering the sacraments to scattered groups of Lutherans. In 1790 he built a home in New Market, Virginia, from which he operated the rest of his life, although he lived in other places

---

5. Many examples of immigrations are cited in E. Clifford Nelson, ed., *The Lutherans in North America*, rev. ed. (Philadelphia: Fortress Press, 1980), 154–55.

6. The English translation is by Charles A. Hay and Henry Eyster Jacobs, *The Doctrinal Theology of the Evangelical Lutheran Church, Verified from the Original Sources by Heinrich Friedrich Schmid*, 3d ed. (Philadelphia: Lutheran Publication Society, 1899). The first and second editions appeared in 1875 and 1888, respectively.

for brief periods. Paul Henkel worked to bring about order among Lutherans. In 1803 he organized the Synod and Ministerium of North Carolina. In 1818 he helped organize the Ohio Synod. In addition, Henkel operated a school for ministerial candidates at New Market, where he trained four of his brothers and five of his six sons for the Lutheran ministry.[7]

In 1820 Henkel founded the Evangelical Lutheran Tennessee Synod. The circumstances behind the creation of this synod indicate how widespread were the tensions between those who would later be called American Lutherans and more confessionally minded Lutherans. David Henkel, one of Paul's sons, had experienced delays in the process toward ordination. The reason given by the North Carolina Synod was his age (he was twenty-four in 1819), but the more likely reason was that the secretary of the synod, Gottlieb Shober, was concerned about Henkel's emphasis on Lutheran particularity. Shober was especially upset about a comment David Henkel supposedly had made, that a marriage between Lutherans and Reformed was like mating cows with horses. Shober almost exercised synodical discipline on the young Henkel. Henkel countered by criticizing Shober for a lack of concern for traditional Lutheran teaching.[8] At the North Carolina Synod meeting in 1819, David Henkel was tried for making statements critical of non-Lutherans and placed on probation.[9]

The 1819 convention that put him on probation was held six weeks early because Shober had convinced the president to change the date so that he (Shober) could participate in the Pennsylvania Ministerium's discussions of the proposed General Synod. Six weeks later, Paul Henkel and his delegates arrived, convened the "real" synod convention, dropped the charges against David Henkel, and ordained him. In 1820 the Henkels attempted to get recognition of their convention. When that effort failed, they withdrew and formed the Tennessee Synod.

This incident was not the only reason for the Henkels' withdrawal. They objected to the doctrinal laxity of the North Carolina Synod. They charged that the synod did not teach baptismal regeneration or the real presence and that the synod was opposed to the Augsburg Confession.[10] What happened to David Henkel gave them added impetus to leave and form a separate synod.

7. Abdel Ross Wentz, *Pioneer in Christian Unity: Samuel Simon Schmucker* (Philadelphia: Fortress Press, 1966), 64.

8. Nelson, *The Lutherans,* 117.

9. *Minutes of the Evangelical Lutheran Synod of North Carolina* (1819), 12.

10. Richard C. Wolf, "The Americanization of the German Lutherans, 1683–1829" (Ph.D. diss., Yale Univ., 1947), 524. See also William E. Hall, "The Formation of the Tennessee Synod," *Lutheran Quarterly* (1954), 57–63.

For a brief time, Paul Henkel had given instruction to Samuel Schmucker's uncles, Nicholas and Peter, and to John George Schmucker. The Henkels and the Schmuckers had very different understandings of Lutheranism, however, and the area around New Market became a battlefield between the two families. When young Samuel Schmucker arrived in the area in September 1820 he wrote of his uncle Nicholas and the local situation: "He is very kind. We have talked over all the circumstance of the town and of New Market. Henkel and his sons persecute instinctively everything that bears the name of Schmucker."[11]

The Henkels, fearing the size and organizational power of such a body, opposed the idea of a General Synod. They believed that smaller synods and congregations were better suited than some ill-defined national body to hear appeals, recognize ordinations, and introduce books. But their chief objection was that the General Synod was never properly grounded in Lutheran doctrine as expressed in the Confessions. Their loyalty to a confessional Lutheranism never wavered. In New Market they operated a printing press and published Lutheran catechisms, hymnbooks, and other religious books. In 1851 one of Paul Henkel's sons, Ambrose, was responsible for the first English translation of the *Book of Concord*. This publication gave many access to the Confessions of the Lutheran church and helped the cause of confessional Lutheranism in America.

Friedrich Conrad Dietrich Wyneken

German immigration to America increased in the 1830s. The immigrants came for many reasons, but an important one was their opposition to the union of Lutherans and Reformed that was being forced upon them in Germany. These immigrants were products of the confessional renewal in Germany; they would be an important influence on Lutheranism in America.

Among the immigrants was a young pastor named Friedrich Conrad Dietrich Wyneken (1810–76). He was born in Verden, Hanover, Germany, the son of a Lutheran pastor. His first formal education was in the local gymnasium. His theological studies were completed at the universities of Göttingen and Halle. Wyneken tutored a young nobleman and then became rector of the Latin School in Brernerford. He decided to go to America after reading in theological journals and church papers of the plight of the Lutheran immigrants. He arrived in America in 1838.

11. Peter Anstadt, *Life and Times of the Rev. S. S. Schmucker* (York, Pa.: P. Anstadt & Sons, 1896), 83.

After a short stay in Baltimore, Wyneken received a commission from the Pennsylvania Ministerium to serve as a missionary in Adams and Allen counties, Indiana. A pastor named James Hoover had served in the area and had organized two congregations in and around Fort Wayne, but he died after only two years of service. Both parishes wanted Wyneken to be their pastor, but he went into western Indiana instead, organizing several congregations in that part of the state.

In many letters to Germany Wyneken expressed concern for the German immigrants. Four missionaries responded and came from Germany in 1840–41. In 1841 Wyneken went to Germany to recruit more workers and to receive treatment for a throat ailment. While there, he gave presentations on the religious life in America, demonstrating the "New Measures" to his audience. Wyneken was an advocate of a confessional Lutheranism and had great appreciation for liturgical forms, which he saw as viable alternatives to American camp meetings and the "new measures."

He remained in Europe until 1843, seeking assistance for the cause of the German immigrants in America. Wilhelm Loehe (1808–72), noted for sending German pastors to America, was especially helpful by organizing the *Nothilfer* (emergency helpers) program. An accelerated pastoral training program was established through which pastors and their families could come to America, receive additional theological education at Fort Wayne, and then go into missionary work.

Wyneken's work, *Die Noth der deutschen Lutheraner in Nordamerika* (*The Distress of the German Lutherans in North America*)[12] deals with the process of Americanization and expresses concern over the religious condition of German Lutherans in America. Published about a year after Wyneken arrived in Germany, it was designed to explain to Germans what was happening to German Lutherans as they settled in America. The earliest edition was printed in the *Zeitschrift fuer Protestantismus und Kirche,* the German church paper published at Erlangen and edited by Professor Gottlieb Christoph Adolf von Harless (1806–79), a noted proponent of confessional Lutheranism. The first American edition appeared in the church paper *Die Lutheranische Kirchenzeitung,* published in 1844 at Pittsburgh by Pastor Friederich Schmidt.

Wyneken began with an emotional appeal for Lutherans to come to the aid of the German immigrants in America. He proceeded to make clear "the misery of your Lutheran brothers in America."

---

12. Friederich Conrad Dietrich Wyneken, *Die Noth der deutschen Lutheraner in Nordamerika* (Pittsburgh: Druckerei der lutherischen Kirchenzeitung, 1844). Translated into English by S. Edgar Schmidt and published by Concordia Theological Seminary Press, Fort Wayne, Ind., 1982. The following quotations are from this translation. A sketch of Wyneken's life can be found in Walter A. Baepler, *A Century of Grace: A History of the Missouri Synod 1847–1947* (St. Louis: Concordia Pub. House, 1947), 53–64.

His first point was that German Lutherans in America were without the blessings of the church. Many who had moved into the cities had fallen into all sorts of vices and had no discipline. Others, who had rid themselves of the bonds of the church, lived in outward respectability but were without God, without church, without hope. The pastors had to concentrate on the people in the congregations, leaving those outside with no one to see to their spiritual needs. Missionaries were needed to reach these people, who often fell prey to "hirelings" who fed them lies. Wyneken described one "self-made clergyman" who was unmasked as a child molester (20). Imposters abounded; people who needed a preacher would take anyone without asking for credentials.

Because there was no one to preach the gospel to the people out on the frontier, impiety was commonplace. Wyneken observed: "Bible and prayer-books are, unfortunately, often also left at home since the people have lost the taste for them through 'enlightenment,' and it isn't even worth sticking out one's hand for the improved catechisms and watered-down hymnals. No preacher comes to shake them out of their earthly striving and thinking, and the voice of the Gospel has not been heard for a long time" (22). Under these conditions, any spiritual longing soon disappeared. Wyneken proceeded to cite several examples of "gross indifference." Hundreds were deprived of baptism, preaching, and the sacrament of the body and blood of Christ. Without sermons, instruction and someone to confirm the children, there could only be one result—German heathens! (27).

> The area in which our German people settle is getting even larger, the number of those suffering spiritual need continues to grow; and it is getting harder and harder to watch over this tremendously large region and help lessen the misery. Therefore my appeal to your hearts: Help in the name of Jesus! Help because the need is ever urgent. What will become of our brethren in ten or twenty years if there is no help? (29)

The second section of Wyneken's work concerned Lutheranism's enemies in America—sects and the Roman church. Wyneken described a number of native sects, of which the Methodists were the most numerous. He then turned to the "New Measures." He described the activities that occurred at protracted meetings—the moanings and groanings, the anxious bench, the "most awful gyrations and gestures." Wyneken commented: "The sects regard these striking occurrences, although they continue to be repeated again and again, as an act of the Holy Spirit; I have however, never been able to overcome a horror for the demonical power at such happenings" (32). Wyneken observed that the Lutheran congregations were suffering because of these practices. "Everything takes its peaceful, quiet course in accordance with the written Word. Suddenly a sectarian preacher comes bursting into the congregation and, with noise, screaming and howling, announces the judgment they must fear if they do not honestly convert" (33).

Wyneken believed such practices were disastrous. They caused people to question their faith, to trust in their own emotions and deeds instead of the promises of God; people ended up confused, wondering if their conversion was genuine. Finally, the congregations were disrupted. Those who had not come to the "new life" were despised and people ended up judging one another and taking sides. The devil had entered the church. Wyneken noted that the sects held the sacraments in contempt, whereas Lutherans understood the sacraments as things that build up the congregation, hold it together and nourish the people. In the sects, baptism ceased to be a cleansing from sin and a washing of regeneration; it became a mere ceremony where one confesses one's faith and repents. Holy Communion was nothing more than a commemorative meal that could be dispensed with. "To them the sacraments are mere signs in the shallowest sense, and infant baptism is decreasing more and more in America, being viewed as an un-Christian abomination, as the main cause of all ruin and death which has broken out over Christianity!" (40).

The Roman church was an enemy because of its solidarity and endless resources. Unlike Lutherans, the Roman church had a surplus of priests. Roman Catholic schools and hospitals were other evidence of Catholicism's strength. Wyneken believed that the Roman church could grow in America because of the freedom there. He also pointed out that the Roman church lumped all other groups together as "Protestants" and then pointed out the inconsistencies of Protestants.

Wyneken saw similarities between the plight of Lutherans and Roman Catholics as both were attacked by Protestants who criticized the doctrines of Holy Communion, baptism, the church, confession, and the Office of the Keys (44). Wyneken observed that Protestants could not distinguish between Lutheran and Roman teachings. Wyneken feared the "Roman threat" and believed that only the Lutheran church could defeat the Roman church.

Lutheranism in America suffered from internal shortcomings and lacked external unity. Pastors were few, and synods were large. Wyneken used the Synod of the West, to which he belonged, as an example, a synod that encompassed four states. Wyneken felt that the General Synod "for the most part, embraces opponents." In commenting on most of the English-speaking Lutherans, Wyneken observed: "While they are enthusiastic about the name 'Lutheran,' they most shamelessly and impertinently attack the teachings of our church and endeavor to spread their false doctrines, chiefly with regard to Baptism and Communion, in sermons, and particularly through their publications and newspapers" (47). Wyneken described these Lutherans as defenders of the "New Measures" and Methodistic in their approach to conversion. In Wyneken's opinion, the seminary at Gettysburg, if it did not change, would become a tool to help destroy the church. He noted the attempts at union between Lutherans and Reformed; these, he felt, could only result in laxity and indifference with regard to doctrine.

Wyneken believed his distress call was a matter of survival. In particular, he feared that the "Methodistic spirit" would soar and infect most of Christendom. America was the battleground, and it was the task of Lutherans in America to halt the missionary efforts of the Baptists and Methodists. He asked his German audience to look to the future. If German Lutherans were unwilling to act, people would fall into the hands of the sectarians and their intoxicating emotions on one hand or the "willing Roman mother" on the other. "The Roman Church also offers enough to keep the flickering eyes of the power of imagination and spasmodically craving emotion occupied, even if it can neither satisfy a Christian's deep longing nor the heart of its deepest needs" (54). Scripturally and confessionally faithful preachers were needed to create a union of orthodox synods. Wyneken noted that a change was occurring in that direction, and he put forth the vision of a unified Lutheranism that would witness to America, Germany, and the world. He advocated sound training of pastors who would work together, follow the old Lutheran worship services, introduce private confession, and affiliate all the congregations with synods.

Wyneken's *The Distress of the German Lutherans in North America* is an often overlooked but perceptive evaluation of the problems that faced German Lutheran immigrants once they reached America's shores. It is a classic statement of the problem of Americanization from one who experienced the phenomenon himself and who ministered to others who were undergoing its tremendous changes.

The immigrants were confronted with a religious climate completely foreign to them. They were in danger of losing faith altogether or falling into the hands of various sects with their strange, un-Lutheran practices such as camp meetings and the carryings-on of revivals.

Wyneken felt that the Lutheran church had adapted to American ways to the point where the immigrant could hardly tell the difference between it and the other American religious groups. He charged the leaders of the General Synod and the Seminary with capitulating to the American religious climate. The General Synod was rapidly becoming just another American "Protestant" church. All Lutheran distinctiveness was gone. In fact, the General Synod was hostile to genuine Lutheranism.

While in Germany, Wyneken became acquainted with Wilhelm Loehe. Loehe heeded Wyneken's plea and was responsible for sending many German pastors to America to minister to the German Lutherans there. Wyneken, in the *Zeitschrift fuer Protestantismus und Kirche,* also attacked the General Synod saying that it was "Methodistic" and was encouraging a union of Lutheran and Reformed churches in America.

These attacks by Wyneken did not go unnoticed by the General Synod. At its meeting in Philadelphia in 1845, the Synod instructed its committee of Foreign Correspondence to prepare an address to the various Lutheran bodies in Europe especially in Germany, calculated to remove false impressions regarding the General Synod's doctrine and practice.[13] The Synod also assigned to that committee the task of preparing "a clear and concise view of the doctrines and practice of the American Lutheran church."[14]

Wyneken represented the Synod of the West at that convention and was an active participant. A resolution rejoicing that the American Tract Society had extended its operation to the German population caused "considerable discussion." Wyneken moved that the resolution be stricken; his motion lost.[15] The report of the committee on Christian Union led to an "animated and somewhat protracted debate." Wyneken opposed a resolution that stated: "*Resolved,* That the idea of a Christian Union upon the basis of the word of God, that will so far harmonized the Church of Christ, as to give success to all the objects of temporal, social and moral happiness, contemplated in the gospel, is an object most truly noble in itself, and deserving the best efforts of purist philanthropy."[16] The resolution passed by a vote of 26 to 21.

In the context of these debates, Wyneken challenged the General Synod to prove the Lutheran character of its doctrine and practice by submitting such works as Samuel Schmucker's *Popular Theology* and *Portraiture of Lutheranism* and Benjamin Kurtz's *On Infant Baptism* and *Why Are You a Lutheran?* to Dr. Rudelback, Professor Harless, and other German Lutheran theologians for judgment regarding the orthodoxy of their contents.[17] He then demanded that the General Synod either renounce the name Lutheran or reject as un-Lutheran the "American" Lutheran views as represented in the writings of Schmucker and Kurtz.[18] Neither of Wyneken's proposals was positively received.

13. *Proceedings of the Thirteenth Convention of the General Synod of the Evangelical Lutheran Church, in the United States, Convened in Philadelphia, May 16, 1845,* 35.
14. Ibid., 54.
15. Ibid., 48–49.
16. Ibid., 58.
17. Baepler, *A Century of Grace,* 63.
18. The *Proceedings* of the 1845 convention do not mention Wyneken's statements, nor

After the convention in Philadelphia, Wyneken severed his connection with the General Synod. He wrote to Loehe: "I should have been happy if, by the acceptance of the second proposal, my character would have been branded in Germany as that of a liar and defamer. However, since the General Synod rejected both proposals, I again had to repeat publicly that she is harboring and nurturing false doctrine. As an honest man and a Christian, I wished to declare war against her, although it may seem silly to her, since I am only one insignificant individual. I desired to tell her in advance that I would do all in my power to oppose her influence, especially that I would warn against her, so that the few in Germany who are on the side of the truth do not bother with her."[19]

In 1848, Wyneken joined the newly formed Missouri Synod. At Philadelphia, Wyneken was virtually a lone voice, but his words were a portent of what was to come.

William Julius Mann

William Julius Mann (1819–93) was an important leader of the confessional party that developed in the General Synod in the 1850s.[20] Born in Stuttgart, Württemberg, Mann attended the gymnasium there; Philip Schaff[21] was his roommate. In 1837 Mann entered the University at Tübingen, where he studied under Christian Ferdinand Baur and Christian Friedrich Schmid.[22] After teaching school for a time, Mann was ordained in 1844. At the urging of Philip Schaff, he emigrated to America in 1845.

When Mann arrived in America, he went to Mercersburg to see Schaff. Mann was interested in occupying the chair of German literature that the seminary there hoped to establish, but the position did not materialize.

---

do they contain the records of any other speeches. Adolph Spaeth, *Charles Porterfield Krauth*, 2 vols. (New York: The Christian Literature Co., 1898), 1:333, says with regard to that convention: "The publications of the American Tract Society, as well as those of the American Sunday-School Union, and the extension of the former's operations to the German population, are cordially indorsed, in spite of the opposition of the staunch Lutheran, Wynecke [sic]." For other accounts see F. Bente, *American Lutheranism*, 2 vols. (St. Louis: Concordia Pub. House, 1919), 1:153 and Baepler, *A Century of Grace*, 62–63.

19. Geo. J. Fritschel, *Quellen und Dokument zur Geschichte und Lehrstellung der ev.-luth. Synode von Iowa u.a. Staaten*. Chicago, 44. Cited in Baepler, *A Century of Grace*, 63–64.

20. The best biographical sources for Mann are the work by his daughter, Emma T. Mann, *Memoir of the Life and Work of William Julius Mann* (Philadelphia: Jas. B. Rogers Printing Co., 1893), and Adolph Spaeth, *Memorial of William Julius Mann* (Philadelphia: Evangelical Lutheran Ministerium of Pennsylvania, 1893).

21. See chap. 2, note 17.

22. Mann, *Memoir*, 32, commented that these men represented the positive and negative teaching at Tübingen and that her father was greatly influenced by Schmid.

Mann left Mercersburg after two months. In December 1845 he accepted a call as assistant at the German Reformed Salem Congregation in Philadelphia.

At that time, Lutheran and Reformed pastors routinely exchanged pulpits. A journal, *Kirchenfreund,* was an organ for both communions. Mann, however, was a Lutheran by birth, confirmation, and conviction; he eventually wanted to have a Lutheran synodical connection. Even while still in the German Reformed Church, Mann was concerned about the phenomenon of "Methodistic revivals." He felt that such events could only produce excitement, not repentance and conversion. Mann especially missed the liturgy, and he believed that prospects for reform in the German Reformed Church were poor.

On September 18, 1850, Mann was elected assistant pastor at St. Michael's and Zion's Congregation in Philadelphia. When Mann applied for admission to the Pennsylvania Ministerium, he said with regard to his former connection with the German Reformed Church:

> This step has been taken out of consideration for a dear friend, who felt assured that I would not be expected to do anything against my conscience and my conviction. With my present knowledge of church matters in this country, there are other and higher considerations which lead me to embrace an opportunity of joining again the Evangelical Lutheran Church; and it is the desire of my heart to serve this church in which I was born, and to which I owe my training and education, as the Lord in His goodness will give me strength and wisdom.[23]

In 1854 Mann was elected senior pastor. He was the fifth in line from Henry Melchior Muhlenberg to serve that congregation, where he remained until 1884.

Mann was active in the Pennsylvania Ministerium. He prepared an explanation of Luther's Catechism, which appeared in 1851. He composed prayers for families and individuals that were appended to the Pennsylvania Liturgy of 1855. He served as chairman of the Ministerium's examining committee and was that body's representative on the board of directors for the Seminary in Gettysburg. From 1860 to 1862, he was president of the Ministerium.

When the controversy over the *Definite Platform* arose, it was Mann who, more than anyone else, took up the cause of confessional Lutheranism against Samuel Schmucker and the *Platform.*

23. Cited in Spaeth, *Memorial,* 23.

Charles Philip Krauth

Charles Philip Krauth (1797–1867) is mainly remembered as the father of Charles Porterfield Krauth, the great confessional Lutheran historian and theologian of the third quarter of the nineteenth century, but the elder Krauth was an important and respected person in his own right. He became involved in the American Lutheran controversy—in many respects against his will.

The elder Krauth was born at New Goshenhoppen, Upper Hannover township, Montgomery County, Pennsylvania. Originally he wanted to study medicine, but eventually he began reading theology under David Frederick Schaeffer in Frederick, Maryland. Later he studied under Abram Reck at Winchester, Virginia. He was licensed to preach by the Pennsylvania Ministerium in 1819 and in that same year took charge of the churches in Martinsburg and Shepherdstown, Virginia.

Besides serving his parishes, Krauth became involved in other activities within the church. During the years 1826–27, he and Frederick Schaeffer edited a paper called the *Evangelical Lutheran Intelligencer* "containing historical, biographical, and religious memoirs, with essays on the doctrines of Luther and practical remarks and anecdotes, for the edification of pious persons of all denominations."[24] In 1826, at age twenty-nine, Krauth was elected president of the Synod of Maryland and Virginia. The following year, he received a call to serve St. Matthew's in Philadelphia.

Best known as an educator, Krauth was regarded as a gifted scholar and considered to have the best knowledge of biblical languages of anyone in the General Synod. In 1833 he was chosen professor of biblical and Oriental literature at the Seminary at Gettysburg, where his colleague was Samuel Schmucker. In 1834 he was elected president of Pennsylvania College, a post he held until 1850.

In addition to the elder Krauth's influence as a teacher, his connection with the *Evangelical Review* caused his voice to be heard throughout the church. Founded in 1849 by William M. Reynolds, this journal was designed to offer a confessional Lutheran position in contrast to Benjamin Kurtz's *Lutheran Observer*. In 1850 Krauth replaced Reynolds as editor.

Krauth had not always taken a confessional stance regarding doctrine. In fact, there is nothing to indicate that his early views and training were any different from those of the majority of Lutheran pastors in America at that time. An early comment made by Krauth exemplifies this: "I find the Lutheran doctrine of the Sacraments hard to accept, in view of my Puritanic training, but I find the Scripture passages quoted in favor of them

24. Spaeth, *Charles Porterfield Krauth*, 1:8.

still harder to get over and explain away, and this I apprehend is the feeling of many who see the truth, but are slow to make a decided and public demonstration of it."[25]

The change in Krauth's views most likely occurred through his reading of theological books from Germany. He was an avid reader who was well acquainted with German publications. Even before he became editor of the *Evangelical Review,* he contributed an article reviewing Schmid's *Doctrinal Theology of the Evangelical Lutheran Church (Evangelical Review* 1, July 1849). After assessing the present theological situation, Krauth commented:

> Our verdict is unequivocally in behalf of the study, the thorough study, of this theology. We would have it thrown over our church with a liberal hand; we would have all our ministers acquainted with the Symbolical Books; we would have them all versed in the distinctive theology of the Church. We would have introduced into our theological schools the study of the Symbols, and didactic and polemic theology so administered as to bring before the view pure, unadulterated Lutheranism.

Krauth described the situation at that time as a confusion of individual views: "our ministers display, in the opinions they entertain, sometimes a decided Calvinistic influence, sometimes an extreme Arminian, sometimes a Pelagian." But he sensed that changes were taking place. "These are signs of the times—they mean that the things which have been, can be no more; that the Church is returning to the sobriety of her better days, and that theology, systematic and biblical, may expect to receive attention such as it deserves."[26] Krauth welcomed Schmid's work, and his review left no doubt as to his sympathies.

Krauth, however, was not attracted to controversy. Even though he came to disagree with Schmucker, the two men maintained a cordial relationship. The elder Krauth was much more concerned about his role as teacher, and it was through teaching that he hoped to influence the church. Krauth's position often proved problematic to him. During the lengthy controversy sparked by the *Definite Platform,* both sides often claimed his support, a situation that caused him much discomfort. In a letter of October 2, 1862, addressed to his friend Professor H. I. Schmidt of Columbia College, New York, Krauth expressed his perplexity over the situation.

> I have three times defined my position and at each time offended both extremes. Some call me a rigid Symbolist, others an extreme New Measures

25. Ibid., 1:18–19.
26. *Evangelical Review* 1 (July, 1849).

man. I am neither. If I say so again I draw down upon me the extremists of both sides. I acknowledge no standard of Lutheranism but the Augsburg Confession. If an American Lutheran is a Lutheran in the United States who regards that Symbol as the only authoritative one, I am an American Lutheran. So have I said again and again.[27]

The elder Krauth's position seems perfectly confessional, and it is obvious that he did not agree with the doctrinal latitude proposed by the American Lutherans. It was his reluctance to get involved in the conflict that caused him to be misunderstood. He continued to write in the *Evangelical Review,* but he did not jump headlong into the fray. In fact, he remained on the faculty of the Gettysburg Seminary until he died. His death occurred at the time of the formation of the General Council, and the elder Krauth grieved over the split that was occurring in the church.

Charles Porterfield Krauth

Perhaps the most interesting of the confessional figures is Charles Porterfield Krauth (1823–1883), son of Charles Philip Krauth. He was born in Martinsburg, Virginia, where his father was pastor. In 1831 he entered the Gettysburg Gymnasium. From 1834 to 1839 he attended Pennsylvania College. In 1839, at age sixteen, he entered the Seminary at Gettysburg, where he studied under his father and Samuel Schmucker. The young Krauth, eighteen, graduated from the seminary in 1841 and was licensed that same year. There is every indication that Krauth at that time shared the theological views of his professors.

During the next twenty years, Krauth served several parishes. He was at Canton, Maryland, from 1841 to 1843, and at Second English Lutheran in Baltimore, 1843 to 1847. The latter parish had prematurely engaged in a building project and was heavily in debt. For one year, starting in 1847, Krauth served the same parishes his father had served, Martinsburg and Shepherdstown, Virginia. In 1848 he moved to Winchester, Virginia, where he remained until 1856. This was followed by two more calls, to English Lutheran in Pittsburgh (1856–59) and St. Mark's in Philadelphia (1859–61).

During these years, Krauth served the church-at-large in many capacities. While a member of the Virginia Synod, he was chairman of a committee that examined and recommended for use the Pennsylvania Synod Liturgy of 1842, which was published by the General Synod in 1847. He was also a delegate to many conventions of the General Synod.

27. Spaeth, *Charles Porterfield Krauth,* 1:19.

When did Krauth change his theological perspective? Beale Schmucker, one of Samuel Schmucker's sons and a good friend of Krauth, stated that the change was complete by the late 1840s. He also related that Krauth's father thought that a copy of *Loci*, by the orthodox Lutheran Martin Chemnitz (1522–86), which he gave to his son, was "the starting point of inquiries and examinations which wrought the change."[28]

Krauth resigned his position at St. Mark's in 1861 to become the full-time editor of the *Lutheran and Missionary*. For the next six years, he presented his views concerning events that were taking place in the General Synod. (For his role in the controversy over American Lutheranism, see chap. 8.)

The four representatives of the confessional opposition to the American Lutherans introduced in this chapter each contributed to the confessional Lutheran cause in his own way. Wyneken arrived prior to the struggle but sounded a warning of what was to come. Mann perceived the threat that the *Definite Platform* posed to a confessional Lutheranism and vehemently protested against it. Charles Philip Krauth was a quiet supporter of the Confessions but was only slightly involved in the battle. His son, Charles Porterfield Krauth, a confessional loyalist, attempted to be conciliatory to the American Lutherans but eventually saw the futility of that stance. He and Mann were prominent figures in the years of struggle after the *Definite Platform* and later became leaders of the General Council.

These men came from a variety of backgrounds and circumstances, but they had in common a commitment to a confessional Lutheran church. They wanted the Lutheran church in America to be distinctly Lutheran. They rejected the American Lutherans' concept of a Lutheranism that was devoid of confessional loyalty, a Lutheranism that was no more than another American Protestant church. The battle lines were drawn for a conflict over nothing less than Lutheranism's very identity.

---

28. J. G. Jennson, *American Lutheran Biographies; or Historical Notices of over Three Hundred and Fifty Leading Men of the American Lutheran Church from Its Establishment to the Year 1890* (Milwaukee, 1890), 424. Spaeth, *Charles Porterfield Krauth*, 1:160, gives the date as 1843.

7

The American—Confessional Conflict, 1849–1857

*D*evelopments that took place during the 1840s within the General Synod indicated it was only a matter of time before there would be open conflict between the American Lutherans and those who were loyal to the Lutheran Confessions. Prior to that time, the American Lutherans controlled the Synod, and their views were generally accepted by clergy and laity alike. Lutheranism had identified itself with the beliefs and practices of American evangelicalism. To the American Lutherans, Americanization meant a general Protestant religion that was concerned only with "fundamental doctrines." Anything that separated Protestants from each other was deemed "nonfundamental" and thus unimportant and expendable.

The shift that began to occur in the 1840s stressed Lutheranism's particularities as greater numbers of more conservative Lutherans came to America and as many clergy began to read specifically Lutheran theological works. The result of this shift was a party within the General Synod that had a very different vision of the shape Lutheranism should take in America—a vision that Lutherans could live in America and be Americans without sacrificing their identity and their religious heritage.

Wyneken's protest at the 1845 General Synod convention in Philadelphia was the first confessional voice heard aloud. At that same convention, a resolution came to the floor: "*Resolved,* That a committee be appointed to prepare and report to the next General Synod, a clear and concise view of the doctrines and practice of the American Lutheran Church."[1] The committee appointed to draw up the requested statement consisted entirely of American Lutheran sympathizers, including Samuel Schmucker and Benjamin Kurtz. At the next meeting of the General Synod, in 1848, the committee asked for more time to prepare its report.[2] When the report was

1. *Proceedings of the Thirteenth Convention of the General Synod of the Evangelical Lutheran Church, in the United States, Convened in Philadelphia, May 16, 1845,* 54.
2. *Proceedings of the Fourteenth Convention of the General Synod of the Evangelical Lutheran Church, in the United States, Convened in New York, May 13th, 1848,* 22.

finally presented in 1850, it closely resembled the Maryland Synod Abstract of 1844, which took a decidedly American Lutheran position. The report was tabled, and the committee was discharged from further duty.[3]

The fact that this official recognition of American Lutheranism failed indicates that changes were occurring within the ranks of the General Synod. Charles Philip Krauth, a professor at the Seminary at Gettysburg, was the presiding officer at that convention. His opening sermon indicates that the theological climate had become more conservative. Krauth began by stating that the time had come for the Lutheran church in the United States to reexamine its position; and then he offered a commentary on the present situation:

> That the orthodoxy of the olden time was gradually lost sight of, that the Confessions were practically superseded, that formal subscription was entirely abandoned, are facts which admit of no controversy. It is true, since the commencement of the era, as it has been called, of the General Synod, the Augsburg Confession has again been brought into notice, and a limited subscription to it enforced; but it cannot be regarded as anything more than an approximate return to the ancient landmarks.[4]

The sermon went on to decry the looseness of doctrine and the ignorance of the Lutheran tradition prevalent in the General Synod. Lutheranism in America had denied its own parentage and had taken for itself "foreign favors." He concluded by advocating, "Let us go back to our father's house . . . let us sit down at his table. . . . They will better suit our appetite than the crumbs which we have gathered elsewhere. . . . It is our duty to exert a conservative influence."[5]

This sermon not only reached the ears of attendees at the General Synod convention; it received wide publicity through the *Evangelical Review,* a journal first published in 1849. Virtually from its initial issue, it called for a change of mind on the part of the General Synod, and it openly challenged the American Lutheran views that had prevailed in the Synod for so long.

The second issue of the *Evangelical Review* carried an article by Charles Porterfield Krauth on the subject "The Relation of our Confessions to the Reformation."[6] This article is important because it is a systematic treatment

3. *Proceedings of the Fifteenth Convention of the General Synod of the Evangelical Lutheran Church, in the United States, Convened in Charleston, S.C., April 27, 1850,* 27.

4. *Evangelical Review* 2 (July 1850).

5. Ibid., 2.

6. This article appeared later, with alterations, in Charles Porterfield Krauth, *The Conservative Reformation and Its Theology* (Philadelphia: J. B. Lippincott & Co., 1871), 201–15, 241–42, 258–61.

of the Confessions written by an American, and it sounded the beginning of the public debate that came to a head with the *Definite Platform* in 1855.

Krauth's chief aim was to place the Lutheran Confessions within the context of the Reformation and to correct certain misunderstandings that had arisen. Unlike those who believed the Reformation was in complete opposition to Rome, Krauth claimed the Reformers built on Rome's truths. The Reformation made no new discoveries, nor did it put forth any new interpretations. Krauth struck out at the anti-Romanism of his day: "There was no fear of truth simply because Rome held it and no disposition to embrace error because it might be employed with advantage to Rome's injury. While it established broadly and deeply the right of private judgment, it did not make that abuse of it which has since been so common."[7]

Krauth dispelled the notion that, because his generation came later, its members therefore knew more and were more advanced; neither did he tolerate the dismissal of an unpalatable doctrine by saying it is a "remnant of popery." Krauth was most pointed when he spoke of the Confessions in the American situation. He saw no conflict between being Lutheran and being American. "Is there a conflict between the two when carried to their very farthest limits? Must Lutheranism be shorn of its glory to adapt it to the times of our land? No! Our land is great and wide and glorious and destined, we trust, under the sunlight of her free institutions long to endure, but our faith is wider and greater and is eternal."[8] There should be no conflict between being a Lutheran and being an American, but if a choice had to be made, the church must come first—"Through my church Christianity, peace with God, redemption in Christ, immortality have been given to me, and therefore I am first a Lutheran and then an American. In my heart these excite no conflict but blend harmoniously together."[9]

Being in the midst of sectarianism should not cause Lutherans to concede their faith. However, the Lutheran church should rid itself of the "pitiful little sectarianism" and assert itself. "Let us not with our rich coffers play the part of beggars and ask favors where we have every ability to impart them. No church can maintain its self-respect or inspire respect in others which is afraid or ashamed of its own history and which rears a dubious fabric on the ignorance of its ministry and of its members."[10] If the church continued in its dishonesty it would fall, and no honest person would lament that fall. Krauth lauded the Augsburg Confession and the role it

7. *Evangelical Review* 1 (Oct. 1849).
8. Ibid.
9. Ibid.
10. Ibid.

had played in the Lutheran church. Then, in light of the situation in the General Synod, he asked a lengthy, pointed question:

> Can we honorably bear the name of Evangelical Lutheran, honestly profess to receive the Augsburg Confession as our creed, and honestly claim to be part of the church of our fathers while we reject, or leave open to rejection, parts of the doctrine whose reception gave our church its separate being and distinctive name, which led to the formation of its confession, which are embodied in its articles and guarded in their condemnatory clauses, and which for centuries our whole church in every official act maintained as principal and fundamental? This is the real question. All others are side issues.[11]

Krauth's article openly supported the authority of the entire Augsburg Confession and was critical of the stance of the American Lutherans without mentioning them by name. The American Lutherans got the message and attacked both the article and the journal in which it appeared. Benjamin Kurtz declared that the *Evangelical Review* was "the most sectarian periodical [he had] ever read." To that charge William Reynolds, at that time the editor of the *Evangelical Review,* responded: "The fact is there is a large body of men in our Church who have no knowledge of her history, no sympathy with her doctrines, no idea of her true character, and whose whole conception of the Church is that of a kind of mongrel Methodistic Presbyterianism, and of this party Drs. S. S. Schmucker and Kurtz are the coryphaei."[12] The battle had come out into the open, and the language used indicated it was not going to be a polite debate. Both sides were zealous in their belief that the future of the church was at stake.

In 1852 *The American Lutheran Church, Historically, Doctrinally, and Practically Delineated, in Several Occasional Discourses* was published.[13] This was a compilation of several of Schmucker's major discourses from a period of a little over ten years. This book was published in order to clarify and defend Schmucker's position and to raise sympathy for the American Lutheran cause, but there is no indication it accomplished that purpose.

In 1853 Schmucker preached a sermon entitled "The Peace of Zion" before the General Synod meeting in Winchester, Virginia. He was well aware that the situation had become more tense, and this sermon was an attempt to calm the waters. Schmucker stated that peace in the church

---

11. Ibid.
12. Cited in Abdel Ross Wentz, *History of the Gettysburg Lutheran Theological Seminary, 1826–1965* (Harrisburg, Pa.: Evangelical Press, 1965), 171–72.
13. For a discussion of the contents of this collection of discourses, see chap. 4.

would be promoted by exercising "scriptural charity or forbearance towards each other, on points of non-essential difference."[14] Among the nonessentials, Schmucker mentioned baptism, polity, and the real presence in the Eucharist. He pleaded that the group might overlook differences on nonessentials "to rise above the atmosphere of personal and of sectarian strife to the pure and vital air of the Gospel."[15]

Schmucker stated that he regarded the Augsburg Confession as a "substantially" correct exposition of the gospel and advocated that the church ought to give "absolute adherence" to the Bible and "fundamental assent" to the Augsburg Confession. He called his audience to labor for unity and peace in order that piety in the churches be advanced. Dead formalities of religion should be set aside, for they are enemies of the peace and prosperity of the church. Schmucker wanted peace, but on terms agreeable to the American Lutherans.

The sermon's pleas for peace were not realized. In fact, Schmucker was to be the chief cause of the upheaval to come.

The 1853 convention was important for another reason: the Pennsylvania Ministerium returned to the fold of the General Synod after an absence of thirty years. One of the Ministerium's delegates was William Julius Mann, who observed: "The spirit was tolerant; but there is a great deal of indefiniteness and obscurity about distinctive Lutheran principles, with a perceptible desire for unity. The Methodistic tendency is declining, and the leaders of the movement are losing influence."[16]

With its return, the Ministerium founded a chair of theology at the Seminary in Gettysburg. Mann was nominated for the position but declined. As he viewed the General Synod more closely, Mann became more skeptical. In 1854, in a magazine called the *Kirchenfreund,* Mann commented: "The hard dogmatic knots of the old Lutheran oak were forced to give way under the Puritan plans. The body was deprived of its leaves and its heart, and the empty skin was filled with whatever was most pleasing, if only the Lutheran name was retained."[17]

In April 1855, Schmucker published his *Lutheran Manual on Scriptural Principles.*[18] There was nothing new in this work. The texts of the Augsburg

14. Samuel S. Schmucker, *The Peace of Zion* (Gettysburg, Pa.: H. C. Neinstedt, 1853), 31.

15. Ibid., 35.

16. Emma T. Mann, *Memoir of the Life and Work of William Julius Mann* (Philadelphia: Jas. B. Rogers Printing Co., 1893), 88.

17. Ibid., 89.

18. Samuel S. Schmucker, *Lutheran Manual on Scriptural Principles: or, The Augsburg Confession Illustrated and Sustained, Chiefly by Scripture Proofs and Extracts from Standard Lutheran Theologians of Europe and America; Together with the Formula of Government and Discipline, Adopted by the General Synod of the Evangelical Lutheran Church in the United States* (Philadelphia: Lindsay & Blakiston, 1855).

Confession were given in Latin, German, and English. The views of the American Lutherans were presented in a clear and concise manner. The most interesting and revealing discussion involved divine revelation. Schmucker set up seven criteria, most of which dealt with reason in relationship to revelation. The overall message was that no revelation can be contrary to reason and that no revelation can teach truths untaught by reason.[19] This principle was consistently applied by Schmucker, which suggests that he may have been more influenced by the Enlightenment than he was aware of or willing to admit. The book was not polemical. It was intended for "moderate men."

The response to Schmucker's book was not what he had hoped. A highly critical review appeared in the October 1855 edition of the *Evangelical Review*. The anonymous reviewer found Schmucker inconsistent because the "errors" Schmucker claimed the Augsburg Confession possessed were, in fact, thoroughly scriptural. Schmucker's rejection of the second part of the Augsburg Confession was deemed "utterly inexcusable" since the second part is important to the understanding of the Lutheran position in relation to the position of the Roman church. The reviewer rejected Schmucker's assertion that the founding fathers of the General Synod shared his position regarding the Augsburg Confession: "And most assuredly there was at that time no development of the idea of an American Lutheran Church as distinct from a German or a European one."[20] The review did more than disagree with Schmucker; it openly questioned his orthodoxy.

The Definite Platform

In 1855 events reached a climax. The General Synod had met in June at Dayton, Ohio, but at that time there was no indication of what was to come. During that convention, the leaders of the American Lutherans met. Benjamin Kurtz and Samuel Sprecher urged Samuel Schmucker to draw up a clear statement for the American Lutherans to use in their various synods.[21]

In September the majority of the pastors in the General Synod received from the publishers Miller and Burlock a small book of forty-two pages entitled *Definite Platform, Doctrinal and Disciplinarian, for Evangelical*

---

19. Ibid., 52–53.
20. *Evangelical Review* 7 (Oct. 1855).
21. An account of these events can be found in Abdel Ross Wentz, *Pioneer In Christian Unity: Samuel Simon Schmucker* (Philadelphia: Fortress Press, 1966), 205–11. Wentz states that Schmucker may have gotten his idea for the *Definite Synodical Platform* from Charles Philip Krauth's sermon of 1850, in which Krauth called for Lutheranism in America to "examine its position and determine its future course."

Lutheran District Synods; Constructed in Accordance with the Principles of the General Synod. The stated purpose of the *Definite Platform* was to provide a more specific expression of the General Synod's doctrinal basis so that other "German churches, which profess the entire mass of former symbols" could be answered.[22] It was one of the most important and controversial documents in the history of Lutheranism in America.

Part I contained the doctrinal basis or creed, followed by a short history in which the conclusion was reached that the Augsburg Confession was the only document that had been universally accepted by Lutherans. It was noted that the General Synod had previously introduced a "qualified acknowledgement" of the Augsburg Confession into its various constitutions and ordination vows.

Certain doctrines in the Augsburg Confession were not considered "fundamental doctrines of Scripture." The Augsburg Confession, it was alleged, contained five errors: (1) the approval of the ceremonies of the mass; (2) private confession and absolution; (3) denial of the divine obligation of the Christian Sabbath; (4) baptismal regeneration; (5) the real presence of the body and blood of the Savior in the Eucharist.

The *Definite Platform* then presented the "American Recension" of the Augsburg Confession, which was nothing more than the Augsburg Confession minus the doctrines "which have long since been regarded by the great mass of our churches as unscriptural, and as remnants of Romish error" (5). The doctrinal basis for the "Recension" was that the Scriptures are the only rule for faith and practice. This statement was followed by the Apostles' and Nicene Creeds. The texts of those creeds remained intact except, in both cases, the word "universal" replaced "catholic."

All the condemnations in the various articles of the Augsburg Confession were stricken. Article X (The Holy Supper of our Lord) merely stated that "Christ is present with the communicants in the Lord's Supper" (11). No mention was made of the presence of the body and blood of Christ. Article XI (Confession) was completely omitted, with the explanation that private confession and absolution had been universally rejected by the American Lutheran church. Article IX (Baptism) substituted "necessary for salvation" with "a necessary ordinance" (11). The conclusion to the "Recension" was completely different from that of the Augsburg Confession. All references to being in harmony with the ancient church were dropped, and stress was placed on the "differences of opinion between us

22. *Definite Platform, Doctrinal and Disciplinarian, for Evangelical Lutheran District Synods; Constructed in Accordance with the Principles of the General Synod* (Philadelphia: Miller & Burlock, 1855), 2. Unless otherwise noted, the following quotations are from the first edition of the *Definite Platform*.

and the Romanists" (19). There was a strong anti-Roman tone in the
"American Recension."

Part II of the *Definite Platform* contained the "Synodical Disclaimer,"
the list of symbolic errors. This section began:

> The extraordinary length of the other former symbolic books as a whole is
> sufficient reason for their rejection as a prescribed creed, even if all their
> contents were believed to be true; because neither the Scriptures nor the
> practice of the early centuries, affords any warrant for an uninspired and
> therefore infallible creed, nearly as large as the entire Old and New Testament
> together. The exaction of such an extended creed is subversive of all indi-
> vidual liberty of thought and freedom of Scriptural investigation. (20)

This was followed by more arguments that Scripture alone should determine
faith. In discussing reasons for rejecting specific articles, however, the
Definite Platform cited not Scripture but popular opinions, "because the
particular doctrine taught in each is regarded as erroneous by the great
mass of the churches in connexion with the General Synod" (20). Nine
more doctrines were rejected by the "Synodical Disclaimer"; among these
were the ceremonies of the mass, baptismal regeneration, private confession
and absolution, the real presence, the Sabbath, exorcism in baptism, forgiving power in the Lord's Supper, and the union of the Two Natures in
Christ.

The author of the *Definite Platform* suggested "for the sake of uniformity,
that any Synod adopting this Platform, should receive it entire, without
alteration" (2). It was also suggested that each synod should adopt a series
of resolutions, among them, "*Resolved,* That we will not receive into our
Synod any minister who will not adopt this Platform, and faithfully labor
to maintain its discipline in his charge" (6). The *Definite Platform* set the
standard of fellowship to minimum terms:

> At the same time, whilst we will not admit into our Synod any one who
> believes in *Exorcism, Private Confession and Absolution,* or the *Ceremonies
> of the Mass,* we grant liberty in regard to the other omitted topics, and are
> willing, as heretofore, to admit ministers who receive them, provided they
> regard them as non-essential, and are willing to cooperate in peace and
> harmony with those who reject them, and to subscribe to this Platform. (5)

Some confusion arose as to what exactly was required as a pledge to
fellowship by the *Definite Platform*. In 1856 a second edition appeared,
which made it clear that the second part of the *Definite Platform*, which
rejected the nine doctrines, was "not a part of the Pledge or Doctrinal
Basis to be individually subscribed" (2d ed., 2). The clarification was

"published by Synod as a Disclaimer of the Symbolical errors often imputed to her" (2d ed., 2) and also "to discourage the views there rejected, and to repel the charge of avowing them" (2d ed., 6).

Reactions to the Definite Platform

Reactions to the *Definite Platform* were not long in coming. The Synod of East Pennsylvania met later in September 1855 and issued a strong resolution against the document. Part of the resolution stated: "We hereby express our most unqualified disapprobation of this most dangerous attempt to change the doctrinal basis, and revolutionize the existing character of the Lutheran churches, now united in the General Synod, and that we hereby most solemnly warn our sister synods against this dangerous proposition."[23]

The church papers took varying positions with regard to the *Definite Platform*. The *Lutheran Observer* carried an article written by "A True Lutheran," entitled "Something to Think About—The 'Definite Synodical Platform.' " It stated that the *Definite Platform* was "the right thing for the age,"[24] and urged its adoption. The *Evangelical Review* took a different view:

> Although so small an affair in form, this brochure of forty odd pages may become a most serious matter; may serve as the entering wedge for splitting and dividing the Lutheran Church in America, not only from her confessions, which stand upon an immovable rock of truth, and from the reviving church in Germany, which begins once more to gather around and endeavor to take its stand upon this rock, after the floods of infidelity have passed over it, but may also be the means of splitting the gradually uniting church here in America, into ten thousand scattered fragments.[25]

The *Lutheran Observer*, under the editorship of Benjamin Kurtz, kept the matter before its readers and encouraged proponents of the *Definite Platform* to state their views. But who was the author of the *Definite Platform*? The original document appeared without an author's name. Everyone suspected it was Samuel Schmucker because his ideas were stated throughout the work. In the December 7, 1855, issue of the *Observer*, the first in a series of articles appeared under the signature "S.S.S." Schmucker

23. *Proceedings of the Fourteenth Annual Convention of the Evangelical Lutheran Synod of East Pennsylvania, Convened in Zion's Church, Lebanon, Lebanon County, Pa. September 21st to 26th, 1855* (Gettysburg, Pa.: 1855), 13–14.

24. *Lutheran Observer* (Sept. 21, 1855).

25. *Evangelical Review* 7 (Oct. 1855).

wrote of the consultations in Dayton that led to the construction of the *Definite Platform,* and then he stated:

> The actual authorship was never intended to be a secret, and is now generally known; yet as the plan was the result of many minds, and the execution of the revision of the Augsburg Confession consisted merely in reprinting the doctrinal articles of that creed unaltered, except the omission of the parts which teach those tenets rejected by the great majority of our American Lutheran churches, it was deemed a dictate of modesty to add no individual names.[26]

Virtually no one was surprised by the admission. Prior to the clarification of authorship, Charles Philip Krauth had written to his son, Charles Porterfield Krauth:

> The American Recension of the Augsburg Confession doesn't seem to go down well. It has received many hard blows. My colleague doesn't disclaim the authorship, so that it has a daddy. A more stupid thing could hardly have been originated. . . . *Quem Deus Vult perdere prius dementat.*
>
> How will it end? I have thought in smoke. But I have all along had fears, and they are strengthened of late, that it will divide the General Synod. It is said that my colleague is determined to press the matter to the utmost. I suppose he thinks that he has drawn the sword, thrown away the scabbard, and now must fight. . . . There ought to be an antidote to the *Observer* somewhere.[27]

Books began to appear in opposition to the *Definite Platform.* The first to reply was a parish pastor, John N. Hoffman, who wrote a small book entitled *The Broken Platform.*[28] Although Hoffman made many good points, especially with regard to Schmucker's rationalistic tendencies, his ranting style did not make him an effective representative of the confessional point of view.

The most formidable and profound reply came from another pastor, William Julius Mann, in a small book entitled *A Plea for the Augsburg Confession.*[29] This book presents a clear picture of the nature of Schmucker's opposition.

26. *Lutheran Observer* (Dec. 7, 1855).

27. Adolph Spaeth, *Charles Porterfield Krauth,* 2 vols. (New York: Christian Literature Co., 1898), 1:372.

28. John N. Hoffman, *The Broken Platform or a Brief Defense of Our Symbolical Books against Charges of Alleged Errors* (Philadelphia: Lindsay & Blakiston, 1856).

29. W. J. Mann, *A Plea for the Augsburg Confession, In Answer to the Objections of the Definite Platform: An Address to All Ministers and Laymen of the Evangelical Church of the United States* (Philadelphia: Lindsay & Blakiston, 1856).

Mann gave the *Platform's* anonymous authors credit for openness in their apostasy with regard to the Confessions. Then he raised a key question. The *Definite Platform* had contended that Luther's teachings were filled with errors; Mann asked, "if Luther mixed truth with error, who can we trust?" (4). He was disturbed by the fact that a person of the old Lutheran faith would not have a place in those synods that had adopted the *Definite Platform*. The *Platform's* denunciation of the old canons was presumptuous, Mann said; to change the doctrinal character of a church was to take an awful responsibility. The fact that most ministers no longer believed in some parts of the Augsburg Confession was not important. "Shall we submit the faith of the Church, the authority of Luther, Melanchthon and a whole crowd of learned and pious men of old and new times, to the views of some ministers, whatever their merits may be, whatever their number, to a 'higher' authority?" (9).

To those who cried "The Bible and only the Bible!" Mann replied that confessions were needed so that the Bible could be interpreted. Lutheranism's particular character ought not to be lost. Mann did not object to those who wanted to examine the Confessions, but those who examined them must not assume that the Confessions were wrong and they were right.

With regard to the first error described by the *Definite Platform* (approval of the ceremonies of the mass), Mann pointed out that "mass" was the general term of reference for the Eucharist. The Augsburg Confession speaks of abuses corrected and assumes agreement in doctrine between Lutherans and Rome. Among the disputed doctrines Mann listed were transubstantiation, the sacrifice of the mass, and reception of the elements under one kind (16–17).

The second error to which the *Definite Platform* pointed to was private confession and absolution. Mann stated that the Lutheran church had nothing to do with the Roman practice of auricular confession in which the person was required to enumerate sins. Confession was retained for the sake of the absolution. Mann asked why the Augsburg Confession should not retain "a most excellent means to bring repentance and consolation nearer to the hearts of sinners" (23). As to the absolution, Mann said, whoever doubts whether the minister of Christ has the right to pronounce absolution in the name of Christ should see what Christ himself said in Matthew 18:18. Mann had no problem with private confession: "We allow a minister to hear a confession from his whole flock. Why in the name of common sense would we regard it wrong in him to hear the confession of individual members thereof?" (24).

The third error listed in the *Definite Platform* was the denial of the divine obligation of the Christian Sabbath. Mann pointed out that the

Augsburg Confession did not specifically speak of the Sabbath. The Roman church had always regarded Sunday as a holy day, and there was no dispute here between Rome and the Reformers. The Augsburg Confession encouraged worship on the Sabbath; what more could be required of it? The *Definite Platform* did not mention a particular dictate of Christ because there was none. The Sabbath celebration came from the apostles rather than Christ. To make Sabbath observance a law, Mann feared, would only result in works-righteousness.

Mann treated the last two alleged errors (baptismal regeneration and the real presence) as a unit. The question to be addressed was the value of the sacraments. Mann was of the firm belief that the *Definite Platform* and the Augsburg Confession were far apart on this question. The Augsburg Confession regarded sacraments as having intrinsic value. The *Definite Platform*, on the other hand, viewed them as signs that may promote piety. The Augsburg Confession stated that, through the sacraments, God works wonders and conveys grace. The *Definite Platform* stated that sacraments, as signs, may edify a person if that person is in the right frame of mind. Because the *Definite Platform* taught that sacraments were only signs, Mann accused it of placing the religion of the New Testament on the same plane as that of the Old Testament. He found it strange that the same person who found a "divine obligation" of the Sabbath should have such a low view of the sacraments. "Surrendering our Lutheran ground in the sacramental doctrine, we have thrown overboard, indeed, her most particular feature, by which more than by anything else, we differ from other churches, and have an originality of our own" (41).

The *Definite Platform* argued that the churches in Germany had rejected the real presence until 1817. Mann asserted that this was because they were infected with rationalism. He repeated that it was rash for the authors of the *Definite Platform* to think that they were right and the Augsburg Confession was wrong. That confession should be defended, not denied. Mann admitted that the church had not always followed faithfully certain rites and usages, and this shortcoming may have weakened the Lutheran church internally. Mann judged the Augsburg Confession to be a sound document based on the gospel as the word of God. He concluded: "There can be no doubt that the propositions of the 'Definite Platform,' if carried out, will not give rest and peace to our Lutheran Church, but that they will produce contention and strife. Let those who raised the question reflect once more, and perhaps the Spirit of God will teach them that their beginning was not a good one, not subservient to the real wants of the Lutheran Church" (47).

In February 1856, a document called the "Pacific Overture" was signed by some of the leaders of both sides in the controversy. This document was designed to bring peace. It read in part:

> *Resolved,* that we, the undersigned, deprecate the further prosecution of this controversy, and hereby agree to unite and abide on the *doctrinal basis of the General Synod,* of absolute assent to *the Word of God,* as the only infallible rule of faith and practice, and fundamental agreement with the Augsburg Confession; and that we will use our best efforts to induce our respective Synods as a sufficient ground for harmonious cooperation among the churches of the General Synod, and that we will persevere in this effort so long as there is any hope of attaining this result.[30]

Among the signers of this compromise were Schmucker and Charles Philip Krauth. The "Pacific Overture" did nothing more than support the doctrinal position that had existed for years in the General Synod. Much doctrinal latitude was allowed, and no limit was placed on debate outside the church papers. Seizing an opening, Schmucker announced that he was drawing up a reply to Mann.

Schmucker's reply was a book entitled *American Lutheranism Vindicated,*[31] in which he argued his cause in much greater detail and with a firm sense of righteousness. Schmucker repeated many of the same arguments he had stated before, especially those regarding fundamental doctrines, creeds, and the confessional documents. He pleaded for charity and understanding in the discussions over the *Definite Platform* and suggested that no one had to agree with the rejection of certain parts of the Augsburg Confession. His opponents were only asked to recognize that the doctrines in question were not essential or fundamental doctrines and to live at peace with those who rejected them.

One of Schmucker's key points was that Lutherans in the past disagreed with parts of the Augsburg Confession. He listed a series of names and singled out George Lochmann, who Schmucker said published an edition of the Augsburg Confession "in which *he made more omissions than are found in the American Recension,* and yet no one found fault with him for doing so" (40). Schmucker also pointed out that the Pennsylvania Synod fifty years earlier did not require assent of its ministers to the Augsburg Confession; and when the General Synod was formed in 1820, it "inserted a clause in her constitution, giving *power both to the General Synod and*

---

30. *Lutheran Observer* (Feb. 15, 1856).
31. Samuel S. Schmucker, *American Lutheranism Vindicated; or, Examination of the Lutheran Symbols on Certain Topics: Including a Reply to the Plea of Rev. W. J. Mann* (Baltimore: T. Newton Kurtz, 1856).

each District Synod to form a new Confession of Faith, for their own use" (39).

Schmucker claimed that the Augsburg Confession was a conciliatory document. The people who wrote it came from Catholic backgrounds, and they could not completely divorce themselves from their past. Even Luther "was a faithful papist until he was upwards of *thirty years* old, when he began to protest against the errors of Rome" (37). The Augsburg Confession is a human creed. Creeds are fallible and need revision.

Schmucker termed the confessional revival nothing more than "Post-Lutheran" or "Ultra-Lutheran" (164). He stated that *"Symbolism is . . . no part of original Lutheranism"* (163). American Lutheranism accepts only the fundamental doctrines, and the "American Recension" was a statement of that fact. Schmucker reiterated each of the points of controversy and did not retract any of his previous positions. He defended American Lutheranism as being the genuine expression of Lutheranism for Lutherans in the United States.

Mann's reply to *American Lutheranism Vindicated* came in the form of a book entitled *Lutheranism in America.*[32] In it Mann laid out the confessional stance of the Lutheran church with admirable clarity. He pointed out that the main problem in the Lutheran church in America was a confessional or doctrinal problem (16). Mann was truly astonished that the liberal party wanted to discard Lutheran doctrine, felt more at home with other denominations, and yet wanted to remain in the Lutheran church. The American Lutherans had given up many of the characteristics of original Lutheranism, particularly Lutheran doctrine and worship, and had instead adopted Puritanism (19). Mann also observed that the American Lutherans' doctrinal position closely resembled that of Zwingli (20–21).

The things that distinguished Lutherans and Reformed in Europe were not to be found in America, Mann noted: "In many places we find instead of the altar simply a table; instead of the gown and bands, a plain black coat; no baptismal font, no crucifix, no paintings, much less the symbol of light, frequently no steeple, no bells; in short, everything which is supposed to have the least leaning toward Romish custom or superstitions, however innocent, appropriate and beautiful in itself is carefully excluded" (26).

Mann described the Lutheran church as having an identity of its own. It is opposed to Rome, but it also stands against wholesale revolution. Luther wanted to purify that which was wrong but also wanted to keep many of the forms and usages as well as the arts of the church. In that

---

32. William Julius Mann, *Lutheranism in America: An Essay on the Present Condition of the Lutheran Church in the United States* (Philadelphia: Lindsay & Blakiston, 1857).

way, he was no Puritan. Mann pointed to Article VII of the Augsburg Confession and stated that the Word and sacraments are essential to the church's life. Mann described Lutheran worship as keeping the old customs that had been in use for centuries. "The statement that the Christians of the first three centuries conducted their worship with Puritanic simplicity is purely imaginary; and those who make it, fabricate a history in opposition to the testimony of history to suit their own predilections" (58). Mann accused Protestantism, which he believed was Puritan in character, of neglecting the devotional side of worship at the expense of preaching. Too much stress was put on the eloquence of the preacher. Mann also mentioned that Luther wanted the Supper every Lord's day (61–62) and kept ceremonies and rites, not because they were Romish, but because they were ancient Christian usages.

Mann regarded the Pennsylvania Ministerium as representative because it was made up of clergy of many different synods and used both German and English in services. It was confessionally conservative and had re-adopted the old Lutheran liturgy. Its weakness, however, was that its practices did not measure up to its statements (87–90). Other synods that Mann considered representative of Lutheranism included the Ohio Synod, the Tennessee Synod, and the Synod of Wisconsin.

The Lutheran church in America was a church in transition. Even the authors of the *Definite Platform* admitted that attitudes toward the Confessions were changing. Mann noted that many members of the clergy had become interested in the *Book of Concord* (94–96). The pastors who had been educated in English did not have the advantage of good theological books, Mann said; their libraries contained the works of American Puritans and of Samuel Schmucker, all un-Lutheran (96–97).

Lutheranism under Muhlenberg was organized around the Confessions, and its worship customs were in most respects strictly Lutheran. Mann was pleased that Schmucker praised Muhlenberg, but he pointed out that Muhlenberg would not agree with Schmucker. What would happen, Mann wondered, if the Lutheran church surrendered to Zwinglianism on the real presence, the doctrines of the Methodists, and the formlessness of the Puritans? The church could still retain the Augsburg Confession, but it would be unable to confess some of the doctrines it contains—and what kind of confession would that be? (134). The church would have to admit that it did not believe its own confession.

For Mann, the mission of the Lutheran church was realized when, in unity, it could boldly confess its faith. That could not happen when there were those, including the "first professor of the first seminary of our Church," who claimed that Luther and the Confessions contain errors. That situation made people feel insecure within their own communion (139). Mann believed the world was getting worse, people becoming less religious. That being the case, it was dangerous to overvalue private, casual emotions and subjective taste—"as if truth was ever revealed in this!" (140). The General Synod was too loose in its doctrine. Pastors were not duty-bound to obey anyone or anything. They could do as they pleased. Mann compared the Lutheran church in America to the many-colored coat of Joseph (142). Such looseness had allowed strange doctrines into the church, as well as a piety that was more Methodistic than Lutheran.

A complete, thorough study of the confessional writings was the only answer to such a condition. Mann admitted it was possible the Confessions might be misappropriated or misconstrued, but they would never be refuted from the Scriptures. A proper connection between past and present was also needed. Mann was not opposed to progress, but he was of the firm conviction that the church must always "hold fast to what is good."

The *Definite Platform* never accomplished what its authors and supporters hoped it would. When it came up for a vote only three synods adopted it, all western synods in Indiana and Ohio, where Samuel Sprecher was very influential. It did, however, bring forward the conflicts between the American Lutherans and the confessional party.

The *Definite Platform* said nothing new. The ideas it contained had been advocated and taught by Samuel Schmucker for years. What was significant was that the *Definite Platform* attempted to make American Lutheranism the doctrinal standard for the General Synod, and it virtually excluded anyone who disagreed with its position.

If the *Definite Platform* had been accepted by all the synods of the church, Lutheranism would have been stripped of its particularites, especially its sacramental theology, and would have been reduced to being another American Protestant church with no distinguishing marks of its own. It was the American Lutherans' stated goal to rid Lutheranism of "remnants of Romish error," which they abhorred and which they believed were obstacles to relationships with their American Protestant neighbors. They wanted to accomplish what they felt the Lutheran Reformers had failed to do. The *Definite Platform* was the last-ditch attempt to accomplish these purposes.

The "Pacific Overture" tried to bring peace to the troubled General Synod, but it was destined to fail because it merely supported the status quo and allowed a wide theological latitude. It was an attempt to keep both the American Lutherans and the confessional party peacefully coexisting within the Synod. In essence, the "Pacific Overture" supported the same policy the General Synod had adhered to and operated under for years.

The significance of William Julius Mann's responses to the *Definite Platform* and to Samuel Schmucker should not be underestimated. His two books, *A Plea for the Augsburg Confession* and *Lutheranism in America*, were clear evidence that it was too late to accomplish reconciliation of the two parties. Mann believed that Lutheranism was grounded in its Confessions, and both of his works were concise statements of the position of confessional Lutheranism. When one compares the *Definite Platform* to Mann's *Plea for the Augsburg Confession,* it is obvious that the two documents and their authors were not even describing the same church.

The controversy over the *Definite Platform* was more than a theological quarrel. The battle was over the question of whether the Lutheran church, as Charles Porterfield Krauth stated, "be shorn of its glory to adapt it to the times of our land." The Americanization issue took the form of a theological debate centered around Lutheran identity in relationship to Lutheranism's existence in America.

Mann's *Lutheranism in America* stands as an insightful commentary on the American religious situation and Lutheranism's place within that context. He saw clearly that the American Lutherans had already accommodated themselves to American Protestantism, the result being a type of Lutheranism that was more Puritan and Methodistic than Lutheran. They wanted an American Lutheran church that was "American" at the expense of the Lutheran heritage as expressed in the Lutheran Confessions—something Mann saw as being unacceptable to any confessional Lutheran.

Mann affirmed that Lutheranism could exist in America without shedding those beliefs that make Lutheranism what it is. His analysis of the General Synod's weaknesses and his proposals for the mission of Lutherans in America could challenge twentieth-century Lutherans, just as they challenged Lutherans of his day. Lutherans could be Americans without making concessions to American Protestantism. Lutherans could keep their confessional identity and be Americans. This was Mann's conviction, and in that conviction he stood in opposition to the views of Samuel Schmucker and the other American Lutherans.

8

From Conflict to
Separation, 1857–1867

*T*he *Definite Platform* was the first in a series of events that would
ultimately lead to the formation of a new synodical body. Many scholars
have assumed that the failure to adopt the *Definite Platform* meant that
the American Lutherans were defeated and the movement itself was good
as dead.[1] Subsequent developments, however, reveal that was not the case.
During the course of the next few years, tensions became greater, finally
leading to parting of the ways between the American Lutherans and the
confessional party. In spite of the *Definite Platform's* apparent defeat, the
doctrinal basis of the General Synod still was influenced by the American
Lutherans' reluctance to adopt a more confessional stance. The General
Synod still reflected its "American" character, and a substantial portion
of the Synod was content with that state.

However, the debates continued. These debates merit documentation
and discussion. Another point of interest is the personal stories of some
of the men involved, particularly Charles Porterfield Krauth. His struggles
and change of mind are central to understanding the events that led up to
the formation of the General Council in 1867. His story demonstrates that,
even after the *Definite Platform's* failure, the basic tenets of the American
Lutherans were alive and well.

J. A. Brown's Protest

No sooner had Schmucker's public debate with William Julius Mann ended
than another challenger appeared on the scene. He was J. A. Brown (1821–
82), pastor of St. Matthew's Lutheran Church in Reading, Pennsylvania,

---

1. Vergilius Ferm, *The Crisis in American Lutheran Theology* (New York: Century Co.,
1927), 344; Abdel Ross Wentz, *Pioneer in Christian Unity: Samuel Simon Schmucker* (Philadelphia: Fortress Press, 1966), 229.

and a member of the board of directors of the Gettysburg Seminary.[2] The challenge came in the form of a pamphlet entitled *The New Theology: Its Abettors and Defenders.*[3]

Brown's stated purpose was to review and scrutinize what he considered to be "New Theology." At issue were two doctrines, regeneration and justification—not nonessentials but "points which enter into the very essence of religion" (15). Brown attacked Schmucker's understanding of regeneration, which was that regeneration only restrains the power of natural depravity rather than destroying it. Another point of Schmucker's "New Theology" that Brown found disturbing was the idea that infants have no predisposition to sin and thus cannot experience regeneration.

Schmucker, in his various publications, had stated that natural depravity means "a disorder of the mental and bodily constitution." Brown accused Schmucker of not taking seriously the moral and spiritual nature of man. Brown asked: "Is it the head or the heart—the bodily or mental, or the moral and spiritual part, that is most diseased? The bodily and mental powers may have suffered sadly in the fall; but has not the *moral* nature suffered the greatest amount of evil?" (23). If Schmucker's position was true, Brown observed, the gospel would be reduced to nothing, and Christianity, instead of being a radical cure for a mortal disease, would be but "a mild and gentle remedy for a slight moral ailment" (24).

Brown was horrified to think that, if Schmucker was right, infants would be excluded from salvation because they had no capability of regeneration. Brown put Schmucker's own language into syllogistic form: "This natural depravity disqualifies its subjects for heaven." "Of regeneration in the proper sense. . . . infants are incapable," *Ergo* — — — — —? — — — —" [sic] (25). Brown meant his readers to draw the logical conclusion, "Ergo, infants are disqualified from heaven." Brown cited several theologians to prove his side of the debate, all Americans and none of them Lutheran.[4]

Brown accused Schmucker of making faith the sole test of justification, to which is added "an entire moral renovation." That made the pardon of individuals dependent on moral fitness. To counter this view, Brown cited the Scriptures[5] and portions of the Lutheran Confessions.[6] The evidence

2. Brown's parents were Quakers. He was baptized in the Presbyterian church in 1841. By 1842, as a result of his contacts at Gettysburg College, he became a Lutheran.
3. This first appeared as an article in the July 1857 edition of the *Evangelical Review* and later in pamphlet form, J. A. Brown, *The New Theology: Its Abettors and Defenders* (Philadelphia: Henry B. Ashmead, 1857). All references will be from the pamphlet.
4. Those cited were Jonathan Edwards, Timothy Dwight, and Archibald Alexander.
5. Rom. 3:28; Rom. 4:4-6; Rom. 3:21; Acts 10:43.
6. *Apology, Art. IV; Formula of Concord, Part I; Formula of Concord, Part II, Art. III.*

of these sources convinced Brown that Schmucker was guilty of Romanism. In contrast, Brown asserted: "We deny that the faith by which the sinner is justified includes a whole catalogue of moral qualifications and religious duties. We deny that any such view of faith is authorized by the word of God, by sound philosophy, or by the standard writers on theology: and we maintain that it is utterly subversive of the most precious doctrine in the Bible—the forgiveness of sins through the blood of Christ to everyone who believes on him" (34–35). By adding obedience, love, and other virtues to faith, Brown claimed, Schmucker had put the believer in a quandary.

> Such a view of justification, even if it were possible, would deprive the penitent believer of all peace of consciousness and solid comfort: as it would lead him, instead of confiding in the all-sufficiency of Christ to cover all his sins, to be prying into his own imperfect and broken obedience to settle the question of his standing before God. If his sins will only be forgiven if he subdues them, and loves and serves Christ, he must be in continual doubt, as to whether his love and service are sufficient to render him a fit subject for divine mercy. (36)

Brown stated that he was neither an American Lutheran nor a symbolist, but one who stood in the middle ground. His only aim was vindication of the truth. He was convinced that Schmucker's position was a "New Theology" that "differs very widely from the theology of the reformers, the old English divines, and modern standard authors in Germany, England, and America" (38).

Samuel Schmucker replied to Brown's accusations in a small tract entitled *Rev. J. A. Brown's New Theology Examined*.[7] What Brown attributed to him, Schmucker said, was really Brown's own theology. He affirmed the General Synod stance that "points left undetermined by the Augsburg Confession are, at least among American Lutherans, regarded as free subjects of private opinion" (5).

Schmucker said that regeneration is a "*radical* and *entire* change, in opposition to a superficial and partial one, and as including '*a new heart*' " (6). It was a radical occurrence that affected a radical change in a person's religious views, religious feelings, and actions. Children were capable of regeneration, Schmucker said, but not infants, "because they neither have, nor can have, any religious views or feelings or actions at all" (7). If

---

7. S. S. Schmucker, *Rev. J. A. Brown's New Theology Examined* (Gettysburg, Pa.: Henry C. Neinstedt, 1857). This tract can be found in a bound copy of miscellaneous papers entitled *Pennsylvania College Papers* in the library at the Lutheran Theological Seminary in Gettysburg.

infants are naturally incapable of such "mental exercises," they cannot experience regeneration—"and what sensible man will deny this?" (8).

Regarding the subject of justification, Schmucker simply repeated what he stated before: "Whenever the returning sinner exercises the FIRST ACT of *living faith,* he is justified" (9). Then Schmucker accused Brown of "a manifest want of acquaintance with Lutheran theology" and advocacy of Calvinism.

Schmucker then turned to the subject of baptism. He insisted that he was in agreement with Lutheran theology in saying that baptism removes the guilt of depravity but not the substance of it. He cited Luther and various Lutheran theologians to prove his point.[8]

In Schmucker's opinion, Brown was "confused and unsystematic" and was, in reality, discussing three topics—regeneration, natural depravity, and justification—and not in order. In his conclusion Schmucker took on a sarcastic tone:

> It is with sincere regret that we have found ourselves called on to make these exposures. We will admit, that for his want of acquaintance with Lutheran theology, some apology may be found in the training of Rev. B. in another denomination, and perhaps in the scanty leisure allowed by his pastoral duties, for general theological study; but ought not the same facts to have taught him, what his numerous misapprehensions have demonstrated to others, that he is not the most proper individual to defend our Zion against real and imaginary foes. (14–15)

In a "Reply to Dr. S.S.S.'s Article,"[9] Brown wasted no time responding to Schmucker's comments. Brown was not at all convinced by Schmucker's arguments, especially his desire for peace; "but if Dr. S.S.S. was so deeply concerned 'for the peace of our Zion,' it would have been better shown by never starting this unhappy controversy" (42). Brown accused Schmucker of a harshness unbecoming a professor of theology.

8. Schmucker cited Johannes-Andreas Quenstedt (1617–1688), an orthodox theologian who was influential on Arndt and some of the other pietists, and S. J. Baumgarten (d. 1757), an eighteenth-century Lutheran divine and a pietist. Another theologian mentioned was Julius Mueller (1801–78), a professor at Marburg and an important theologian in the negotiations that led to the Prussian Union. In his *Die Christliche von der Sünde* (vol. 1, 1839; vol. 2, 1844) he interpreted the fact of sin as the assumption of an extraterrestrial fall occasioned by a free act of decision on each individual. For more information on Mueller, see F. L. Cross, ed., *The Oxford Dictionary of the Christian Church* (New York: Oxford University Press, 1966), 932–33.

9. This reply follows the text of the pamphlet edition of Brown's *The New Theology,* 40–72.

Schmucker was the one who was really confused, Brown alleged. He had Lutheran sources available to him, Brown said, but used American sources so that he would not be accused of Symbolism. Schmucker used those same American sources and cited them to his students, according to Brown.[10] He accused Schmucker of regarding sin, regeneration, and justification as unimportant. "Perhaps Dr. S.S.S. does not regard clear views of sin, regeneration and justification, as very important to the faithful and successful preaching of the Gospel. It is said, that he is fond of preaching on War, Slavery, the Laws of the Universe, Natural Theology, and kindred topics; leaving to humbler intellects the treatment of sin, repentance, faith, justification, and other Christian doctrines" (48).

Brown was disturbed by Schmucker's use of psychological terms in dealing with the doctrines under debate. He pointed out that the Symbolical Books (Lutheran Confessions) do not use the term "mental" when speaking of original sin; he said that Schmucker had reduced sin to a "disorder." Brown was willing to admit that there was some agreement between him and Schmucker over the question of regeneration, but the main issue remained: could children who were incapable of regeneration in life be regenerated in death?

Brown thought that Schmucker was a rationalist. With regard to regeneration, Brown pointed out that the Bible represented it as "being born again, being renewed, and being partakers of the divine nature." Schmucker's "change of habits," however, was only "reformation" rather than "regeneration" (67). As to justification, Brown concluded that Schmucker was advocating that sinners must first be sanctified before they could be justified, a reversal of the order of salvation. In addition, Schmucker tied works to justification and made justification depend on them. Brown commented: "The point is the *condition* of a sinner's pardon or justification. Dr. S.S.S. distinctly affirms that without certain things on the part of a sinner, 'it is impossible for him to obtain pardon or to be justified.' If the sinner cannot be justified without them, they must be conditions of his justification" (70).

The Brown-Schmucker exchanges radiated more heat than light, but they were important. The fact that Brown was not, by his own admission, a member of the confessional party indicates there was some opposition to Schmucker elsewhere in the General Synod. Brown instituted heresy charges against Schmucker but was dissuaded from carrying the process

10. It should be pointed out that Brown never attended the Seminary in Gettysburg but studied theology under J. G. Morris and Benjamin Kurtz. See Abdel Ross Wentz, *History of the Gettysburg Theological Seminary, 1826–1965*, 2 vols. (Harrisburg, Pa.: Evangelical Press, 1965), 397.

to a conclusion by Charles Porterfield Krauth, a former student of Schmucker's who was later one of the first professors of the breakaway seminary in Philadelphia and one of the founders of the General Council. Krauth felt that his former professor should not suffer such an act of disgrace. Brown, ironically, succeeded Schmucker as professor at the Seminary in Gettysburg when Schmucker stepped down in 1864. Brown was elected president of the General Synod in 1866 and served on the seminary faculty until 1879, when he resigned because of ill health.

Years of Continued Conflict, 1859–1864

The publication of the *Definite Platform* brought into the open the differences between the American Lutherans and the confessional party. Responses continued to be made in print for the next two years.

Even after the battle of the publications was over, there were signs that all was not well within the General Synod. The problem was that nothing about the Synod itself really changed. The doctrinal stance of the Synod remained unaltered. The American Lutherans were not formally repudiated; in fact, they retained positions of leadership.

One illustration of this unchanged state is a sermon entitled *The Mission of the General Synod,* preached by Simeon Harkey, an American Lutheran, before the General Synod in 1859 and published the same year.[11] Harkey's text was Isaiah 60:22. He gave a short history of the General Synod and asked: "What is the mission of the General Synod?" His first point was that the General Synod had "a special work to promote brotherly love and fellowship in the Lutheran Church, as much as the *whole* church" (6). This statement clearly indicates that Harkey saw the General Synod as reaching out beyond itself to other American Protestant groups. Doctrine was not considered to be important. Love was the prime consideration. Harkey proclaimed, "But we want *love* in the Lutheran Church, as much as orthodoxy: yes, a thousand times more than what some men call orthodoxy" (6). Tensions between North and South were becoming evident, and Harkey urged "the promotion and practice of brotherly love" as a preventive measure against division.

The mission of the General Synod was to unite all Lutherans in the United States. Harkey acknowledged that many varieties of Lutherans existed, but he insisted that the General Synod could accommodate them

11. Simeon W. Harkey, *The Mission of the General Synod: A Sermon Preached in the English Evangelical Lutheran Church, Pittsburgh, Pa., May 19, 1859, at the Opening of the Nineteenth Convention of the General Synod of the Evangelical Lutheran Church in the United States* (Philadelphia: Henry B. Ashmead, 1859).

all. The General Synod was able to be so inclusive because it "cannot and does not require perfect *unity* or *uniformity* in all points of doctrine" (10). This liberal stance allowed for individual judgment, something Protestants prized. The General Synod also had no uniformity of liturgical, educational, and practical matters: "So it would be a great advantage to us Lutherans to have everywhere the same Hymn Book, Catechism, Liturgy, and customs and usages. But still no man's conscience must be burdened, nor dare these things be made in any wise compulsory. The want of uniformity here must be no obstacle to our union,—here we can 'agree to differ' " (11).

Harkey dealt with the matter of the Augsburg Confession at length. He affirmed that the General Synod had "adopted it as to *fundamentals,* and to these she requires unqualified subscription" (12). Harkey acknowledged that objections had been raised about the distinction between fundamental and nonfundamental doctrines because they could mean different things to different people. He dismissed these objections as "quibbling." The stance of the General Synod is: "In essentials unity, in doubtful matters liberty, in all things charity" (13).

It was imperative that all Lutherans in America unite because of an increase in the number of sects. Lutheranism had never produced a sect, Harkey pointed out, but he was fearful that if unity could not be achieved on the ground of the General Synod, such a sin would occur. Unity would also bring about growth and success; neither could happen if Lutheranism were divided into synods that quarreled with each other. Harkey's vision was of a unified Lutheranism that would take its place in America.

> There is a new phase of humanity being developed in this country, and especially in the West. America is not, and never will be, a nation of Englishmen, nor of Germans, nor of French, Scotch, or Irishmen, nor of Swedes or Norwegians; no, never any one of these, or any other individual nation; but it will be a *new race* out of a union of all these elements; a new development of humanity by a mixing up and commingling of all these, re-cast and re-moulded by our American institutions. (16)

If Lutheranism was to participate in this destiny, all national distinctions needed to be removed. In Harkey's opinion, that could only be accomplished by a unified Lutheran church.

The mission of the General Synod was to evangelize and Americanize the foreign Lutheran population. By Americanize Harkey did not mean that the immigrants should give up their customs. "In fact, they *must* retain enough of their own habits and customs to make them feel comfortable and happy in their new homes" (18). Nor should they be made to give up their own languages. Americanization meant relating to American institutions; "And as one nation, we must have one common character, object and aim—one form of government, and one set of institutions—in a word, all people coming to this country must become *Americanized*—must adapt themselves to our country and its institutions in Church and State" (19).

Harkey wanted Lutherans to be Americanized within their own church rather than to end up in another of the many religious groups that existed in America. He wanted the immigrants in the Lutheran fold, but that fold should allow for differences in nonfundamentals. Unity, in the sense of harmony among the members, was clearly more important than doctrine, and nonfundamental doctrines should not get in the way of the overall mission of Lutheranism.

Harkey gave some attention to the language question. Although the immigrants should not have to give up their native language, to be truly American they would have to adopt English, simply because English was the language of America. The church should help that process along by offering hymnbooks, catechisms, newspapers, and periodicals in English.

Only a Lutheran church unified under the banner of the General Synod could effectively conduct home missions. Harkey pointed to the Methodists' work with Germans—German Lutherans at that! Unity was needed to counteract that sort of intrusion. He called on Synod to raise large sums of money to help carry out the cause.

Harkey's last point was that it is the General Synod's mission to maintain a high standard of piety. His language shows that he did not want the General Synod to move to extremes, but remain in the center. Harkey advocated "A piety that is zealous and warm on one hand, and uniform and solid on the other—equally removed from wild fire and fanaticism, as well as stiffness and cold formality" (27). Preaching to a General Synod that was anything but unified, Harkey closed his sermon with a passionate plea for unity:

> O! if I had a voice like an angel's trumpet, I would make this truth sound and re-sound throughout the whole Church: Cease, Oh cease from your controversies and disputes about non-essential points of doctrine and practice, and labor with all your might for the conversion and salvation of immortal souls! Give up your mistrust of each other, your hard feelings and bitter speeches against each other, and come let us strive together to bring a lost world to Christ. Let us lift high the banner of vital piety and true holiness, and spend all our energies to marshal all our people under it. Then our church will be safe. (27)

Harkey's sermon makes it clear that the theological situation in the General Synod had not changed. Plenty of latitude was still allowed and was considered desirable. Harkey's sermon also gives a clue to what Americanization meant—to adapt to America and its institutions, in both church and state. The General Synod, with its emphasis on allowances for disagreement on nonfundamental doctrines and its emphasis on the right to private judgment, was the right church for Lutherans to achieve unity. Only a church body such as the General Synod could accomplish a Lutheran mission in America. Quibbling over doctrine would only hinder the good works that needed to be done.

Two statements by William Julius Mann, Schmucker's main critic during the controversy over the *Definite Platform,* reflect the tensions within the General Synod. In 1855 Mann commented on the condition of the Synod:

> Certainly the name is the most characteristic feature of the General Synod. It is simply used as a watchword for a party, and being less concerned about the Lutheran character of the doctrinal principles thus adopted, some take their correctness for granted without further examination, while others even revel in the delightful confidence of having corrected the Lutheran Church. The majority of pastors have never made an independent study of the dogmatical peculiarities of the Lutheran Church. They are, according to American custom, completely dependent on the views of the teachers to whom they owe their theological education. If these teachers themselves have strayed away from the peculiarly Lutheran doctrine, anything is offered as Lutheran doctrine, that with the slightest modification might just as well go forth into the world under any other name.[12]

Mann attended the General Synod meeting at Pittsburgh in 1859. His reaction to the events there was pointed: "In the General Synod there was apparently much willingness to concede, but there were no concessions."[13] Mann observed a synod internally struggling; yet nothing had changed.

That same year, Samuel Schmucker published his *Evangelical Lutheran Catechism.*[14] Some samples will serve to show that this catechism reflects the same basic position as the *Definite Platform.* In Part XVI ("The Great Change, or Conversion") the question (215) is asked: "Is the practice of the Romanists to confess to the priests and receive absolution from them Scriptural?" The answer given is: "Neither the Savior nor his apostles ever instituted such a rite, and such a pretended absolution is utterly worthless. All believers have access to God through Christ, and can obtain pardon if

12. Adolph Spaeth, *Memorial of William Julius Mann* (Philadelphia: Evangelical Lutheran Ministerium of Pennsylvania, 1893), 32–33.

13. Emma T. Mann, *Memoir of the Life and Work of William Julius Mann* (Philadelphia: Jas. B. Rogers Printing Co., 1893), 91.

14. Samuel S. Schmucker, *Evangelical Lutheran Catechism, Designed for Catechumens and the Higher Classes in Sabbath-Schools* (Baltimore: T. Newton Kurtz, 1859).

they sincerely seek it, without the mediation of priest or minister. Yet penitents and Christians may properly converse with the ministers of Christ on their spiritual interests, and receive their instruction and advice" (85–86).

Schmucker held firm on his rejection of baptismal regeneration (Question 286). In the section "The Holy Supper of our Lord," Schmucker did not deal with the real presence except to deny "that Romish doctrine, that the bread and wine are changed into the body and blood of Christ" (Question 301). For bread to become body and wine to become blood "contradicts common sense and reason, as well as the testimony of the senses" (115). No reliable figures can be found regarding the circulation of this catechism, but it indicates that Schmucker had not renounced his previous opinions and that the General Synod was still under his influence.

Another example of the state of the General Synod at this crucial juncture can be seen in the proposed liturgy that came before the Synod in 1864.[15] Samuel Schmucker was the chair of the subcommittee that formulated the various worship orders. Many of the critics of the American Lutherans had called for a return to historic Lutheran liturgical forms. The orders proposed for the General Synod were, liturgically and theologically, reflective of American Protestantism.

The order for public worship was as follows: anthem by the choir; scriptural benediction; salutation or invocation; reading of a confessional prayer with the Lord's Prayer, and either Creed or Decalogue; reading of the Scriptures; announcement and reading of the first hymn; extemporaneous general prayer; reading of the second hymn; sermon; closing prayer; collection and notices; closing hymn and doxology; and the benediction (*Proposal Liturgy,* 1). Between the first hymn and the general prayer, there is a rubric that reads, "If the previous exercises were performed at the desk, the minister now ascends to the pulpit" (1). This would seem to indicate that no altar was used.

The orders for special services also give evidence of non-Lutheran tendencies. Baptism is always referred to as an ordinance rather than a sacrament. The stated purpose of confirmation is "to conduct the instruction as to awaken the unconcerned to a sense of their lost condition, to conduct inquiring souls to the Savior, and to train them all to become consistent and active members of the Church of Christ" (52). Here, as in other places, the need for conversion is stressed.

The opening line of the Service of Communion reads, "Christian friends, we are here assembled to prepare for the worthy communication of the

---

15. *Proposed Liturgy of the Evangelical Lutheran General Synod, Reported by the Subcommittee of the General Liturgic Committee of the General Synod at York, Penna., May 4th, 1864.*

dying love of that Redeemer . . ." (59). This sets the theme for the service and indicates that the Supper is seen as a memorial of the death of Christ. The elements for the Supper can be ordinary bread or unleavened bread and grape juice or wine (62). Like baptism, the Lord's Supper is referred to as an ordinance.

The Communion Service has a Zwinglian flavor; for example, "To those who in living faith receive the outward symbols of his body and blood, he vouchsafes the most lively assurance that he dwelleth in them, the hope of glory" (64). The address to the communicants contains a long account of the suffering and death of Christ, emphasizing that the Communion is a memorial of Christ's death—a prominent theme in Zwingli's eucharistic theology. Finally, the invitation to Communion includes "all who are members in good standing of other Christian denominations" (67). This indicates the practice of open Communion without concern about the doctrines communicants might hold.

These proposed orders of worship were designed to impart uniformity and orderliness to worship in the General Synod. These orders did not follow traditional Lutheran liturgical orders. They did, however, reflect the theological position of the American Lutherans. They are yet another indication that Samuel Schmucker had not lost his influence in the General Synod as a whole.[16] Nothing had really changed since the days of the *Definite Platform*. Profound differences still existed, and it was only a matter of time before those differences would result in a complete split.

Charles Porterfield Krauth's Journey

Of all the figures associated with the *Definite Platform* controversy, Charles Porterfield Krauth's is the most interesting. His early pro-confessional article in the *Evangelical Review* has been noted (see chap. 7). In the wake of the *Definite Platform,* the young Krauth wrote the "Pittsburgh Declaration," which was accepted by the Pittsburgh Synod at its meeting at

16. The account of the General Synod's actions regarding the proposed liturgy can be found in the *Proceedings of the Twenty-first Convention of the General Synod of the Evangelical Lutheran Church in the United States, Assembled in York, Pa., May, 1864.* The full subcommittee did not meet until the convention was in session. Schmucker did virtually all the work on the proposed liturgy. When a vote of the subcommittee was taken, only G. F. Krotel voted against it. On May 4, Schmucker distributed copies of the proposed liturgy to the convention. On May 10, Schmucker presented the subcommittee's report. The Synod received the report and resolved to refer the proposed liturgy to the district synods and churches for comments. A committee of five was appointed to receive comments and make adjustments. The committee members were Schmucker, H. N. Pohlman, J. G. Morris, Samuel Sprecher, and Theophilus Stork, all American Lutheran sympathizers.

Zelienople, Pennsylvania, in 1856. Two statements of this declaration are especially noteworthy:

> That while the basis of our General Synod has allowed a diversity in regard to some parts of the Augsburg Confession, that basis never was designed to imply the right to alter, amend, or curtail the confession itself.[17]
>
> That while we do not wish to conceal the fact that some parts of the doctrine of our confession in regard to the sacraments are received in different degree by different brethren, yet that even in these points, wherein we, as brethren in Christ, agree to differ till the Holy Ghost shall make us see eye to eye, the differences are not such as to destroy the foundation of faith, our unity in labor, our mutual confidence, and our tender love.[18]

These statements indicate that, although Krauth was opposed to the *Definite Platform,* he desired peace within the church and was willing to continue to work with those with whom he disagreed.

In 1857 Krauth wrote a series of three articles in the *Lutheran and Missionary.*[19] The first article was entitled "The General Synod." Krauth began by stating the obvious—that the General Synod was in a state of anxiety, and such a state was not good for the church. Krauth was of the opinion that the General Synod should do something to resolve the differences that prevailed in the church. To continue the present situation would only paralyze and demoralize the Synod.

Krauth recalled that the General Synod had begun in the midst of crisis, when rationalism had taken hold in Germany and the various sects beckoned in America. In response to these conditions, the General Synod was founded as a distinctively Lutheran body. Krauth commented: "When the General Synod became completely organized by the acknowledgment of the doctrinal Articles of the Augsburg Confession as a standard of faith, it was the only *voluntary* body on earth pretending to embrace a nation as its territory, and bearing a Lutheran name, in which the fundamental doctrines of Lutheranism were the basis of union" (1:384).

In the second article, "The Doctrinal Basis of the General Synod," Krauth assumed that the General Synod had a doctrinal basis and was orthodox. He then contended that the General Synod never proposed to be a union of all Protestant or evangelical denominations but simply the

---

17. Cited in Henry Eyster Jacobs, *A History of the Evangelical Lutheran Church in the United States* (New York: Charles Scribner's Sons, 1897), 427.

18. Ibid., 428.

19. The complete texts of these articles can be found in Adolph Spaeth, *Charles Porterfield Krauth,* 2 vols. (New York: Christian Literature Co., 1898). All citations are from this source.

evangelical Lutheran synods in the United States. Thus, its basis was *Lutheran*.

Krauth's solution to the problem of dissension was that the General Synod should assert its original doctrinal position. He was referring not to the entire *Book of Concord* but only to the Augsburg Confession, and then only the first twenty-one articles. Only insofar as these articles embrace fundamental doctrines should such an affirmation be made. Finally, Krauth defined correctness in doctrine in terms of *substantial* agreement (1:386).

Krauth made the case that the General Synod chose the Augsburg Confession because it was commonly accepted by all Lutherans, but he was careful to point out that it was the Confession of 1530 and not Melanchthon's "Variata" of 1540 that had been accepted. Krauth maintained that the first twenty-one articles of the Augsburg Confession, by their constitution, were obviously credal; the remaining articles related disputed points with the Roman church at the time of the Reformation. Because these latter points were not credal, the General Synod made no specific mention of them. The first twenty-one articles were specifically mentioned, Krauth explained, because it was anticipated there might be differences of opinion regarding them; in the articles concerning abuses, it was assumed there would be little discussion.

Referring to the General Synod's formula of licensure and ordination, Krauth argued that the Synod simply accepted the articles as doctrines. On the question of doctrines, Krauth accepted the term "fundamental" as relative, but he maintained that the term needed to be defined. As far as Krauth was concerned, it is not up to the individual to define what is fundamental, for that could only result in chaos of opinion. "The Church, and not the individual, then, is to be our guide to the meaning of the word" (1:391).

Krauth demonstrated that the term "fundamental" could not be used in the sense Protestants had used it because there were many doctrinal differences among Protestants, and Protestants held views contrary to many Lutheran teachings. Baptism and the Lord's Supper were two among many examples. Krauth commented: "Now, that in which Protestants differ without ceasing to be Protestants, cannot be fundamental to the Protestant system. If the word 'fundamental,' then, in our Formula is used relatively to Protestantism, it would allow within the bosom of our Church all the differences which divide the Protestant world—a suicidal commingling" (1:393). Krauth called "delusive" the notion that the combined strengths of the various Protestant groups could accomplish great things.

Some ministers in the General Synod could not give an unlimited subscription to the Augsburg Confession, Krauth admitted, and it was this class of ministers who were active in establishing and helped to sustain the General Synod. Other ministers rejected no portion of the Augsburg Confession but were uncertain about some parts. They were wondering which direction they should go. A third group of ministers received every part of the Augsburg Confession but would not cut themselves off from others on account of doctrinal issues. This was obviously the camp to which Krauth belonged.

Which direction would the General Synod take? Krauth advocated that affirmation should be made only on the *substantial* correctness of the Confession, for all were agreed on that. Members should be allowed the freedom to receive or reject what is not substantial. He admitted this was a middle-of-the-road proposal that would satisfy neither the rigid symbolist who regarded it necessary to accept every part of the Augsburg Confession nor the "schismatist" who regarded it necessary to reject portions of the Confession. What the church in the United States wanted was neither of these classes but an evangelical Lutheranism broad enough to embrace both. In 1857, that was the Lutheran church envisioned by Charles Porterfield Krauth.

Krauth's third article was entitled "The Duty of the General Synod in the Present Crisis." Krauth began this article by stating that the General Synod could not take a higher or lower position on doctrine than it was presently doing, but that the present formula needed to be restated and defined. He recalled the 1850 sermon in which his father had said that too much liberty was allowed in the General Synod's subscription. The younger Krauth reasserted his previous position, that the church decides what are fundamental doctrines of Scripture. Using Article X of the Augsburg Confession ("On the Lord's Supper") as an example, Krauth proceeded to show that fundamental doctrines have nothing to do with Protestantism or even Lutheranism, but only with the Word of God. "A man must, if he accepts the Formula, either maintain that the *Scripture* doctrine of the Lord's Supper is non-fundamental or that this Scripture doctrine being fundamental is taught in a manner substantially correct in the Tenth Article of the Augsburg Confession" (1:405). Krauth pointed out that the term "presence" is used throughout Article X in reference to Christ's presence in the sacrament. Those who reject the term are condemned by Article X; thus a Zwinglian interpretation is clearly rejected. The General Synod must decide how to handle Article X. Some would regard the present state of ambiguity as desirable, but Krauth would have no part of that: "The present posture of affairs in our Church, we think, demonstrates that we must either clearly state what is its meaning, or see the Church worn out with intestine strife" (1:406).

Krauth offered three suggestions. First, the General Synod should recognize no ecclesiastical body that does not believe the Scriptures to be the word of God, the only infallible rule of faith and practice. Second, the General Synod should recognize no synodical body as Lutheran that does not make the Augsburg Confession, "unmutilated and unchanged," its confessional affirmation. No synod has the right to issue a recension of that Confession. To allow such a thing would result in as many denominations as there were synods. Third, the General Synod should make it clear that its licentiates and candidates for ordination, while affirming the Augsburg Confession, are neither affirming nor rejecting the other "symbolical books."

Although he differed with Schmucker, Krauth wanted to maintain peace in the General Synod. It has been noted that he defended Schmucker against J. A. Brown's charges of unsound doctrine. Brown had concentrated on the doctrines of natural depravity, regeneration, and justification. In this regard, Krauth made a curious comment: "Dr. Schmucker does not hold views fundamentally erroneous on the points in dispute, but that there are sentences, especially in his later works, which are not in accordance with the form of sound words; in short, that he is sound, though not all that he has written is" (1:410). This conciliatory statement reveals that, for Krauth, peace in the Synod was most important; he believed that the American Lutherans and the confessional party could peacefully coexist in the General Synod, in a spirit of charity and tolerance.

Krauth's response to the petition of the Melanchthon Synod to join the General Synod was another example of his conciliatory stance. This synod had come into existence in 1857 under the leadership of Benjamin Kurtz as a result of the controversy over the *Definite Platform*. The "Declaration of Faith" unanimously adopted by the Melanchthon Synod accepted, without reservation, the position of the *Definite Platform*. Much debate accompanied their application for admission to the General Synod in 1859. Finally, they were granted admission with the following recommendation: "We would fraternally solicit [the Melanchthon Synod] to consider whether a change, in their doctrinal basis, of the paragraph in regard to certain alleged errors, would not tend to the promotion of mutual love, and the furtherance of the great objects for which we are laboring together."[20] It was Charles Porterfield Krauth who proposed the Melanchthon Synod's acceptance.

Although Krauth was not in agreement with the doctrinal stance of many in the General Synod and thought a more definite stance on the part of the

20. *Proceedings of the Nineteenth Convention of the General Synod of the Evangelical Lutheran Church in the United States, Assembled in Pittsburgh, Pa., from the 19th to the 26th of May, 1859,* 11.

Synod desirable, he remained conciliatory. He used his position as editor of the *Lutheran and Missionary* to defend the confessional Lutheran stance in the hope that by persuasion he could gradually change the character of the Synod.

At this juncture, Krauth could still be described as a moderate. He insisted that he was not an "Old Lutheran" but advocated a Lutheranism that "is moderate in its tone, free from the spirit of false exclusiveness, and makes no pretensions which have any show of extravagance."[21] In an editorial, Krauth even stated that Lutheranism in America must be American.

> We are "American Lutherans." We accept the great fact that God has established our Zion in this western world under circumstances wholly different from those in which her past life has been nurtured. New forms of duty, new types of thought, new necessities of adaptation, are here to tax all her strength, and to test how far she is able to maintain her vital power under necessary changes of form. The Lutheranism of this country cannot be a mere feeble echo of any nationalized species of Lutheranism.[22]

In that same editorial, Krauth qualified what he did *not* mean:

> *And yet, we are not American Lutherans,* if to be such, means that we are to have a new faith, a mutilated confession, a life which abruptly breaks with all our history, a spirit alien to that of genuine Lutheranism of the past. An American Lutheran Church, which has no right to claim as a part of its heritage the immortal names, and holy memories of the past, a new sect in this land of sects—God save us from this.[23]

In the early 1860s, Krauth began to believe that faithful adherence to the truth was essential for the church to be unified, and that was not the case with the General Synod. During this period, he wrote:

> Our Church in the General Synod has not breathed the spirit of outspoken Lutheranism, at least has not felt as our early fathers felt, the necessity of plain words on disputed points. With no hierarchical centre, no liturgical service as in the Episcopal Church, with a Congregationalism tending in its elements to independency, and robbing us of strength of government, we have had hardly anything to hold us together but our name and our history; and detaching these, as we have largely done, from their vital doctrinal

---

21. Spaeth, *Charles Porterfield Krauth*, 2:36.
22. Cited ibid., 2:37.
23. Cited ibid., 2:38.

connexion, we have exposed ourselves to the hazards of division and dis-
solution. If principle did not demand more doctrinal unity, our interests
would. We must have it, or our experiment in this country will be a failure.
We will have it, and with a forbearance mingling itself with honesty, we
shall have it, not at the price of a rent and bleeding Church, but in our
Church, then truly united.[24]

The Civil War brought about the same chaos in the church that was
afflicting the nation. In 1862 the Southern synods were absent from the
regularly called General Synod convention. They finally met at Concord,
North Carolina, on May 20–26, 1863, and formed the General Synod of
the Evangelical Lutheran Church in the Confederate States of America.
Doctrinal differences played no role in their leaving. Most of the members
of the Southern synods were more conservative on social issues, in this
instance slavery, than they were with regard to doctrinal questions.

The event that finally precipitated a crisis was the admission of the
Franckean Synod to the General Synod in 1864. The Franckean Synod
had never accepted the Augsburg Confession. Their "Declaration of Faith"
was devoid of any reference to particular Lutheran doctrines. When confronted with this, the Franckean delegates stated that they assumed, by
virtue of membership in the General Synod, that they would be accepting
the General Synod's confession of faith. They were instructed to formally
adopt that confession at their next meeting. The resolution to accept the
Franckean Synod resulted in a heated debate. When the vote was taken,
the Franckean Synod was admitted by a vote of ninety-seven to forty. The
Pennsylvania Ministerium's delegates protested that, in admitting the Fran-
ckeans, the General Synod had violated its own constitution. When their
position was not recognized, the Ministerium delegates, citing the conditions of their reentry in 1853, withdrew to report to their body.[25]

The moment of truth finally came for Charles Porterfield Krauth. On
July 13, 1865, in an article in the *Lutheran and Missionary* entitled "The
Aimless Battle," he published a recantation of his former "crudities and
inconsistencies" with regard to the subject of fundamentals. In a remarkable
bit of candor, Krauth said:

We do not feel ashamed to confess that time and experience have modified
our earlier views, or lead us to abandon them, if we have so modified or
so forsaken them. . . .

24. Cited ibid., 2:57.
25. *Proceedings of the Twenty-first Convention of the General Synod of the Evangelical
Lutheran Church in the United States, Assembled in York, Pa., May, 1864*, 19.

In Church and State the last years have wrought changes, deep and thorough, in every thinking man, and on no point more than this, that compromise of principle, however specious, is immoral, and that however guarded it may be, it is perilous; and that there is no guarantee of peace in words where men do not agree on things. . . .

To true unity of the Church is necessary an agreement in fundamentals, and a vital part of the necessity is an agreement as to what are fundamentals. The doctrinal articles of the Augsburg Confession are all articles of faith, and all articles of faith are fundamental. Our Church can never have a genuine internal harmony, except in the confession, without reservation or ambiguity of these articles, one and all. . . . This is our deep conviction, and we hereby retract, before God and His Church, formally, as we have already earnestly and repeatedly done indirectly, every thing we have written or said in conflict with this our present conviction. This we are not ashamed to do. We thank God, who has led us to see the truth, and we thank Him for freeing us from the temptation of embarrassing ourselves with the pretence of a present absolute consistency with our earlier, very sincere, yet relatively immature views.[26]

This frank retraction[27] reveals that Krauth had come to believe that one could no longer be neutral, that a peaceful coexistence between the American Lutherans and the confessional party was no longer possible. Subsequent events showed that Krauth acted out his conviction.

The Seminary's Founding at Philadelphia

Even before Charles Porterfield Krauth issued his retraction, he took a step that moved him farther from the General Synod. He, along with Charles F. Schaeffer and William Julius Mann, formed the faculty of the newly founded seminary in Philadelphia.

In 1864 Samuel Schmucker resigned his position as professor at the Seminary at Gettysburg. The Pennsylvania Ministerium wanted the position to be awarded to Krauth, but J. A. Brown, noted for his criticisms of Schmucker, was elected instead. This action intensified the animosity between the Ministerium and the General Synod, and the Ministerium decided to establish its own seminary.

The question of whether to establish a new seminary was not a new one. As far back as 1842, the Pennsylvania Ministerium had sought connection with the Lutheran seminary in Columbus, Ohio, rather than Gettysburg. In that instance the language question was the main issue.[28] Al-

---

26. *Lutheran and Missionary* (June 13, 1865).

27. C. F. W. Walther later stated, in his memorial notice after Krauth's death, that Krauth's declaration was "an imperishable monument of the uprightness and candor of his convictions." See Spaeth, *Charles Porterfield Krauth*, 2:114.

28. The best source for the history of the Philadelphia Seminary is Theodore G. Tappert,

though the Ministerium endowed a professorship at Gettysburg after it rejoined the General Synod in 1853, the arrangements proved unsatisfactory. In 1859 five students from the Ministerium withdrew in protest of the theological environment at Gettysburg, and a proposal was made to shift the Ministerium's professorship to another locality. In 1860 C. F. Welden, president of the Ministerium, proposed that a new seminary be established, both to increase the number of ministerial candidates and to ensure that students would be trained in sound doctrine. In May 1864 Charles W. Schaeffer, nephew of the professor of German at Gettysburg and president of the Ministerium, voiced the same concerns.

On May 25, 1864, the Ministerium took formal action to establish its own seminary in Philadelphia. Charles F. Schaeffer was designated the German professor, Charles Porterfield Krauth the English professor, and William Julius Mann "intermediate professor," meaning he was to teach in both languages.

The *Lutheran Observer* ridiculed the whole enterprise. The editor stated that graduates of the new seminary would be taught "symbolic orthodoxy" and "narrow, unfraternal, and denominational exclusivism," "formal ritualism" and "anti-revivalism." "There the Old Lutheran, obsolete doctrines . . . are to be recalled from their grave."[29]

Krauth reflected on the situation at the Seminary at Gettysburg: "It is most unnatural and dangerous that in the same communion, and under the same roof, one set of students should be taught to regard as Romish abominations and dangerous errors what others are taught to consider as the very truth of God."[30]

On October 4, 1864, at a service held at St. John's English Lutheran Church in Philadelphia, the faculty for the new seminary was formally installed. The charge was given by Beale M. Schmucker,[31] who stated that the object of the seminary was twofold. The first object was to provide German-speaking pastors, but theological instruction was to be in both German and English; the second was to provide ministers who would teach

---

History of the Lutheran Theological Seminary at Philadelphia 1864–1964 (Philadelphia: Lutheran Theological Seminary, 1964). Tappert states that the use of English was far less uniform in the Pennsylvania Ministerium than in other synods. By 1828 the Ministerium's minutes were printed in both German and English. As late as 1862 the Ministerium was, in actuality, bilingual in character.

29. Cited in Tappert, *History,* 31.

30. Cited ibid.

31. Beale M. Schmucker (1827–88) was a son of Samuel Schmucker. Although he studied under his father, through reading the *Book of Concord* and other confessional Lutheran literature, he adopted a more conservative position with regard to the Confessions, siding with Krauth, Mann, and the other leaders of the confessional party within the General Synod. He was one of those instrumental in forming the General Council in 1867.

the doctrines of Holy Scripture as set forth in the Confessions of the Lutheran church. Schmucker stated: "We do not believe that the Confessions of the Lutheran Church are merely substantially correct, or correct with reference to truths necessary to be believed in order to the soul's salvation alone; we believe that they are in entire accordance with the teachings of the divine word."[32]

The reply to the charge was given by Charles Porterfield Krauth. Krauth set forth the importance of the creeds, the Scriptures, and the Confession of Faith (Lutheran Symbols). To place oneself under these does not deny the right of private judgment; but private judgment does not allow one to lapse into error; nor can it be arbitrary. "The right of private judgment is not the right of Church-membership, not the right of public teaching, not the right of putting others into an equivocal attitude to what they regard as truth."[33] Krauth went on to state: "When we confess, that, in the exercize of our right of private judgment, our Bible has made us Lutherans, we neither pretend to claim that other men should be made Lutherans by force, nor that their private judgment shall, or will, of necessity, reach the results of ours. We only contend, that, if their private judgment of the Bible does not make them Lutherans, they shall not pretend that it does."[34] Krauth concluded: "We concede to every man the absolute right of private judgment as to the faith of the Lutheran Church. If you have abandoned the faith of the Church you may not use her name as your shelter in attacking the thing she cherishes, and in maintaining which she obtained her being and her name."[35]

These statements by Beale Schmucker and Charles Porterfield Krauth pointedly stated the purpose of the new seminary. They also clearly attacked the American Lutherans' doctrinal misrepresentations made in the name of private judgment. The founding of the Seminary at Philadelphia was the first official act that would signal a break from the General Synod. It was only a matter of time before members of the confessional party would take a decisive step to go their own way.

The Separation, 1866–1867

The years 1866–67 brought the conflict to its conclusion. By this time many significant events had taken place. Following his resignation in 1864,

---

32. *Addresses Delivered at the Installation of the Professors of the Theological Seminary of the Evangelical Lutheran Church, Philadelphia, October 4th, 1864* (Gettysburg: Aughinbrugh & Wible, Book & Job Printers, 1865), 6.
33. Ibid., 16.
34. Ibid., 17.
35. Ibid.

Schmucker was no longer a professor at the Seminary in Gettysburg. That same year the new seminary in Philadelphia opened. In 1865 Krauth made his famous retraction. In 1866 Benjamin Kurtz, one of the leaders of the American Lutherans and the editor of the *Lutheran Observer,* died.

One possibility for reconciliation came after the Pennsylvania Ministerium withdrew from the General Synod convention in 1864. The following amendment was offered on the articles referring to the admission of synods:

> All regularly constituted Lutheran Synods not now in connection with the General Synod, receiving and holding with the Evangelical Lutheran Church of our fathers, the Word of God so contained in the canonical Scriptures of the Old and New Testaments, as the only infallible rule of faith and practice, and the Augsburg Confession as a correct exhibition of the fundamental articles of the Divine Word, and of the faith of our Church founded upon that Word, may, at any time, become associated with the General Synod, by complying with the requirement of this constitution, according to the ratio specified in Art. 2d.[36]

This amendment was sent to the District Synods for action. It represented a more confessional direction regarding the doctrinal basis of the General Synod. The reception of this amendment was quite positive, even on the part of the Pennsylvania Ministerium.

Four synods rejected the amendment: the Hartwick Synod, the Franckean Synod, the Melanchthon Synod, and the Central Synod of Pennsylvania. On his deathbed, Benjamin Kurtz signed a strong statement of opposition. He complained that such a concession to the symbolists was only the beginning, and eventually the General Synod would be forced to accept the entire body of symbolical books without exception or reservation.[37] The *Lutheran Observer* sided with the opposing synods claiming that any endorsement of the Augsburg Confession must be moderate and liberal. The *Observer* stated: "There is no greater madness than that of laying down a subscription which brands as traitors to Lutheranism four-fifths of the most evangelical and devoted portion of the native Lutherans of this land."[38]

The General Synod convention held at Fort Wayne, Indiana, in 1866 proved to be the event that would make any attempt of reconciliation between the American Lutherans and the confessional party impossible. Samuel Sprecher, one of the leaders of the American Lutherans, was the

36. Cited in Spaeth, *Charles Porterfield Krauth,* 2:133.
37. Ibid., 2:135.
38. *Lutheran Observer* (Nov. 17, 1865).

president of the General Synod and would preside over the convention. Evidence indicates that the stage was set so that the Pennsylvania Ministerium delegates would be excluded. Sprecher, in a letter to Samuel Schmucker dated February 12, 1866, criticized the Ministerium for its many years of absence from the General Synod. He also criticized its constitution, which gave its delegates the right to withdraw and report to the Ministerium if an issue was deemed to be a violation of the Ministerium's constitution. Sprecher concluded the letter by saying, "My present feeling is that I have the right to refuse to receive the certificates of their delegates."[39] On the way to the Fort Wayne convention, Samuel Schmucker told his son Beale that many "prominent men" of the General Synod "had carefully considered the situation, and that they had resolved that the Pennsylvania Ministerium should no longer be connected with the General Synod." Then Beale Schmucker said of his father: "He calmly reviewed the position on both sides, and gave reasons why it was better for peace and unity that this course should be taken, and being assured of the support of a majority of votes, the action was decided on."[40]

The General Synod convention opened on May 17, 1866. The opening sermon was preached by Samuel Sprecher. Charles Porterfield Krauth's reaction to the sermon was anything but positive. For Krauth, it was proof that nothing had changed. In reviewing the sermon in the *Lutheran and Missionary,* Krauth decried Sprecher's contention that Lutheranism was a process rather than a system of doctrines.

> Lutheranism may successively mean everything and anything which the craziness of an abuse of the right of private judgment may cover with the pretenses of Protestant investigation. Lutheranism may be Unitarian, Pelagian, Calvinistic, Baptist, Arminian, as the current shifts. Provided only that nothing in the way of "writings or creeds of men come between them and the examination of the Bible," twenty men may reach twenty different results, and all are equally good Lutherans.[41]

At the convention, Sprecher ruled that, because its delegates left the General Synod convention in 1864, the Pennsylvania Ministerium had in effect withdrawn from the General Synod. Therefore, the credentials of the Pennsylvania Ministerium's delegates were rejected. When the matter reached the floor, Sprecher's ruling was sustained by a vote of seventy-seven to twenty-four.

39. Cited in Spaeth, *Charles Porterfield Krauth,* 2:156.
40. *Lutheran and Missionary* (Dec. 27, 1884).
41. *Lutheran and Missionary* (Aug. 23, 1866).

A three-day debate followed centering on the Ministerium's right of reservation, which had enabled the walkout of 1864 to take place. Some compromises were proposed but rejected. The Ministerium defended its right of reservation; the General Synod leadership demanded that the Ministerium give it up. Finally, the Ministerium's delegates left.[42] A protest was lodged against the action of the General Synod by W. A. Passavant, a delegate of the Pittsburgh Synod, and signed by twenty-two delegates from eight synods.[43]

The Ministerium met June 7–9 in a special session at Lancaster, Pennsylvania for consideration and adoption of its revised constitution. On June 10, the regular meeting of the Ministerium declared its connection with the General Synod dissolved. The following resolution was adopted:

> That a committee be now appointed and be charged with the following duties:
>
> 1. To prepare and issue a fraternal address to all Evangelical Lutheran Synods, ministers and congregations in the United States and Canada, which confess the *Unaltered* Augsburg Confession, inviting them to unite in a convention for the purpose of forming a union of Lutheran Synods.
>
> 2. After consultation with the members of other synods, to determine and announce the time and place of such convention, the time to be, if possible, within the current year [1866].[44]

On August 10, 1866, the Fraternal Address was issued. Charles Porterfield Krauth was the principal author. The address stated that the General Synod was not Lutheran, nor could it fulfill the need for a clear Lutheran witness in America. One portion of the address is worth noting because of its vision for Lutheranism in America.

> With our communion of millions scattered over a vast and ever-widening territory, with the ceaseless tide of immigration, . . . with the diversity of surrounding usages and of religious life, with our various nationalities and tongues, our crying need of faithful ministers, our imperfect provision for . . . the urgent wants of the Church, there is danger that the genuinely

42. For an account arguing the case for the Pennsylvania Ministerium, see *The Synod of Pennsylvania and the Late Convention at Fort Wayne, Ind. 1866* (Philadelphia: Jas. B. Rodgers, 1866). This pamphlet argues that the Ministerium never intended to leave and that Sprecher's ruling was unconstitutional. For conflicting interpretations by historians see Jacobs, *History*, 455–70 and Abdel Ross Wentz, *A Basic History of Lutheranism in America* (Philadelphia: Fortress Press, 1964), 145–49.

43. Those synods were New York (4), Pittsburgh (5), Ohio (4), Iowa (3), Northern Indiana (3), Minnesota (1), Hartwick (1), and Illinois (1). Spaeth, *Charles Porterfield Krauth*, 2:160.

44. Richard C. Wolf, ed., *Documents of Lutheran Unity in America* (Philadelphia: Fortress Press, 1966), 140–41.

Lutheran elements may become gradually alienated, that misunderstandings may arise, that the narrow and local spirit may overcome the broad and general, that the unity of the Spirit in the bond of peace may be lost, and that our Church, which alone in the history of Protestantism has maintained a genuine catholicity and unity, should drift into the sectarianism and separation which characterize and curse our land.[45]

In connection with the Fraternal Address, Krauth also published a set of Theses on Faith and Polity. In this detailed document Krauth carefully argued for a particular Lutheran identity and a unity that is witnessed to through the "general Creeds" and "official Confessions." In Article VIII of the Theses on Faith and Polity, Krauth referred particularly to the Unaltered Augsburg Confession in its entirety, including the errors it condemns. In Article IX Krauth went beyond the Unaltered Augsburg Confession and included all the other confessional documents.

IX. In thus formally accepting and acknowledging the Unaltered Augsburg Confession, we declare our conviction that the other Confessions of the Evangelical Lutheran Church, inasmuch as they set forth none other than its system of doctrine and articles of faith, are of necessity pure and scriptural. Preeminent among such accordant, pure and scriptural statements of doctrine, by their intrinsic excellence, by the great and necessary ends of which they were prepared, by their historical position, and by the general judgment of the Church, are these: the Apology of the Augsburg Confession, the Smalcald Articles, the Catechisms of Luther and the Formula of Concord, all of which are, with the Unaltered Augsburg Confession, in the perfect harmony of one and the same scriptural faith.[46]

Krauth knew that if the Lutheran church was to be strong and was to give forth a vital faith in America it would have to have a solid foundation— the Scriptures and the Lutheran Confessions, whole and intact. Without such a foundation, the errors of the General Synod would be repeated and Lutheranism would become nothing more than another American sect.

The convention to form the General Council of the Evangelical Lutheran Church in America met at Old Trinity Church at Reading, Pennsylvania, December 11–14, 1866. Never before had such a wide representation of Lutherans in the United States gathered at one place. The synods represented were: Pennsylvania, three from Ohio, Wisconsin, Michigan, Pittsburgh, Minnesota, Iowa, Missouri, Canada, New York, and the Norwegian Synod. The Augustana (Swedish) Synod was represented by letter. Krauth proposed

45. Ibid., 62–63.
46. Ibid., 145–46.

his Theses on Faith and Polity.[47] They were discussed and adopted by the convention and would form the basis of the Constitution of the General Council.[48]

The first official convention of the General Council opened in the Church of the Holy Trinity, Fort Wayne, Indiana, November 20, 1867. Krauth preached the opening sermon, based on Zechariah 4:6–7, entitled "The General Council. Its Difficulties and Encouragements."[49] Krauth acknowledged that the different nationalities and sections of the country that were represented had their own difficulties, but these difficulties would be met by representing a true Lutheranism "which is the servant of no nationality, language, or section."[50]

Krauth attempted to strike a delicate balance regarding ecclesiastical authority. He pointed out that there should be no form of an authoritarian council that would force its will on congregations. The Council was made up of synods, which were "congregations of congregations." The unifying factor of the Council would be faith: "The more inflexible our faith is, the more yielding is our charity; the more intolerant our faith is, the more enduring is our love; and this we believe to be the spirit of the body."[51]

Krauth's sermon represented both the struggles of many years and the hope that Lutheranism in America would be truly Lutheran. Years of intense debate over Lutheran identity and the hard choices that led to a separation from the General Synod had brought him and many of his hearers to this moment in Lutheran history. The formation of the General Council was a landmark opportunity. In 1867 hopes were high that a Lutheran church could be established in America that would be truly Lutheran and would be a worthy witness to the Lutheran faith in America. A letter written by William Julius Mann to his friend Philip Schaff expresses well the goals of the founders of the General Council.

> Whatever is worth doing, is worth doing well, and if we want to be Lutherans we will be consistent *ex animo* Lutherans and not Lutherans with the mere sham of the name. These were my thoughts concerning the convention in Reading. It is the greatest nonsense to attempt in behalf of the Lutheran Church to run a race with Methodists or Presbyterians, as our new-Lutheran brethren, who bear the name are doing, proclaiming it as the most glorious

47. For the full text see Wolf, *Documents,* 143–48.
48. The Constitution of the General Council of the Evangelical Lutheran Church in America is found in Wolf, *Documents,* 148–52.
49. The entire text of this sermon can be found in Spaeth, *Charles Porterfield Krauth,* 2:183–89.
50. Ibid., 2:184.
51. Ibid., 2:188.

feature of the Lutheran Church, that she had no character of her own, but could be turned and twisted, in life and doctrine, like a wet rag or a nose of wax.[52]

The reasons for the separation were clear. Those who formed the General Council concluded it was no longer possible to remain in the General Synod and be truly Lutheran. Mann was pointed in stating that Lutheranism should retain its own identity and not try "to run a race with Methodists or Presbyterians." Lutheranism in America should be Lutheran and nothing else.

When the *Definite Platform* was issued in 1855, issues between the American Lutherans and the confessional party were brought into the open. Most of the initial reactions to the *Platform's* proposals contained more emotion than substance—William Julius Mann's two works being exceptions.

As the disputes between the American Lutherans and the confessional party intensified, the issues became more clearly defined. The writings of members of the confessional party, especially those of Charles Porterfield Krauth, show a marked depth in their analysis of the problems. A consensus began to emerge regarding solutions. A vision for the future of the Lutheran church in America was being formed. Krauth is a classic example of a person whose position evolved as a result of the debates and events around him.

The main question was the extent to which the American religious climate would influence Lutheranism. Both sides agreed that Lutheranism had a place in America; the differences were over the extent to which Lutheranism should be "Americanized." One interesting point needs to be made: the language question was of little concern in the debates over American Lutheranism. The major issues involved doctrine and practice: would Lutheranism be true to its confessional stance, on all points; or would it surrender to such things as "Methodizing tendencies," revivals, and the Zwinglian sacramental theology that pervaded American Protestantism?

For the confessional party, confessional integrity initially meant recognizing all twenty-one articles of the Augsburg Confession as containing fundamental doctrines. These should be accepted because they were the Lutheran church's witness to the truth, based on the church's reading of the Scriptures. That being the case, there was no allowance for private judgment on these matters. As time went on, that definition was expanded to include the condemnations in the Augsburg Confession and finally all

52. Quoted in Spaeth, *Memorial of W. J. Mann*, 42.

the confessional writings that make up the *Book of Concord*. The confessional party also expressed the desire for the traditional Lutheran liturgical service as a further expression of Lutheran distinctiveness.

Such a vision could not be realized within the confines of the General Synod. Although the *Definite Platform* had been rejected, the American Lutherans still retained their influence and most of the positions of power. This suggests that many members had rejected the *Platform* for reasons of peace and not because of total disagreement with its position. Krauth's retraction, which came after much personal struggle, shows that he finally concluded that peaceful coexistence of the two parties was impossible. When the parting of the ways finally came in 1867, no one who had followed closely the bitter conflicts of the previous decade was surprised.

Conclusion

Unfinished Issues Regarding Confessional Identity

The American Lutheran controversy ended with the formation of the General Council in 1867, the climax of a struggle that lasted almost twenty years. The underlying issue in the controversy was the Americanization of the Lutheran church—specifically, the theological and liturgical form Lutheranism should take in America.

The American Lutherans advocated that the Lutheran church should possess characteristics similar to those of their Protestant neighbors in America. These characteristics included the practice of revivals, an essentially Zwinglian view of the sacraments, and an informal liturgy. The American Lutherans held liberal views regarding the Lutheran Confessions. They accepted only certain portions of the Augsburg Confession and claimed that, ultimately, the Bible was the only rule of faith. The confessional party, on the other hand, argued that the Lutheran church should adhere to both the Scriptures and the Confessions, should not give up its particularities, and should continue to maintain a unique identity in America.

Every religious community that cares about its identity has to struggle to preserve that identity. This means that its identifying marks must retain their integrity and importance for the life of the community. The kind of struggle over identity recounted in this book can take place within any religious community. In the ongoing struggle to maintain a group's identity, there are always those who advocate a compromise of some sort—often, ironically, in the name of preservation of the community.

Charles Porterfield Krauth's Summary

The issues between the two groups are summarized in a series of articles entitled "American Lutheran Church vs. Evangelical Lutheran Church in America," written by Charles Porterfield Krauth. These articles appeared in the *Lutheran and Missionary* in 1866.[1] According to Krauth, the American Lutherans were intent on molding a new form of what they called Lutheranism—a form they were free to alter or amend in whatever ways they saw fit, according to their own judgment.

Krauth contended that there is only one way in which the term "American Lutheran Church" can be read, and that is that the Evangelical Lutheran Church has an existence *in America.* "American" has nothing at all to do with changing the Lutheran doctrinal position. There should be no doctrinal differences between the Lutheran church in nineteenth-century America and the Lutheran church at any other time and place. "There is no such thing as an 'American Lutheran Church' in any other true and honest sense than this—that there is an Evangelical Lutheran Church in America, which, in the doctrines of the Gospel and in the right administration of the Sacraments, is one with the Evangelical Lutheran Church everywhere else" (106).

On the basis of that principle, Krauth made several points. First, no church in America called itself "American"—not even the General Synod. Second, no one could point to a book, pamphlet, or prayer in which the "American Lutheran Church gives any *authorized* account of itself" (107). Third, Krauth argued that many Lutherans who were also American repudiated the idea of an American Lutheran Church.

Krauth's fourth point was that those who claimed to be American Lutherans said they believed that the Bible is the only rule of faith; but that made them no more Lutheran than it made them Episcopalian, Presbyterian, Baptist, or Methodist. In his fifth point, Krauth observed that, when interpreting the Bible, the American Lutherans used reason to shed light on God's word. Here Krauth made a differentiation: "In genuine Lutheran principles of interpretation, reason is simply a witness on the facts; in American Lutheranism it is a judge upon the law" (107). In other words, reason becomes a law unto itself. Genuine Lutheranism, Krauth maintained, accepts the words of Scripture literally and does not try to force reason on the Scriptures. By contrast: "When in defiance of the law of language 'American Lutheranism' pretends that 'is' can mean 'is like,' it simply kills the whole Word of God" (108). Krauth was here referring to the disputes about the real presence of the body and blood of Christ in the Lord's Supper.

Krauth's sixth point was that since the American Lutherans had different principles of interpretation than the Lutheran church, they reached different conclusions. They "have no centre of unity whatever, except that they

1. Adolph Spaeth, *Charles Porterfield Krauth,* 2 vols. (New York: Christian Literature Co., 1898), vol. 2, gives a good summary of the points made in the articles. The following citations are from the summary.

agree in rejecting in greater or smaller measure, the doctrines of the Lutheran Church" (109). Krauth saw among the American Lutherans a wide range of views. "Among them have been strong Calvinists, although the predominant tendency is to a very low Arminianism, and to Pelagianism. They have no Confession of Faith" (109). The *Definite Platform* had been rejected by many American Lutherans, Krauth said, because no one could tell what it really meant.

In his seventh point, Krauth said that the American Lutherans claimed to identify with historical Lutheranism, but had adopted the very teachings Lutheranism had condemned. Krauth listed several "defenders of the faith," all of them Lutherans—Chemnitz, Spener, Francke, Claus Harms, Muhlenberg—and also referred, without giving names, to many others in America. Krauth said that the American Lutherans judged people as "wretched symbolists," but then tried to hide behind the very church those "wretched symbolists" defended.

The eighth and last point was that American Lutherans had given the church nothing of practical value—nothing good that was not already present in the faith before American Lutheranism made its appearance. Krauth believed that American Lutheranism would end up being nothing more than a sect.

Krauth ended his series by pointing out several defects in the American Lutheran Church. It was not *American,* because its fundamental principles had been previously asserted by various European "errorists." It was not *Lutheran,* because it denied the Lutheran faith. It was not a *Church,* because it had no separate organization, no name, no creed, and no history.

Krauth's conclusion was that this "new apostasy" would fail. What Lutheranism had meant for the last three hundred years, it would mean for the next three hundred years. " 'American Lutheranism' carries its death in its name. The name it tries to float on is really a millstone about its neck, and it will sink to the bottom" (112).

Krauth minced no words in his condemnation of American Lutheranism. He clearly saw the differences between the American Lutherans and the confessional party. One wanted to Americanize Lutheranism so that it would conform to the American religious climate, which was dominated by Protestantism; the other held out the vision of a Lutheran church that would be distinctively confessional and offer that witness in America. Krauth contended that Lutherans could be Lutheran and live in America. They should not capitulate to the American Protestantism that surrounded them. Krauth's and the General Council's vision for a unified confessional Lutheranism in America was a worthy goal. Krauth, however, may have been too optimistic in his assumption that American Lutheranism would become a new sect or "sink to the bottom."

The General Council's vision did not completely come to pass. Many of the synods that originally showed interest in the General Council never joined; others left after a short period of time. In the General Council itself the desired results did not always occur. Although the General Council had a conservative stance regarding the Lutheran Confessions, that stance was not always reflected in the life of the parish. Luther Reed, considered to be the father of the Lutheran liturgical movement in America, met head-on with that reality. At the time of his first call to a parish in 1895, twenty-eight years after the formation of the General Council, he encountered essentially the same worship practices that had been prevalent before the time of the synodical split. Communion was infrequent, private confession and absolution were nonexistent, vestments were not used, a small table replaced the altar, and there was no formal liturgy.[2] Lutherans still struggled with their identity.

Americanization and Religious Identity Today

Many years have passed since the American Lutheran controversy. In the meantime, America has gone through several wars. American society has changed drastically, and technological advances have made the nineteenth century seem distant and remote. Lutherans, like members of every other religious group, have had to adjust to the realities of the late twentieth century.

The most significant question today may well be not only what it means to be a Lutheran but what it means to be a Christian in twentieth-century America. We are no longer immigrants coming to a new land. The initial difficulties of Americanization have been dealt with by each denomination, sometimes well, often not so well. Decisions made in the last hundred years continue to affect both individual Christians and whole church bodies. For example, the doctrine of predestination is rarely emphasized in the Presbyterian church; Americans prefer to believe that their fate lies in their own hands. Revivals, once common among Methodists, are now rare; middle-class Americans are uncomfortable with unbridled emotion. The decision to deemphasize once-important doctrines and practices has changed the character of these churches. The Roman Catholic Church, on the other hand, has chosen not to modify its stand on birth control in response to the American desire for smaller families. This decision not to accommodate has also had significant consequences.

2. Thomas L. Edge, "Great Men of American Lutheranism: Luther D. Reed," *Una Sancta* 23:4 (Christmass, 1966), 12.

Today, Christians are confronted with a myriad of social, ethical, and moral issues: war and peace, life and death, technological progress, environmental concerns, medical ethics, racial and sexual equality, and economic and social justice. Many of these issues are new to our generation. Each issue is complex; none has easy answers; all require some degree of compromise. The magnitude of these issues may tempt us to ignore the theological dimensions in order to address the practical concerns.

Religious groups are confronted by an ever-changing society. As they consider the social, moral, and ethical questions cited above, they must consider the theological questions if they are to maintain their identity. America continues to be a religiously pluralistic society; today the variety of religious groups is even greater than one hundred years ago. The older religious groups (Roman Catholics, Presbyterians, Lutherans, Methodists, Episcopalians, and Baptists) remain. Many new groups (Pentecostals, fundamentalists, Eastern religions) are now active in America. America presented a confusing religious climate in the nineteenth century; today that climate is even more complex. How to act and what to believe are challenges that face American Christians today. What kind of responses should these challenges evoke?

Avery Dulles, a Roman Catholic theologian, addresses the issue of Americanization in a recent article, "Catholicism and American Culture: The Uneasy Dialogue."[3] What does Americanization mean for Roman Catholicism? American culture is so diverse, it is not easy to find any common denominator. Dulles uses the term "consumerism," to describe modern American culture, and he contends that the traditional work ethic has been undermined by the quest for affluence and sensory gratification. The church's task is to address American culture with the gospel.

Dulles favors liberal and neoconservative Catholicism as opposed to traditionalism and radicalism. Both the liberals and neoconservatives believe that the church can build into its structure such American traditions as freedom, personal initiative, open communication, and active participation. These things can be sources of renewal. On the other hand, both liberals and neoconservatives would warn that the church must guard against the dangers of accommodation; when the church simply echoes prevailing opinions and values, the church has nothing to say. "A church that no longer issues a clear call for conversion is only dubiously Christian."[4] Dulles's point is that traditional Catholicism has convictions and priorities very different from those embedded in contemporary American culture.

---

3. Avery Dulles, "Catholicism and American Culture: The Uneasy Dialogue," *America* (Jan. 27, 1990), 54–59.
4. Ibid., 59.

What Dulles says of Roman Catholics also applies to Lutherans. Both religious bodies are the product of immigration. Both have a particular theological identity. Neither is a part of the American Protestant establishment. What Dulles calls the "uneasy tension" is always present. When does adaptation become total accommodation? When does a religious body accommodate to the point where it no longer knows who and what it is? The challenges of Americanization and of maintaining religious identity will continue to confront Roman Catholics and Lutherans.

The Unfinished Issues for Lutherans

Clearly, the issues of Americanization and maintaining a group's religious identity are complex. Any church that seeks to remain true to its history and confessions and yet respond to contemporary problems could have an identity crisis.

The American Lutheran controversy is an example of an Americanization struggle, one that involved Lutheranism's very identity. The debate regarding the form Lutheranism is to take in America is not finished. It is as alive among Lutherans in America today as it was in the mid-nineteenth century. Unfortunately, Lutherans do not always realize that the issues of Americanization and religious identity are ever-present and are a part of the various decisions they make.

Two issues will not receive detailed attention here—the proposals of some feminists concerning God-language and the question of episcopal succession. I regard the God-language issue as a matter of concern for the church catholic, not just Lutherans. Proposals for "nonsexist" references to God, Christ, and the Trinity constitute an all-out assault on traditional Christianity. There is, however, something positive in the face of this assault. I hope that the issues raised by feminists will cause serious theological reflection, done ecumenically, on the teachings the church has affirmed, but perhaps taken for granted, over the centuries.[5]

As for the other issue, Lutherans are a divided house when it comes to the issue of episcopal succession; some Lutheran jurisdictions have bishops in succession, while others do not. I believe episcopal succession is for the church's *bene esse* (well-being). George Lindbeck has forcefully argued: "It is to [the] episcopally unified church . . . that all the major Christian traditions owe their creeds, their liturgies, and above all their scriptural

---

5. An excellent collection of essays on this subject is Alvin F. Kimel, Jr., ed., *Speaking the Christian God: The Holy Trinity and the Challenge of Feminism* (Grand Rapids: Wm. B. Eerdmans Publishing Co., 1992).

canon. If the latter are unexpungable, why not also the episcopate."[6] There is no absolutely compelling reason for not having bishops in episcopal succession. If Lutherans who do not presently have it should adopt it, this would be a great step toward healing the breach that occurred in the sixteenth century and be a contribution to the unity of the whole church.

In the past decade, the uneasy balance between loyalty to the Lutheran Confessions and accommodation to American culture has appeared once again to shift toward accommodation. One example of accommodation is the understandable but often overzealous desire for ecumenism. On January 7, 1986, Bishop David W. Preus of the American Lutheran Church presented a paper entitled "Lutheran Ecumenical Identity . . . Unity in Reconciled Diversity"[7] to the annual Mid-winter Convocation at Luther Northwestern Seminary in St. Paul, Minnesota. Preus began his talk with the following thesis: "It is time for Lutherans to make a course correction in relations with other Christian churches. Traditionally Lutherans have tended to be more zealous in defending the truth of the gospel than expressing the unity wrought by the gospel. Now it is increasingly apparent that Lutherans should not play truth and unity off against each other, but should let their expressions of unity emerge from their grasp of the truth."

Bishop Preus spoke approvingly of the various ecumenical dialogues in which Lutherans have been engaged, but his main thrust was to advocate that Lutherans should enter into pulpit and altar fellowship with the Presbyterian Church USA, the Reformed Church in America, and the Cumberland Presbyterian Church. Such a move, he believes, is desirable under the rubric of "unity in reconciled diversity." What this means is "Lutherans need not insist on complete doctrinal agreement before welcoming altar and pulpit fellowship with other Christians. Agreement in the gospel and the sacraments does not require total doctrinal agreement."

Preus included a brief historical survey that indicated that he was aware of the controversies that occurred between Lutheran and Reformed during the Reformation period. Preus believed these differences were no longer reasons for separation, but gave no historical evidence to show why. He assumed that circumstances had changed.

In assessing the situation in America, Preus stated: "U.S. Lutherans are no longer immigrants adrift, uncertain of their place or polity in a new land. We are here, rooted, American, with a tradition that gives us stability and identity in the Christian family. . . . We are friends, neighbors, colleagues, and family members with Christians of other denominations."

6. George Lindbeck, "The Church," *Keeping the Faith: Essays to Mark the Centenary of Lux Mundi,* ed. Geoffrey Wainwright (Philadelphia: Fortress Press, 1988), 199.

7. David W. Preus, "Lutheran Ecumenical Identity . . . Unity in Reconciled Diversity" (Paper delivered at Luther Northwestern Seminary, January 7, 1986).

Lutherans, Preus said, should be willing to enter into such relationships because of the pluralistic nature of American society. Anyone should be invited to the Lord's Table except "those who deny the presence of the forgiving Lord Jesus Christ." The meaning of "presence" was not explained. A second reason for establishing pulpit and altar fellowship, Preus said, was that some congregations had already taken this step. The national Lutheran bodies should follow the lead of these congregations.

This proposal called Lutherans to abandon their traditional insistence on agreement on the sacraments. Preus suggested that both sides accept "the mystery of the Lord's presence," which could include the Lutheran concept of "real" presence and the Reformed concept of "spiritual" presence. Disagreement over the "mode" of Christ's presence can be allowed to stand.[8]

Preus's proposal resembles Samuel Schmucker's *Fraternal Appeal*. Unity can take place on the basis of what is agreed on; differences can be ignored. But it was precisely the "mode" of Christ's presence in the Eucharist that caused divisions during the Reformation and still causes division today. *What* is given in the consecrated elements is still a vital question. The words spoken by Christ when he instituted the Supper are still cause for controversy; this controversy cannot be settled by ignoring those words. The American Lutherans wanted Lutheranism to surrender the doctrine of the real presence. Bishop Preus asks us to travel down a road where that doctrine would be compromised. Some of the very doctrines the Lutheran Reformers rejected would be allowed.[9] If this were to happen, the doctrine of the real presence would soon be alien to Lutheran vocabulary or, at best, become a belief held by a minority within the Lutheran church.

Robert Jenson cites a "flaw" in ecumenical discussions regarding the Eucharist. When discussing the presence of Christ, difficulty arises about what constitutes a person. Jenson poses the following questions: "Is a 'someone' indeed not a 'something'? Can a person be present where no body is present? And if this necessary embodiment of person be granted, can there be a body that is not somehow an object, a something?" These

8. Preus's position is in agreement with the recommendations of the Lutheran-Reformed Dialogue Commission. See James E. Andrews and Joseph A. Burgess, eds., *An Invitation to Action: The Lutheran-Reformed Dialogue Series III 1981–1983* (Philadelphia: Fortress Press, 1984), 4–6. This commission recommended pulpit and altar fellowship between Lutherans and Reformed in spite of the fact that "there is no question that there has been and still remains a difference in understanding between Lutheran and Reformed doctrine on the *mode* of Christ's real presence in the Sacrament" (115).

9. For the Lutheran view of the Eucharist, see Hermann Sasse, *This Is My Body: Luther's Contention for the Real Presence in the Sacrament of the Altar* (Minneapolis: Augsburg Publishing House, 1959).

questions are pivotal in the Lutheran–Reformed discussions; they must be faced and not simply be set aside.[10]

Another example of a challenge to Lutheran identity in America is a recent book by Paul Kuenning, a retired Lutheran pastor from Milwaukee. In *The Rise and Fall of Lutheran Pietism*,[11] Kuenning is concerned with the church's social involvement in American society. This book attempts to connect the pietistic movement to the social activism of many Lutherans in America, particularly Samuel Schmucker. Kuenning tries to refurbish Schmucker's generally negative reputation by underscoring Schmucker's participation in the various social causes of his day.

Kuenning believes the pietists were right in asserting that conduct is more important than doctrines and confessions. He laments that the pietistic activism, which extended from Muhlenberg's day through Schmucker's, was stifled by the doctrinal controversies that came in the middle of the nineteenth century.

According to Kuenning, pietists equated conversion with being "born again," an experience that required a change of heart and tangible evidence of such a change. Kuenning maintains that Schmucker and the other pietists were "moderates" in relationship to the "New Measures," but he does not explain what might differentiate a "moderate" from other practitioners of revivals. Kuenning says: "From New York to Georgia and as far west as Ohio, wherever Pietism prevailed, revivalism and conversion were normative aspects of American Lutheranism for the first century and a half of its existence."[12]

Pietists were convinced that Lutheran believers shared with all evangelical Christians a belief in the same fundamental truths of the Bible. Such common agreement enabled Christians to cooperate in various voluntary organizations such as Sunday schools, temperance groups, and Bible societies, in order that American society might be subject to positive Christian influence. Kuenning is impressed with the "ethical activism" of Schmucker and the other Lutheran pietists, an activism that took the form of revivals, ecumenical activities, and missions.

Kuenning highlights Schmucker's work on behalf of the abolition of slavery. In fact, he suggests that the negative reaction to the *Definite Platform* may have been due to Schmucker's activism, particularly in the abolitionist cause, as much as doctrinal reasons.[13] Kuenning claims that

---

10. Robert W. Jenson, *Unbaptized God: The Basic Flaw in Ecumenical Theology* (Minneapolis: Fortress Press, 1992), 32.

11. Paul P. Kuenning, *The Rise and Fall of Lutheran Pietism: The Rejection of an Activist Heritage* (Macon, Ga.: Mercer Univ. Press, 1988).

12. Ibid., 84.

13. Ibid., 175–78. Wentz takes a similar position; Abdel Ross Wentz, *Pioneer in Christian Unity: Samuel Simon Schmucker* (Philadelphia: Fortress Press, 1966), 320.

collusion between Southerners and Old Lutherans in the North resulted in a policy of silence regarding slavery. He also believes that one reason for opposition to the Franckean Synod was that group's strong abolitionist stance, not their rejection of the Augsburg Confession, which Kuenning says they accepted.

Kuenning puts forth five reasons why a recovery of the pietistic legacy is desirable. First, renewal and reception of that legacy could enhance what Kuenning calls "the inherent richness and diversity" of Lutheran theology and practice. Second, a recovery of pietism could help dialogue and co-operative endeavors with Protestant evangelicals, which Kuenning views as a rising force in America. Third, pietism can furnish Lutherans with an ethical theology. Kuenning attacks the "rigid two kingdoms confinement" and previous Lutheran theology for its lack of emphasis on deeds. Fourth, pietism can contribute to Lutheranism's ecumenical endeavors. Finally, it will contribute to an "optimistic eschatology," which emphasizes the re-alization of the kingdom of God on earth as a prelude to its fulfillment in history.

Kuenning's work cannot be accepted uncritically, particularly his gen-eralizations about pietism and confessional Lutherans. It is an incorrect generalization to claim that pietists were always active in the social arena while conservative confessional Lutherans cared little for the problems of society. What is most troubling, however, is his uncritical acceptance of the doctrinal positions of Samuel Schmucker and the other American Lu-therans, positions that could have deprived Lutheranism of its identity and might have led to its destruction. For Kuenning, social action is finally more important than doctrinal fidelity. For him, the real gospel is to be found in deeds, not creeds. Every benefit Kuenning believes will come from a recovery of pietism relates to social action and human works, and has little if anything to do with God's actions through the Word and the sacraments, the heart and essence of the church. Correct doctrine and charitable actions need not stand in opposition to each other. The church can be and should be concerned for both.

Final evidence that the issues of Americanization and religious identity are far from over is the so-called church growth movement. This movement is many-sided. Some advocates of church growth argue that, in order to grow, churches must maintain high standards in regard to both doctrine and moral conduct. These standards provide direction to people and mean-ing to life.[14] By contrast, church growth movement advocate David S. Luecke, a Lutheran Church–Missouri Synod pastor, contends in a book

14. This is the observation of Dean M. Kelley, *Why Conservative Churches Are Growing* (New York: Harper & Row, 1972).

entitled *Evangelical Style and Lutheran Substance* that Lutheranism must compete to get more members in the American religious "free market" environment.[15]

Concerned over declining membership in the Lutheran church, Luecke proposes to counteract that decline by offering strategies for church growth. By "church growth" Luecke means growth in numbers—especially attracting people who have no church affiliation. He says that Lutherans can attain such a goal by employing a certain "evangelical style" without sacrificing "Lutheran substance." The challenge is "learning new subtleties of communicating the gospel to American cultural subgroups that are becoming more diverse" (57).

Luecke feels that the Lutheran church has a strong theological and liturgical foundation, which speaks well to its members, but these words and actions do not necessarily speak to or get the attention of people who are not of Lutheran background. Luecke views people outside the church as consumers, people who are seeking some meaning to their lives. These consumers have needs; the church ought to assess those needs and attempt to meet them. Taking his cue from the business world, Luecke says that the Lutheran church should package its "product offering" to gain acceptance and attendance.

Luecke holds up the evangelicals as an example from which Lutherans can learn. These evangelicals have a high commitment to the authority of Scripture for people's faith and life, but they are also "experiential" in their style, which is characterized by warmth and enthusiasm. Luecke cites a wide range of examples of church growth, from the Seventh-Day Adventists to Jerry Falwell's Thomas Road Baptist Church to Robert Schuller's Crystal Cathedral.

With regard to sacraments, Luecke admits to the centrality of baptism and the Lord's Supper, but he thinks that increased contact with evangelical church style can show Lutherans "new sacraments." Although baptism and the Lord's Supper should remain central, "this style can show how sacramental thinking might be extended, that is, how God's presence can also be recognized through other forms of combining the Word of His promises with what believers can touch, feel, and experience" (85). It is clear that Luecke's vision of the church moves away from the traditional sacraments to other forms. These forms relate to subjective human experience, whereas the traditional sacraments emphasize the objective presence and action of God. Luecke does not believe that church growth can be accomplished

---

15. David S. Luecke, *Evangelical Style and Lutheran Substance* (St. Louis: Concordia Publishing House, 1988).

through highly developed liturgical forms. In fact, he associates liturgical renewal with a decline in church membership (86).

The influence of the evangelicals on Luecke is evident in his stress on decision and conversion, which he calls "touchpoints." He feels these emphases have much to offer the Lutheran church and can only improve the Lutheran church's "evangelism techniques." Luecke realizes that a stress on decision and conversion makes Lutherans uneasy, but they should not have major reservations about this, "for decision-oriented practitioners of evangelism are usually quite clear on *sola gratia* as they look for response to God's promise" (83).

Luecke's assessment of the Lutheran church in America is as follows; "The New Lutherans today seem headed in the direction of further assimilation into the theological orientation and the agenda and style of mainline Protestant churches. They tend to look to liturgical practices and social action to set the style for their modernized piety. Neither of these two emphases, however, appears very well related to infectious church growth at this stage of religious life in America" (91). Luecke's prescription for church growth is that church life should be simple and democratic. This means that such things as scholarship, centralized authority, tradition, liturgies, and "carefully worded confessions" should not receive great attention. Churches should be "popular," meaning "of the people." Luecke speaks positively of certain aspects of pietism, especially its emphasis on the priesthood of all believers. The Office of the Ministry is recognized, but, in the last analysis, the people should have the say as to what happens in the church, and whatever means can attract new members into the church should be employed. Luecke states that the democratic form of church life has been characteristic of American religion; in order to succeed in America, the Lutheran church should adapt itself to that form.

Luecke's proposals undermine Lutheran confessional and liturgical integrity. In spite of his talk about "Lutheran substance," there is finally much that is not Lutheran in them. His emphasis on decision and conversion is more reminiscent of revival meeting techniques than the Lutheran doctrine of justification. In spite of his invocation of *sola gratia*, Luecke is open to the charge of Pelagianism, which advocates that salvation comes, in part, as the result of human effort, whether it be through techniques that are employed or human decision. The Lutheran emphasis that God, through Christ [alone], justifies sinners and brings salvation is compromised if not absent. In Luecke's scheme, the sacraments are reduced to being marginal. In the church Luecke envisions, infant baptism in all likelihood would eventually become the exception and adult baptism the norm. The Lord's Supper would be infrequently celebrated, and a symbolic meaning of that sacrament would eventually replace the doctrine of the real presence. Traditional liturgical forms would quickly disappear and be replaced by a simpler service. If the Confessions no longer have binding authority and the liturgical tradition is discarded, anything can happen, all in the name of democratic structures and growth in numbers. In the last analysis, Luecke's proposals contain the potential for the collapse of all Lutheran doctrinal and liturgical substance and the destruction of the Office of the Ministry. Growth in members is an admirable goal, but sacrificing one's identity is not the way to achieve it.

David Truemper, a theology professor at Valparaiso University, discusses the church growth movement and its implications for confessional Lutheranism, particularly with regard to liturgy, in an article entitled "Evangelism: Liturgy *versus* Church Growth."[16] Truemper notes that Lutheranism is no longer a subculture religion. He adds:

> In some respects, the worst fears of many are being realized: with the waning of German or Scandinavian culture among the immigrants has come the waning of confessional integrity at the theological and doctrinal level. The challenge of Americanization remains, and it remains as a vulnerable point. The lack of a broadly based understanding of the catholic liturgical principles to which the confessional writings commit us works to reduce the level of discussion about tensions between evangelism and liturgy to one of taste or style, areas in which no appeal to absolutes are allowed and no application of objective criteria are tolerated. (30)

Against the church growth movement advocates of accommodation, Truemper argues (rightly) that for the church of the Augsburg Confession, it is the liturgical assembly gathered around Word and sacrament that is "the fundamental expression of the church's existence." He then states: "Our confessional tradition is shaped by a view of the church's nature and work that is, at bottom, liturgical. What is the church? It is the liturgical assembly. Where is the church? Where the gospel is preached and the sacraments are done. What should the church do? Assemble the faithful around the gospel proclaimed and sacramentally enacted" (32).

Confessional Lutheranism does not oppose evangelism, but evangelism must come in its proper order. Truemper comments: "The liturgy of word and sacrament is the end (goal, purpose) of the church's existence. It is not a means to another end. The church exists to worship God, to give to God God's due, to acknowledge God as God. The church does not worship

---

16. David G. Truemper, "Evangelism: Liturgy *versus* Church Growth," *Lutheran Forum* (Feb. 1990), 30–33.

so as to recruit members; it recruits members so as to form them into worshippers" (32). If this form of the church growth movement were to have its way, all that is distinctly Lutheran would either disappear altogether or be presented simply as one option among many. Lutheranism needs to evangelize people, but in that process it must present itself for what it is, openly and honestly. It should not compromise itself and thus fall into the trap of the American marketplace mentality. Every church wants to grow, but at what price?

Preus's ecumenical proposal, Kuenning's stress on social action, and Luecke's emphasis on church growth have one thing in common: though they would no doubt protest the contrary, they ask the Lutheran church to divest itself of its confessional and liturgical heritage and make compromises on things that concern its very identity. Although not totally identical to the proposals of the American Lutherans in the mid-nineteenth century, their proposals are similar. The Lutheran church is, in some respects, reliving the American Lutheran controversy today.

The Lutheran church is defined by its particular confessional stance and liturgical life. If these are downplayed, ignored, or discarded, there is nothing left that is specifically Lutheran and anything is possible. If the Lutheran confessional and liturgical moorings disappear, then Lutherans can enter into communion with anyone, Lutherans can cease to be concerned about theological differences and engage in all kinds of social action, and Lutherans can use all sorts of devices and techniques to get people in the door. Yet, in that process, the Lutheran church will take on a new identity; it will be Lutheran in name only.

As long as Lutherans are in America they will have to respond to the issues of Americanization and maintaining their religious identity. Knowing this, they can find wisdom and guidance for the future by examining events of the past, in this instance the American Lutheran controversy. Lutherans had made adjustments to the new land in which they found themselves. They cast off their state church connections, adopted (in varying degrees) the use of the English language, and allowed for democratic procedures in carrying out their affairs. Most of these adjustments had already been made by 1850, when the American Lutheran controversy was in its early stages. Hence, these did not become points of contention in the controversy.

The essence of the issue was Lutheranism's theological identity. Lutherans possess a particular theological heritage, expressed in the Augsburg Confession and the other writings that comprise the Confessions of the Lutheran church. The question within the General Synod became: What are Lutherans to be when confronted with the American religious situation, dominated at that time by Protestantism? The American Lutherans wanted

Lutheranism to be a part of that Protestant milieu, and they wanted to participate in the various Protestant societies that were engaged in the cause of "Christianizing" America. That meant giving up certain Lutheran theological positions so that Lutherans might more closely resemble their Protestant neighbors. The American Lutherans, with such influential leaders as Samuel Schmucker, held the majority view in the General Synod through the first half of the nineteenth century.

When the confessional party became more visible after about 1850, they advocated that Lutheranism should remain uniquely Lutheran, true to the Reformation heritage; for them this was Lutheranism's witness in and to America. The leaders on this side of the controversy, particularly William Julius Mann and Charles Porterfield Krauth, argued emphatically that Lutherans could live in America without having to sacrifice their faith in the process. The Lutheran church could (and should) exist in America and be Lutheran. It did not have to resort to being an American Lutheran Church.

Samuel Schmucker and the American Lutherans represented a faction that had totally adapted itself to America. It was their view that Lutheranism was essentially no different from American Protestantism. They were challenged, in turn, by a varied group—some immigrants, others American-born—who saw Lutheranism's identity and future in terms of a truly confessional Lutheran church. The American Lutherans wanted to blend into the American religious culture; the confessional Lutherans advocated that Lutheranism should provide a distinctly Lutheran witness in America and to America. They wanted Lutheranism to be another unique force in America's religious life.

History teaches us lessons. The American Lutheran controversy can provide guidance to the Lutheran church in the twentieth century as it struggles with the ongoing question of what it means to be Lutheran in America. The Lutheran church, as a confessing movement in the church catholic, has an integrity of its own, and that integrity ought not to be compromised. The Lutheran church has a particular view of the gospel, communicated through Word and sacrament and expressed in the liturgy, and it must hold on to these things in order to be faithful to and maintain its identity. The Lutheran church is called to be what it is in America and not try to imitate someone else. The Lutheran church has a vital theological heritage to offer Americans, and the only way it can offer an effective witness in this land is to maintain the integrity of that heritage.

The participants in the American Lutheran controversy cared enough about truth and the Lutheran church's future in America that they were willing to fight over the vital issues involved in that controversy. That is refreshing to see, especially in contrast to the theological indifference that seems so prevalent in much of Lutheranism in America today. If theological discussion occurs at all, it often quickly deteriorates into a conflict of opposing personal opinions, with no attention paid to the objective nature of a given issue. The Lutheran bodies involved in the merger that formed the Evangelical Lutheran Church in America seem intent on avoiding theological controversy at all costs; this may indicate that organizational matters are deemed more important than theology, and that unity, even if it is uneasy, must be maintained.

The issue of what it means to be the Lutheran church in America is still with us and always will be. We ought to care about this issue at least as much as did our forebears. As Lutherans, we owe that to our heritage, but, most of all, we owe that to Christ and his gospel, which the Lutheran church has, at its best, affirmed boldly and without reservation.

Index